STRESS AND STRATEGY

STRESS AND STRATEGY

Shirley Fisher

STRESS RESEARCH UNIT,
DEPARTMENT OF PSYCHOLOGY,
UNIVERSITY OF DUNDEE.

LAWRENCE ERLBAUM ASSOCIATES, PUBLISHERS
London   Hillsdale, New Jersey

Lawrence Erlbaum Associates Ltd., Publishers
Chancery House
319 City Road
London EC1V 1LJ

British Library Cataloguing in Publication Data

Fisher, Shirley
Stress and strategy.
1. Stress (Psychology) 2. Stress
(Physiology)
I. Title
155.9   BF575.S75

ISBN 0-86377-031-2
ISBN 0-86377-035-5 Pbk

Typeset by Multiplex Techniques Ltd
Printed and bound by A. Wheaton & Co. Ltd., Exeter

To Reg Pittman
for constant encouragement
in the writing of this book

Acknowledgements

I would like to thank Mr A. Wilkes, Department of Psychology, University of Dundee, for encouragement in the writing of this book. I would like to thank Professor Ray Over, Department of Psychology, La Trobe University, Melbourne, Australia, Professor C. Jin, University of Beijin, Peoples Republic of China, and Dr Norman Loveless, Department of Psychology, University of Dundee, for reading and commenting on selective aspects of the manuscript.

The research on homesickness quoted in this book is supported by funds from The Economics and Social Science Research Council and the Manpower Services Commission.

I would like to thank Mrs Patricia McKillop and Mrs Marilyn Laird for typing the manuscript, and Mrs Maureen Sneddon for help with diagrams and figures.

Contents

Introduction

This book is designed for intermediate and advanced students of psychology. It should be of interest to students in related disciplines in the social sciences and medicine who are concerned with stress and its relationship with human health and efficiency.

There have been two main aims in writing this book. The first is to provide a basis for understanding stress and its effects on health and efficiency. The second is to develop and extend a new synthesis of ideas about stress in terms of control, strategy, and the implications for health.

There already are a number of useful accounts of the general effects of stress on biological and psychological systems. Most notable are two books: The first by Cox (1978) views stress from psychological and physiological perspectives; the second by John Jung (1978) sets the concept of stress in the context of general motivational research.

In addition, there are more specific texts which provide empirical and theoretical accounts of a range of environmental stresses and their effects on efficiency (Broadbent, 1971; Poulton, 1970). More recently, a book of readings by Hockey (1983) has brought the research literature on environmental stress up to date.

In the area of social psychology and social medicine there has been an increased interest in the way life events affect people, in terms of the risk of mental and physical disorders. Many readings provide useful summaries of research in aspects of life stress and health. Most notable for providing a comprehensive basis for understanding life events, threats, and the effects on people are the contributions of Lazarus (1966, 1968) and Mandler (1975). More recently, Fisher (1984a) and Langer (1983) have provided accounts of how the presence or absence of control is a possible factor, which determines whether events are perceived as stressful and what the effect on mental health is likely to be. This book to some extent represents a further development of this idea. Recently Lazarus and Folkman (1984) have explored ideas about coping in a clinically oriented context.

Finally, there are many books devoted to the developing area of stress at work (Cooper, 1982; Cooper & Smith, 1985). A notable development is that stress at work may relate to high demand but low jurisdiction or control. These ideas developed by Karasbek (1979) are discussed by some of the contributors in Cooper and Smith (1985).

OUTLINE OF THE APPROACH TAKEN

A fundamental aspect of the book is concern with the association between stress, control, and the implication for strategic responses; it represents a further development of ideas from an earlier publication (Fisher, 1984a). There is increasing reference in the social, clinical, and applied research literature to the idea that when there is control, adverse effects of stress are reduced. In contrast, helplessness in conditions of loss of control is a precondition for depression.

In spite of the considerable interest in perceived control, there has been relatively little attempt to understand the relationship between stress and control in any detail, and hardly any attempt to consider the psychological processes that must be involved. However, there is developing interest in how the perception of control might influence mental and physical health and there is a large, disparate research literature addressed to various aspects of instrumentality, predictability, or responsibility as factors in the response to stress. Additionally there is a developing literature evolving from learning theory on the detection of contingency between successive events including response and outcome. Much is now known about how stresses affect personal competence. There is a need for a textbook for students that systematically brings some of these issues together. Fisher (1984a) attempted to draw together some of the main findings in these areas. In this second book the aim is to present a synopsis of some of these ideas for the intermediate and advanced student.

A new aspect of this book has been to develop the ideas about coping strategies in stress in terms of the attempt to gain control by various means. Discussion of the use of strategies in stress leads to consideration of the issue of whether a person is truly free to use different strategies or whether life experiences and stressful conditions create constraints on structure and in turn restrict the range of available strategies. This issue is one with important implications for therapy. A person may not be free to select effective strategies in cases of personal crisis. This would suggest that interventions are more likely to be useful than self-help. However, if structural constraints also reflect deeper aspects of personality, it may not be possible to prescribe an effective strategy unless it is compatible with these constraints.

ORGANISATION OF THE BOOK

The first part of the book is concerned with reviewing evidence on the effects of various aspects of control on the perceived response to stress. The availability of instrumentality, predictability, or responsibility, affects the responses of animal populations to noxious stimulations. In human beings, tolerance and choice may be influenced not only by these aspects but also by the overall attitude a person has about what is sometimes referred to as "experimenter demand" or what the experimenter is looking for. Equally, even in very simple conditioning experiments, evidence suggests that human beings respond strategically, noting contingent events and perhaps manifesting responses which reflect instructions or personal bias as to what is required. The evidence provides some hint that human beings might behave strategically in situations involving personal proficiency.

Evidence reviewed subsequently is concerned with how, in all the complexity of life situations, human beings decide whether or not control is possible. The ability of people to make sense of contingent relationships between events and outcomes is generally poor. It seems that the memory load involved in building internal statistical models of actions and outcomes in the real world, is too great. Various "rule of thumb" techniques may be used for the assessment of control and in some cases where the individual assesses the frequency of evidence of one kind as compared to another across a series of trials, there are important sources of bias. The operation of bias will lead to unrepresentative models in cognition; a person may be assessing his potential for control from an inadequate model. These issues and the evidence for the conclusion that the internal models of control may be biased is discussed at length in Chapter 4.

Bias in thinking about the possibilities for control is seen as being of central importance as an influence in decision making in life situations. "Locus of control" is a phrase generally taken to mean an ideological attitude with regard to whether events are externally controlled (fate, powerful others) or internally controlled (personally determined). Recent research evidence reviewed in central chapters suggests that "locus of control" is not described by a single dimension. The idea is developed that there may be different worlds or "domains" of control with different associated methods of exercising control. Individuals may be expected to vary in the domains within which they seek control. Some may favour personal skill, whereas others may favour social or political control. Thus, a life event which is stressful may be tackled in one domain of control by one individual but in another by a different individual. Faced, for example, with the stress of a dying relative, one person may concentrate on trying to make that person better by personal effort (buying special food, medicines, etc.); another may seek to buy extra medical help or persuade a remote friend to help find a way into a specialist clinic, etc. The status, wealth, and experience of a person may lead to favoured modes of response. Only when these modes are seen to fail will a person consider other ways. Some life events may occur in which only certain modes of response will be successful. The competent person is the one who matches his strategy with an "ideal" strategy. For example, a person who fears that his/her house will be torn down for a motorway, would perhaps do better to concentrate all efforts on the local authority concerned, than try to defend the house with trenches and barricades, if the long-term aim is to preserve the house.

These issues are important because beliefs and attitudes concerning control may determine whether stressful life events are challenging and beneficial to a person or negative, with adverse effects.

In order to exercise control in any domain selected, a person must be competent. Stressful circumstances act to influence levels of competence. There are two central chapters (Chapters 6 and 7) concerned with the way in which competence is affected by stress. In these two chapters, models of stress and performance are considered. The student is first presented with an account of the details of and difficulties with the arousal model. Then there is an account of resource-based models in which stress is assumed to increase mental demand. "Composite" and "state" models are then considered.

A theme that persists throughout the book is that stress imposes problems, in that it involves a mismatch between *reality* or the *state of the world* and what is *desired*. This is an approach based on principles of homeostasis; stress creates the conditions of imbalance. The individual seeks to rectify this and restore equilibrium. It is argued that in theory this should lead to strategic responses because the ingredients of a situation define a range of possible actions which could be taken. A person in stress might be considered to be engaged in contemplating actions and outcomes rather as a chess player confronts the position of the pieces on the chess board and works out his moves. Fisher (1984a) argued that such contemplations provide the basis of worrying.

Stress may be conceptualised as circumstances which create a mismatch as described above, but might arise as the result of an existing mismatch which cannot be corrected. To illustrate this distinction: Loud noise might be thought of as creating a set of environmental conditions which the individual finds uncomfortable and seeks to avoid (mismatch between reality and what is desired). By contrast, unexpected failure to control the steering of a moving car results in the perception of unsuccessful action and *creates* a precondition for stress. One issue of importance is whether a person is truly free to think in an ideal, logical, way about these sorts of situations. In Chapter 11, we consider the way in which responses might be structurally determined. Firstly, *stresses might constrain responses*. Secondly, *cognitive styles might prevail to determine features of response*. In a stress scenario, it might be the case that a person becomes too distressed to ask the logically necessary questions. Equally, personality factors may excercise constraint. These issues, which should be of interest to those who are interested in therapeutic aspects of mental health, are developed in the latter part of the book.

It is argued that these decisions and the perceived outcomes are part of the struggle for control and ultimately determine the probability of mental and physical health on a short- or long-term basis. A "marionette model" is developed, which assumes that previous life events and cognitive styles exercise constraints on the use of strategies. If the constraints operating still allow a person to produce strategies effective for a particular situation, then even a potentially threatening encounter could have positive connotations. Conversely, if the constraints which operate restrict decision making and favour decisions which will not be effective for a particular stressful encounter, then the probability of poor outcome, perceived helplessness, and ill health, is increased. These issues are considered in the control model of stress and illness in Chapter 12.

Since this book is written with the advanced student of psychology as well as researchers in mind, we have attempted to provide more detailed accounts of experimental evidence and to provide a detailed coverage of important models and theories. However, the book also concerns the development of ideas from a previous book (Fisher 1984a) and leads to the notion that loss of control in stressful environments may lead to protracted stress experience, increased risk of pathological states of arousal, and increased risk of illness. In Chapter 12 an attempted synthesis of ideas is provided and a model of stress and illness is developed.

1 Stress: A Problem of Definition

1. THE UMBRELLA TERM OF "STRESS"

The term "stress" is an umbrella term for an increasingly wide variety of conditions, responses, and experiences. A fundamental problem for any writer or researcher concerned with stress and its effect on behaviour is to attempt to find an adequate definition.

There have been a number of attempts to provide comprehensive definitions of stress; each has its own problems; each is inadequate in some respects. A useful initial classification of these approaches is in terms of stimulus variables, response variables and internal variables, usually termed independent, dependent and intervening, variables, respectively.

A. Definitions Based on the Independent Variable (Stimulus Features)

A definition of stress in terms of the independent variable has the advantage of giving "out-thereness" to stress variables. Stress is assumed to be a condition of the environment. The environment could be physical or psychosocial. On first consideration, such an approach seems to provide a reasonable basis for classifying stresses. The only problem is to provide a definition of what constitutes a *stressful* as compared with a *non-stressful* condition of the environment. The obvious solution is to assume that stress is merely an intense level of stimulation and that it is the level, or intensity, which is the distinguishing factor. Thus stress could be seen as an "intense level of everyday life": It is too high a level of temperature, too high a level of noise, too high a level of stimulation. Stress is merely a level on a dimension of stimulation that will eventually result in pain. However, this definition does not account for ways in which *absence of stimulation* might be stressful. Greater generality can be given if it is assumed that *extremes* rather than excessive stimulation are stressful. Such a bipolar conceptualisation allows isolation and lack of stimulation also to be stressful.

The responses that characterise the behaviour of an individual under stress can be seen as part of an attempt to avoid or escape extreme conditions of the environment. Characteristic physiological changes can be envisaged as part of the attempt to mobilise resources in order to avoid exposure. Cannon (1932, 1936) was the first to hypothesise that physiological changes associated with exposure to stress formed part of a homeostatic response pattern designed to mobilise sugar and oxygen resources resulting in the release of energy. Extending this notion, behavioural changes could be seen as the *result* of underlying changes in physiological systems associated with the provision of energy.

There are two ways in which a definition of stress in terms of the independent variable accounts for the variety of response patterns that characterise the individual confronted by stress. First, the external condition could be thought of as exerting a force or pressure. The response is then seen as part of strain causing breakdown or damage. Physiological and behavioural responses to stress are then envisaged as malfunctions in relation to too much pressure. The extreme result of increasing malfunction might be mental breakdown and disorder, but there would be no clear indication of what form disorder might take.

A second approach involves the hypothesis of *homeostasis*: Stress is an invasion of the organism's normal range of comfort; it is a state of discrepancy. The organism is essentially hedonistic, avoiding pain and seeking pleasure. It therefore mobilises resources in a way designed to attenuate exposure or, if possible, to terminate the stress: The form of the response and its success determines whether the result is perceived as challenging (positive) or distressing (negative).

Some problems with a definition of stress in terms of the state of the independent variable are: (1) that there is an implicit assumption that what is stressful for one person will also be stressful for another; (2) there is no simple way of deciding on what is the limit of tolerance, or at what point a level becomes stressful. Cut-off points may differ for different individuals and be subject to range effects produced by previous experiences, including stressful experiences. This is best illustrated by the engineering model developed by McGrath (1974) in which force or pressure (stress) is exerted by an environment and the response reveals the strain. The total effect is transactional, depending as much on the structure or property of a material as it does on characteristics of the stimulus. Moreover, the effect of stress may be cumulative; a structure may first show no change but later crack or crumble, although the same force is exerted throughout.

B. Definitions Based on the Dependent Variable (Response Features)

Response-based definitions might be thought at first to have many advantages. A substance or person can be deduced to have been exposed to stressful conditions if signs of strain are present. This is like saying that "intelligence is that which intelligence tests test"—stress is that which is responded to by behaviour characteristic of stress. The view has the advantage that personal meaning and so-called neurotic sources of fear are included: If a person responds to the presence of an apple by stressful response patterns, then by definition an apple is a source of stress.

A problem is that it may be difficult to define and distinguish responses that are part of the stress response from those that are not. The original view of the physiological response to stress developed by Selye (1956) was that it was an undifferentiated state of heightened arousal and hormone activity. On this view it would be relatively straightforward to conduct a test to determine which of two hidden individuals was experiencing stress, by measuring physiological or behavioural response levels. However, more recent research has tended to emphasise both stimulus-specific and person-specific response patterns and the possibility of fractionation between different arousal systems (see Lacey, 1967; Lacey, Bateman, & Van Lehn, 1953). Thus it may be necessary to define which "end-organ" responses, as part of a total pattern, are signs of stress, and which are not. A person may sweat for reasons other than being under stress, and sweating alone as an end-organ response would not provide an adequate definition. The presence of circulating stress hormones such as catecholamines (adrenaline and noradrenaline) or corticoid hormones (cortisol) could provide the basis for a definition, but there is a time course associated with the production and excretion of these hormones and the time of assessment may well determine the level. Also, characteristically, the human response to stress can occur in advance of an actual event, or may appear in reflective thought when an event such as a tragic loss has passed. Therefore the stress response may be dissociated in time from the source of the problem.

Finally, a further difficulty arises from the fact that a number of dependent variables change in stress and that one variable (the controlling variable) may change to protect a second variable (the controlled variable). Therefore different impressions may be given of whether or not stress is occurring. A useful illustration is in terms of the bodily responses to raised temperature. In human beings, as environmental temperatures rise, the mechanism of sweating comes into operation to help maintain stable bodily temperature. If *sweating* were measured, an impression of a changed response to raised temperature would result. However, if *body temperature* were measured, a change might be less easily detected.

C. Interactional Definitions of Stress

Increasingly, the main approach to the conceptualisation of stress is interactional or transactional. In simplest terms, it is assumed that mental state or structure determines the presence or absence of stress. Thus, as in engineering, where physical structures differ in their capacity to resist external force without showing signs of strain, so in human beings mental structures determine the degree to which stresses are perceived. A useful example is of a study by Symington et al. (1955), which showed that autonomic arousal increased in the case of dying patients who were conscious and not in those who were unconscious. Clearly the presence or absence of the capacity for thought was a determinant of response; the simplest possible equation involves the idea of mediating appraisal processes concerned with dying.

There are various models which have developed the importance of intervening mental activities as important factors in determining stress. The simplest interactional approach is non-specific about the nature of the intervening processes. There is a mediating psychological structure which provides a basis for interpretation of evidence and leads to the classification of that evidence as stressful. Recent interactional approaches however, do provide reasons rather than merely advocating intervening structures.

McGrath (1974) proposed a demand–capacity model in accordance with which the environment imposes demand on the individual but this is only stressful if the individual *lacks the capacity to meet that demand*. Implicit in this definition is the idea that the individual perceives his capabilities and can make such an appraisal either before he engages the problem or during the scenario created by the problem once he has engaged it. McGrath formulates a set of propositions which he argues provides a conceptual structure for envisaging stress. The focal organism or "actor" can be at a number of system levels—individuals, groups, or organisations. There are then four classes of events. The first class is *demand* imposed by the environment. The second is *reception* (recognition or appraisal by the organism) and this creates *subjective demand*. The third is the *focal organism's response*, whether it is physiological or behavioural. Finally there is the *consequence* of response or results of action. The psychological structure of the individual is seen to be potentially influential at any one of these four stages. For example, individuals may be differentially sensitive to different aspects of the environment, differ in the way demand is perceived, have different subjective assessment of personal capabilities and limitation, or different perceptions of outcome. Essentially, stress is seen to be a relationship between the environment and the organism across these four classes of events.

An earlier approach by Lazarus (1966) provides a foundation for understanding the underlying processes in these four interactional stages. Lazarus
distinguished primary, secondary, and tertiary appraisal processes in a potentially stressful situation. Primary appraisals are concerned with interpreting
and coding the problem. Secondary appraisals are concerned with the possible response to perceived demand. Tertiary appraisals are concerned with
the assessment of the consequence of response. These three types of appraisal are implicit in McGrath's distinctions.

An interactional view is also provided in an approach linking the state
of the independent variable to coping, by Welford (1973). Welford
hypothesises that an inverted 'U' function relates efficiency in a person's
performance to level of demand, which is in turn determined by the level
of stimulation on a scale from tolerable to extreme. Implicit in the Welford
model is the notion that at high levels of demand, coping resources are
ineffective. Thus, with increasing levels of demand, the probability of imbalance between demand and effective capacity increases. In other words,
an individual faced with extreme conditions is less likely to perceive that
he has the necessary responses to cope. This provides the basis for an
interactional view in which the state of the independent variable is a part
determinant of the existence of stress.

Cox has provided the basis for a four-stage transactional model of stress.
The main principle of the model is that stress is a personal, perceptual
phenomenon rooted in psychological processes (Cox, 1978, p.18). Feedback
components are emphasised and a cyclical process is envisaged. Again,
there are identifiable stages similar to those provided by McGrath. Demand
is determined by the external environment but also by internal needs which
may be physiological or psychological. A second stage is determined by the
perception of demand and *perceived coping ability*; imbalance at this stage
creates the conditions of stress. *Methods of coping available to the individual*
constitute a third stage. The fourth stage is concerned with the consequences
of coping and it is suggested that stress only occurs when the organism's
failure to meet demand is important; in other words, there must be provision
for some priority weighting attached to failure. Finally, the model includes
the notion of feedback at all stages so that the consequences of failure
influence the perception of demand, the perception of the capacity to cope,
and the cost attached to failure. The model could be argued to be transactional in the sense that a greater contribution is made by the psychological
structure of the individual, than is envisaged in a purely interactional model.
McGrath (1976) added a further principle to the main principles described
in 1974, and this brings his model closer to a transactional model. He
argues, on the basis of findings by Lowe and McGrath (1971), that the
closer perceived demand is to perceived capacity, the greater will be the
stress. However, Cox finds it implausible to suppose that large imbalances
such as might be created by disastrous situations are not stressful, and

proposes that stress is likely to be a 'U'-shaped function of imbalance between demand and capacity. Thus, very small *and* very large imbalances would be considered stressful.

Fisher (1984a) argued for a more analytical approach to the nature of mediating cognitive processes centred on the perception of personal control. There are two distinguishable paradigms that provide the context for judgements about stress. The first is when a person is coping with a task in the presence of an adverse condition which might be considered stressful. The second is when a person copes with a task but then begins to fail under conditions where success matters. Under these circumstances, the task itself creates the precondition of stress. In both cases the intention or ambition that dictates behaviour is important. Miller, Galanter, and Pribram (1960) were the first to introduce the idea that behaviour is purposefully organised by means of plans. Contained in the blueprint for the plan is the consequence that should be achieved. In the case of the first of the two paradigms above, the purpose may be to attenuate, terminate, or minimise the effects of stress. In the case of the second paradigm the purpose might be re-establish control of the task perhaps by extra compensatory effort when competence is perceived to be low.

This may provide a basis for the definition of stress in terms of personal control: Stress exists when conditions (internal or external) deemed unpleasant cannot be changed. This will occur when demand exceeds capacity, as in the McGrath formulation. An extra element may be the *cost* of exercising control; if there is only a minor imbalance then a person may decide to expend effort because reversibility of the circumstances he dislikes are within reach. On the other hand, a large imbalance may incur too much cost to correct. The cost of no action must be weighed against the cost of action.

2.   THE LINKS BETWEEN STRESS AND THE PERCEPTION OF CONTROL

A. Control as a Factor in Stress

If control is assumed to be a factor which determines stress level then a number of propositions follow. Firstly, the individual should choose and be shown to benefit from being given the means for control (instrumentality). Secondly, the benefits should be greater than would be expected on grounds of predictability only. Thirdly, perceived control should have effects equal to but not greater than objective control. Conversely when a person has control but does not know it, the effect should be the same as when there is no control. Fourthly, individuals must be equipped with the mental resources to determine whether control is possible (otherwise the gains should be no greater than is determined by chance). Fifthly, individuals shown by objective measures to experience high levels of threat should be shown by independent criteria to experience low perceived control. Sixthly, since animals respond to threat with behaviour and physiological activity characteristic of human beings experiencing similar threats, then the propositions listed above should apply to animals.

In the presentation of evidence in succeeding chapters, the interested student might consider whether these propositions are fulfilled or whether the hypothesis that control is a critical factor in stress remains a speculative assumption with intuitive appeal. It is hoped that in succeeding chapters some of the evidence on which these propositions are formulated will be made explicit.

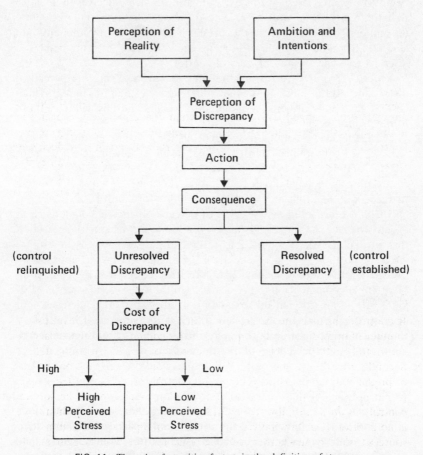

FIG. 1.1   The role of cognitive factors in the definition of stress.

B. A Model of Cognitive Factors in Stress and Control

Figure 1.1 provides a basic conceptualisation of a definition of stress in terms of perceived control over unpleasant environments. This conceptualisation assumes that stress is a change in homeostatic balance resulting in temporary or permanent perceived loss of control. The formulation provided will account for the stressful response to sudden life-threatening or noxious environmental conditions as well as for circumstances where the individual's own failure creates or exacerbates the perception of stress. The conceptualisation is based on ideas developed by Fisher (1984a).

The two fundamental ingredients are the perception of reality (the state of the external or internal world) and ambition. If the way reality appears is discrepant with the way a person would like it to be (perception of discrepancy), action is selected to rectify the situation. The individual may begin to perceive stress at this early stage if he also perceives in advance that there is little he will be able to do about the situation. Accidental encounters, life changes, or the presence of noxious environments are assumed to produce a state of homeostatic imbalance, creating perceived *discrepancy* which represents loss of control.

Action is required to restore the situation by resolving the perceived discrepancy. If this fails and the individual perceives that this matters (high cost), then a state of perceived high stress occurs and this will have input to the arousal system.

The reader will readily perceive that this formulation has much in common with a conceptualisation of normal problem-solving activity. Fisher (1984a) argued that stressful conditions are special classes of problems confronting an individual. For this reason stress may be seen as challenging by those who feel that they have the capability for control.

It will also be noted that the role of perceived personal competence as a factor in reaction to potential threats is underlined. A person who perceives that he has the skills required to resolve the discrepancy is in a quite different position from the person who perceives the loss of appropriate skills. Therefore, this conceptualisation of stress emphasises the perception of personal competence as a major factor in the response to stresses of all kinds. If we are to gain understanding of how an individual reacts and copes with short- or long-term, laboratory or life stresses, it is necessary to understand how the perception of personal competence, the main building block for the perception of control, is affected.

C. Stress, Control, and Strategic Response

A notion to be explored in later chapters is that there are different kinds of control that can be operated in different circumstances. Equally, there are different strategies or means of exercising control. Some strategies may be effective for the purpose intended; others may have adverse consequences for the individual. Mental disorders may arise from either failure to operate effective strategies or the operation of strategies which are partially effective but which carry unforeseen costs for the individual.

An important issue developed towards the end of the book is whether a person is free to choose from a selection of strategies or whether as he progresses through life, he is increasingly constrained by mental structures. Additionally, stressful conditions may act to constrain structure because cognitive processes on which selection or execution of strategies depend are changed. In these conditions a person may be less free to find effective coping techniques.

These are complex issues and we cannot pretend that they will be easily resolved. However, they are very interesting issues and there are implications for the approach of counsellors and therapists concerned with those facing life crises, mental disorder, or even physical ill health.

As this analysis develops towards the end of the book, it may be arguable that we are not in a strong position to test the propositions of the control model of stress nor to assert with total confidence that control should be part of the transactional definition of stress. In real life situations, having control does not mean pressing a button; it is more likely to involve making the best decisions to obtain a result consistent with aims. A person may appear to relinquish control quite willingly as when a dentist or doctor is consulted. However it could be argued that this is strategic behaviour because any person without dental skills and facilities should not tackle his or her own tooth care; allocation of this task to a skilled expert may be a powerful aspect of the exercise of control.

2 Stress and Control

"Control" is a complex term generally taken to imply power or mastery over the environment. The perception of control is based on facts in cognition. An individual may utilise these facts to decide whether he can attenuate or terminate situations which are disliked or threatening.

In spite of the popularity of the notion that the level of control might affect the reaction to all kinds of events such as life events and accidents as well as being a factor in stress at work, there has until relatively recently been very little serious attempt to understand the complexity of the relationship between stress and control in any detail. There is, however, a research literature involving work with both animals and human beings that brings three issues into focus. The first is whether having control is really stress-reducing on all occasions. The second is whether benefits are due to having control as compared with increased predictability. The third is whether all individuals elect to have control over what happens to them.

Before these issues can be considered, it is necessary to examine some of the complex issues that experimental studies with animals and human beings have addressed. These studies are presented in some detail for the student not only because it is believed that the issues raised serve to illustrate the complexity of the topic, but because they raise important issues as to whether control is a necessary condition for the creation or amelioration of stress.

There are two main issues addressed by the sections in this chapter. The first is whether the availability of control does indeed reduce the effect of a stressful exposure in animals and people; the second is whether, if it does so, the effect is due to the perception that control is possible or whether it is due to *enhanced predictability* of the noxious events. An interesting aspect arising from the first issue is that having responsibility for the exercise of control may *create a different source of stress*. Thus, how control is operated may be as critical as whether control is available at all.

1.   ANIMAL STUDIES OF THE PREDICTABILITY AND CONTROL OF NOXIOUS STIMULATION

Work with animals exposed to treatments of electric shock has provided a major contribution to the understanding of the importance of the *availability of instrumental responses* that facilitate avoidance or escape of noxious stimulation, as a major factor in determining a number of reactions indicative of stress. The research literature contains an interesting contradiction: Although the weight of evidence suggests that absence of an appropriate instrumental response (helplessness) results in more stressful symptoms than conditions where a response is available, studies with "executive" monkeys (see following text) suggest that the reverse might be the case.

Early studies with rats by Mowrer and Viek (1948) showed that when hungry rats could turn off the electrification of the grid on the floor of the cage by leaping into the air, they were more likely to approach and eat food 10 seconds before each shock than were rats who were yoked to the executive animals (in that they received the shock the executive animals failed to avoid). The yoked (helpless) groups showed much more disruption of the previously learned positive responses to food. Thus it seemed that having instrumentality available decreased the fear of anticipated shock. Although Miller (1963) pointed out that the animals with instrumental responses could systematically learn to minimise the pain produced by shock by reducing contact with the floor, it could still be argued that such behaviour gave the animal a form of control not available to the yoked animals.

Against the view that instrumentality provides a basis for the reduction of adverse effects of shock, studies on primates by Brady et al. (1958) suggested that it might *increase* stress. Monkeys who could avoid shock by pressing a lever every 20 seconds developed gastrointestinal ulcers, whereas the yoked controls did not. Weiss (1968) criticises the design of these experiments on the grounds that the monkeys who were given instrumental control ("executive monkeys") had been selected on the basis of their ability to learn avoidance responses on pre-experimental trials. Evidence cited by Weiss (1968) from a study by Sines et al. (1963) suggests that rats susceptible to ulcers are those who show rapid learning of avoidance responses.

Work by Weiss (1968) with albino rats showed that those who could avoid shock delivered to the floor of the cage by leaping up to a platform were less vulnerable to the effects of stress than those who were helpless. The design was such that having escaped, the animal would then be pushed gently back on to the floor of the cage again (a situation over which there was no control). Body weight and stomach lesions provided the criteria of stressful response. The yoked animals with no control over shock showed a *greater decrease in body weight* (largely because of failure to gain weight after the stress sessions), in comparison with the avoidance condition group. The differences were apparent after only one exposure to the stress situation.

In a second experiment the stress levels were increased because animals were restrained in small tubular cages and the duration of the stress session was 20 hours; the principal variable under study was the *severity of stomach lesions*. Avoidance responding by the avoidance group occurred on an average of 35% of the trials. Both avoidance and yoked animals lost more weight than non-shock animals. The yoked, helpless animals developed more extensive lesions than avoidance and non-shock animals. Again, the increased vulnerability of the helpless animal was confirmed.

There are some important points of difference with the studies by Brady and colleagues. Firstly, Brady used primates and there was some degree of preselection. Secondly, the sessions used by Brady were conducted for different work schedules over a period of days, whereas the Weiss study involved durations of up to, but no greater than, 20 hours.

A later study by Weiss (1971a) investigated the effect of warning signals in circumstances where the animals could avoid or escape shock. This was partly instigated because of the executive monkey results. In the design used by Brady and colleagues, shock was not preceded by a warning signal. The design was such that the animal avoided shock by means of a response but had no warning to provide the necessary information about the imminence of shock. Therefore the animal was required to make a temporal discrimination about when shock would occur and then respond appropriately. Weiss (1971a) argued that "having to maintain a coping response in an unsignalled shock situation might be more stressful than being unable to perform any effective response (p. 1)." In Weiss's study, there were three different kinds of warning signal and "no shock," "executive," and yoked (helpless) groups. In the first warning signal condition a tone preceded shock by several seconds. For those with avoidance facility, the warning signal indicated that a coping response was required. For the yoked group, the signal would merely warn of the possible occurrence of shock (depending on the behaviour of the executive animal). In a second condition no signal preceded shock. This was the Sidman-type avoidance task as used by Brady and colleagues. In the third "progressive signal" condition, warning tones increased in frequency and amplitude leading up to the shock. Weiss argued that this provided an external clock providing the animals with more information to predict shock. The occurrence of ulcers and steroid concentration in the blood provided the two dependent variables used as an index of stress.

Confirmation that the provision of feedback which is relevant ameliorates the stress is provided by the fact that avoidance groups in the progressive signal condition benefited most.

In all three signal conditions, avoidance-escape animals showed less extensive gastric ulceration than yoked groups. The largest difference was found for the progressive-signal condition. However, avoidance-escape animals developed more ulceration in the no-signal condition than in the signal condition. Although the degree of severity of ulceration was not greater than for the yoked groups, the effect does confirm that the circumstance of Brady's executive monkeys may have been particularly stressful. Finally, even for the yoked groups the no-signal condition produced more extensive ulceration than the signal condition, thus confirming the ameliorating effects of warning signals.

Therefore, although the presence of the instrumental means for avoiding shock reduced its stressful properties, the presence of a warning signal had a further ameliorating effect. The results point to a need to understand the role of psychological factors in conditions associated with stress. Predictability and avoidability/escapability are critical factors in this respect. Weiss (1971b) located two critical variables: the *number of coping responses* and the *amount of appropriate feedback*. The number of coping responses was found to covary with the tendency to ulceration and the relationship was monotonic.

Appropriate feedback was found to be a critical factor in that if responses immediately produce stimuli that are relevant to the stressor, ulcerogenic stress will not occur. Successful avoidance produces circumstances in which such feedback is not received. On the other hand, escape does provide a sudden change in feedback. In the above experiment, provision of the progressive-signal condition provided relevant feedback because any response made terminated the tone and provided information necessary for the perception that the instrumental response was functional.

Fisher (1984a) has emphasised the possible importance of the provision of stress-relevant feedback as a factor in the perception of control. Avoidance strategies are likely to be associated with high anxiety and in some cases, distress, because appropriate feedback is not present.

The animal studies involving the presence or absence of instrumentality suggest that control is a strong factor which ameliorates the response to stress. Warning signals (predictability) also have an ameliorating effect. The findings that both responsibility *and* helplessness have stressful properties can be reconciled by the analysis that suggests that it is the provision of feedback about effectiveness that is important. Brady's monkeys were, because of absence of relevant feedback, effectively helpless: It is perceived authority that counts even in animals.

2. HUMAN STUDIES OF THE EFFECTS OF PREDICTABILITY AND CONTROL

In the wider psychological research literature the importance of authority as an aspect of control is clear. Lazarus (1966) defines control in terms of reversibility; a person has control if he can reverse a state of affairs. In turn, this implies that there is an *available means* of avoiding, attenuating, or terminating a condition perceived as undesirable or unpleasant and that there is competence in this respect. Competence and control may be very closely linked; the former is a precondition for the latter.

White (1959) defines competence as an organism's capacity to interact effectively with its environment and argues that competence in the widest sense is positively sought. Diamond (1939) developed the notion that higher animals have sensori-neural systems which demand stimulation and which force the environment to *provide* stimulation. On this formulation there is *motivation towards creating changed consequences* by means of activity. The term "felt control" (White, 1959) additionally implies that competence is represented in cognition in such a way that it can be experienced. This raises the important point that the exercise of control is appraised during or after an experience and can be used to generate advance predictions about future potential. The belief in a capacity to put knowledge into effect adequately without generating errors and lapses is an important determinant of felt control: An individual may know that he *can* drive a car but may believe himself to be a bad driver because of the errors he makes from time to time. The perception of errors and slips may colour the impressions gained about control for particular situations.

There are three very useful reviews of the complex experimental literature on how the presence or absence of control influences the response to unpleasant circumstances. They are those of Averill (1973), Miller (1979), and Thompson (1981). These authors develop different definitions and descriptive classifications of control and their contributions in this respect will be examined later.

The main features of experimental studies concerning the effects of control in human subjects involve manipulations of variables such as exposure to loud noise, or electric shock. Dependent variables are usually reported experiences, tolerance, performance on a concurrent or subsequent task, and physiological responses.

One paradigm that provides evidence of the importance of control involves self-administration of noxious conditions. It is assumed that if a person delivers unpleasant stimulation to himself, he has control over it. He could reverse or postpone the decision to self-present shock, although it could be argued that the agreement he makes with the experimenter to take part in the experiment reduces control: He cannot reverse the decision on all trials because he would no longer be taking part. Early studies by Haggard (1943) showed that self-administered shock resulted in smaller skin conductance changes than experimenter-induced shock and was perceived as less unpleasant. In addition, the response to shock was more readily extinguished and subjects were more aware of contingencies. A problem with interpreting this result is that self-administration confounds *control* with *predictability*. The individual can prepare to receive stimulation and even operate a strategy for reducing its effects.

Experimental studies have demonstrated a marked preference for certainty and predictability even when there is no association with adverse conditions. However, Berlyne (1960) indicated that highly repetitive conditions lead to boredom and unpleasant experiences associated with raised arousal. Therefore, predictability may in some circumstances lead to changes that imply raised stress levels.

Pervin (1963) carried out a detailed study of the role of prediction and control in conditions of threat, in order to try to partition the effects of control and predictability. Control was manipulated by either allowing the subject to control the application of electric shock bursts (S-control), or allowing the experimenter to have control (E-control). There were three conditions of predictability (signal; no signal; inconsistent signal) provided by means of three different lights which indicated when the shock would occur. The subject had one switch that produced shock and another that did not, but which allowed shock to be E-controlled. The data collected included: (1) preferences—the subject was asked to indicate which of the conditions was preferred; (2) pain ratings; (3) anxiety ratings; (4) subjective reports of experiences; (5) reaction times for decisions.

Results showed that largely in terms of personal assessment, there was preference for S-control. A number of reasons were provided: (1) subjects imagined that shock duration might be shortened; (2) greater correspondence between switch and shock was assumed to reduce surprise; (3) mastery, freedom, and choice were seen as desirable. Those subjects who disliked control reported that: (1) it resulted in conflict about whether to press the switch or not; (2) it increased concentration on anxiety-producing signals; (3) it represented unnecessary punishment of the self.

Preference was also expressed for predictable shock occurrence. Subjects reported that they could prepare for shock by developing an attitude of acceptance towards it or by bracing the limb physically. They could also rest in no-shock conditions. By contrast, absence of predictability led to conflicting expectations and experience of surprise, frustration, anger, and depression. Predicting no-shock and receiving shock was perceived as most painful. Predicting shock and receiving no-shock was perceived as "disturbing" and the subject was left with no release of tension. In the inconsistent signal condition, subjects reported seeing the warning light as "tricky" or "malicious."

Pervin reports that the differences between S-control and E-control were small. Most of the effects were in terms of *self-reported preferences*. The greatest difference occurred at the beginning of the experiment and for the no-signal condition. Thus the effect of control may have interacted with anxiety. Overall, Pervin emphasises *psychological meaning* and suggests that a feeling of mastery is preferable.

With regard to predictability, the rating data indicated that what was important was the relationship between the prediction and the event: Lack of predictability was perceived as unpleasant and disturbing. However, predictability became less preferable and less anxiety-reducing with increasing trials. The effect is interpreted by Pervin to mean that complete predictability is more desirable in new, highly threatening situations but less desirable in repetitive, less threatening situations, and underlines the role of circumstantial factors as moderators of predictability effects.

As mentioned above, the problem with the Pervin study is that the aversiveness of various combinations of levels of predictability and control was really only evident in terms of subjective reports of preference, anxiety ratings, or pain ratings. There was no evidence of benefits on physiological response.

Emphasis was given to individual differences in preference by Ball and Vogler (1971); subjects were given an initial choice of being self-shocked or machine-shocked. Preference was assessed in terms of whether subjects developed a consistent pattern of self-shocking or machine-shocking. In addition, once a subject had developed a consistent pattern in a chosen condition, he was given the choice of continuing with it but at the cost of receiving two shocks in quick succession rather than one. Shock intensity was adjusted so as to be painful but not unbearable. After seven randomly delivered shocks had been presented, a subject was given an instruction of how to self-deliver shocks and was allowed to experience self-shock. The subject was then given the choice of self-shock or randomly delivered machine-shocks.

Of 39 subjects, 25 chose self-shock in preference to machine-shock and 21 of these subjects claimed that it was to avoid uncertainty. Those 25 subjects were then given a choice between single machine-shock and double shock which was self-delivered. In spite of the penalty of experiencing twice the shock, 7 subjects preferred to continue with their original self-shock choice.

The strong preference for self-shock over machine-shock cannot easily be interpreted in terms of whether control or predictability is the critical factor because self-shock confounds predictability and control. However, the study contributes useful information about possible reasons for accepting machine-shock conditions for those who chose to do so. Out of the 11 subjects who chose machine-shock originally, 4 subjects were prepared to accept the double-shock penalty rather than change (Ball & Vogler, 1971).

One subject reported that it was "enjoyable" and the remainder that although the shock was painful they were "curious" and preferred the excitment of random delivery. In a post-test interview one subject, who was religious, indicated that machine-shock was consistent with a personal philosophy of enduring pain in life; suffering was a form of acquiescence to God's will. A second subject reported trying to be belligerent: "I was trying to foil you. It was a contest and to give in would have been a concession (p. 1200)." The authors comment that the subject saw the test as a sign of toughness and his self-esteem was at stake. The authors also point out that forcing the experimenters to play their hand enables a subject to be assured that he is not as vulnerable as he fears he may be. He demonstrates a degree of control by setting the time and place of confrontation. The authors cite the novel *Cool Hand Luke* (Pearce, 1965), where the hero submits to brutal tests of ability to survive punishment. For Luke the worst punishment is bearable if the unseen tormentor can be confronted. Control is gained by *precipitating* the encounter. In an autobiography by Dolgun (1965) of his experiences as a victim of interrogation procedures in the Soviet Union during Stalin's regime, a similar theme is echoed, in that Dolgun implies that he gains esteem and satisfaction from controlling the behaviour of the guards. Fisher (1984a) termed this "control by irrelevant means" since there was no control over (relevant) sources of deprivation and punishment.

In the study by Ball and Vogler (1971), one of the subjects who had opted for double machine-shock responded "I am very resistant to authority. I thought that you wanted to see if I could take self-shock when the machine began to give me two shocks (p. 1201)." Yet another observation by a subject who found it hard to decide between double machine-shock and single self-shock was "I did not like being put in a robot position (lever pushing) (p.1202)."

Some of the subjects who found it difficult to decide between self-shock and machine-shock reported that the two alternatives were equally unpleasant. However, a few of these subjects did not accept the instructions as valid and continued to experiment with contingencies to see if there was a way of escaping shock entirely. One subject reported choosing double machine-shock because "I thought that by taking double shocks the experiment would end in one-half the time (p. 1202)." Yet another subject evolved a different logic for machine-shock: "The possibility of not getting shocked exists if you do not do it to yourself (p. 1202)."

The authors of the study refer to these reported strategies as "deviant" and emphasise that investigation of the reasoning involved shows sources of reinforcement involving idiosyncratic and distorted views of the experiment. This raises the important point that the perception of control may depend on *personal meaning attached to a particular situation*. Individuals may perceive a situation in terms that will enable them to accept the worst or find an interpretation which makes the worst palatable; or may seek out the worst in order to gain long-term advantages. In even simple threatening situations, what appears like loss of control, passivity, and helplessness may be a *yet more subtle form of the exercise of control*.

Preference for predictability has also been examined in the context of delayed stimulation. Badia et al. (1966) used a design in which a warning was followed by electric shock after a short or long delay. Subjects showed a verbal and behavioural preference for short delays. Maltzman and Wolff (1970) used a structured forced-choice situation to investigate the preference for short versus long delay in the presentation of noxious levels of white noise (100 dB). Immediate presentation involved noise delivery 1 second after the word "now." Delayed presentation of the noise was 15–25 seconds later, with an average of 20 seconds. In one condition, subjects were asked to listen to the noises because they would be asked to judge them later; in another condition no such instruction was given. A main purpose of the experiment was to record the galvanic skin response (GSR) evoked by noxious stimulation in the immediate and delayed conditions, in addition to personal preferences. The results showed that most, but not all, of the group (36 out of 40 subjects) preferred *immediate* noise to delayed noise. Of the four who did not, two subjects favoured the delayed condition. Mean preference ratings overall were 1.75 (immediate) and 2.93 (delayed) on the pleasant–unpleasant scale and were significantly different. There was a smaller GSR for the short delay (mean GSR 1.61) as compared with the long delay (mean GSR 2.06).

The authors admit that the immediate and delayed conditions differ in that in the delayed condition, the delay is variable. They quote an unpublished study by Overbaugh which showed that with a *fixed* 20-second delay, 19 out of 20 subjects prefer the immediate condition. Three possible explanations of the preference for immediate noxious stimulation are considered. The first is that the delayed condition allows anxiety levels to rise because the subject predicts the noxious event and induces raised emotionality in himself as a consequence. The second explanation is that a short delay permits the individual to develop *preparatory responses* which reduce the aversive nature of the noise in a way that the long delay does not. In the study by Ball and Vogler (described above) one subject described a preference for predictable shock because he could brace his leg. Perhaps the long delay introduced more uncertainty, thus reducing the possibility for such preparatory orienting action. Maltzman and Wolff (1970) finally propose a third hypothesis which is preferred: They assume that the "now" signal evokes an orienting response which distracts from the effects of the noise, whereas the "later" signal loses such an inhibitory effect because of the time delay. "In other words, paying attention to one event distracted from, inhibited attention and the accompanying emotional disturbance induced by a second event, the noise (p. 79)."The "focus of attention" explanation is an interesting one; it could be part of a strategy to avoid being affected by the noise or it could be automatically engendered by the conditions of the experiment and not consciously perceived. Although in neither case (immediate or delayed) does the subject have physical control over exposure to very loud noise, it could be argued that the basis for attentional control is provided. The sustaining of attentional control is more difficult in the delayed than in the immediate condition simply because of the fact that it has to be sustained for longer.

The indication that subjects do not have to *operate* the instrumental means of control in order for instrumentality to be effective is provided by Glass and Singer (1972). Firstly, their studies showed that at least for human subjects the mere belief that there is a means for exercising control over noxious stimulation, should it be required, is a *sufficient condition for amelioration* of the effect of the stress. Secondly, the studies showed that it was possible for the amelioration to be evident not at the time, but *afterwards*. In other words, the effect of having had control may carry over to produce benefits later.

The studies were concerned with the effects of noise on tasks such as number comparisons, addition, and letter search. The tasks were administered in four conditions of noise distraction produced by combining foreign-speaking voices, mimeograph machine noise, and a typewriter. One group received noise levels of 110 dB for 9 seconds at the end of every minute of the session. A second group received the same noise exposures but at random intervals. Two other groups received the same fixed or random noise levels but at 56 dB (see Glass, Singer, & Friedman, 1969). The effect of the loud noise was to produce distraction effects initially, which became less marked with time. There was an interaction with task complexity; physiological measures showed that the more complex tasks had greater effects associated with the noise. However, after the noise exposures subjects were presented with two further tasks. One was a coping task designed to be frustrating. Subjects had to trace over all lines in each of four designs without being allowed to lift the pencil from the paper or trace over any line twice. Two of the conditions were insoluble. The second task was a proof-reading task. Ten errors were presented on each of seven pages of an essay. These were to be detected during a 15 minute period.

The two tasks provided different dependent variables. The tracing task was designed to measure persistence. It was found that subjects who had previously received noise at random intervals made fewer attempts to solve the problem than those who received no noise or noise at fixed intervals. Thus, the experience of uncontrollable unpleasant stimulation has a carry-over effect to a new situation with a different task.

3. ISSUES CONCERNING THE EFFECTS OF
CONTROL ON AVERSIVE STIMULATION

A. Control Typologies

The main issue of importance is the extent to which the presence or absence of control affects the response to stressful conditions. Related is the issue of the different types of control that may be operated in different situations. Instrumental control achieved by depressing a switch or lever is markedly different in character from, for example, making a decision about a situation. Terms such as "jurisdiction" and "discretion" (see Broadbent, 1983; Fisher, 1984a; Karasek, 1979) provide more subtle labels for control as operated in real life.

Three reviews (Averill, 1973; Miller, 1979; Thompson, 1981) have sought to provide descriptive typologies of control as well as providing useful accounts of research findings.

Averill (1973) distinguishes "behavioural control," defined in terms of the availability of a response that can modify objective characteristics; "cognitive control," which involves the processing of relevant material to reduce stress; and "decisional control," as the choice between different possible courses of action.

Miller (1979) identifies "instrumental control" where a "person is able to make a response that modifies the aversive event (p. 287)," and points out that the response can be active or passive and can involve avoidance or escape. A variant of instrumental control is "perceived instrumental control"—subjects believe that control is being exerted over the aversive event but objectively this is not the case. The second type of control is defined as "self-administration" where a subject delivers noxious stimulation of himself. Both instrumental control and self-administration are conditions where control and predictability are likely to be confounded. The third type of control distinguished by Miller is "potential control," in which a person believes he has control available but refrains from using the response. This features in the paradigm used by Glass and Singer described above; a switch for terminating the noise is available but not usually used (see Glass, Singer, & Friedman, 1969; Glass, Rheim, & Singer, 1971).

Miller makes some useful distinctions concerning the psychological differences between these categories of control. In the case of instrumental control, control and predictability may be confounded. In the case of *perceived* instrumental control, Miller points out that perceived control may be varied, but differences in predictability are minimised because the stressor occurs independently of responding. A point worth making in this context is the difference between subjective and objective reality. If the subject believes there is control, then events should seem subjectively predictable. Fisher (1984a) has argued that predictability may be a building block in the perception of control in complex situations. Certainly it could be argued that it is a necessary if not sufficient condition for the perception of control.

Thompson's typology of control evolves from detailed consideration of difficulties with the Averill and Miller typologies (Thompson, 1981). Averill's typology is argued to be unsatisfactory in that "cognitive control" does not refer to control at all and use of the term is tautological because cognitive control is "that which reduces long-term stress." Therefore, by definition it is stress reducing. There is no reason to suppose that information gain per se is a form of cognitive control. Averill's use of the term "decisional control" is argued by Thompson to be less than useful—firstly, because participants are argued to have decisional control for ethical reasons; secondly, because decisional control involves choice and is considered to be a form of behavioural control. Miller's typology is argued to be useful methodically but not psychologically distinct. Thompson illustrates this by pointing out that instrumental control (the ability to make an appropriate response) is equivalent to potential control if the response option is not exercised.

Thompson (1981) introduces a four-category typology to circumvent the objections she lists. Firstly, there is behavioural control, defined as a "belief that one has a behavioural response available that can affect the aversiveness of an event (p. 90)." Behavioural control involves terminating or reducing the intensity or duration or changing the timing of an event. Secondly, there is cognitive control, which is "the belief that one has a cognitive strategy available that can affect the aversiveness of an event (p. 90)." The diverse assortment of cognitive strategies are argued by Thompson to be in need of typology. She favours a distinction between *avoidant strategies* and *non-avoidant* or *sensitising strategies*. The former are concerned with ignoring or denying the existence of the event. The latter focus on the event involving heightened sensitivity and rumination. Thirdly, there is information which is delivered to the potential recipient of the noxious event. Different information manipulations lead subjects to react differently to stressful events: "it is probably not useful to think of information as one conceptually homogeneous variable, since there is no reason to expect that these different forms of information will have the same effects on stress (p. 91)." Finally, "retrospective control" is defined in terms of "beliefs about the causes of a past event (p. 91)." Retrospective control as defined by Thompson is a form of attributional analysis about the cause of the event.

In reviewing the research literature on the effects of control of various kinds on stresses such as shock, thermal pain, cold water, pressure, loud noise, photographs of unpleasant events, and intelligence test administration, Thompson combines the forms of control (behavioural, cognitive, informational, and retrospective) with the timing of control in relation to the noxious event (anticipatory period, impact, past event). Summarising across a wide research literature Thompson concludes that behavioural control can: (1) reduce the aversiveness of an event; (2) reduce pre-event anxiety; (3) reduce anticipatory arousal; (4) reduce interference on tasks performed concurrently; and (5) influence the post-event effects of experience. Thompson's review of the evidence suggests that there is no reliable effect on experienced painfulness or stressfulness of the event. This is not in keeping with the results of Pervin (1963), reviewed previously, which indicated that S-controlled shock was associated with changes in preference and less self-rated anxiety, although differences were not large.

"Cognitive control" is argued by Thompson (1981) to have positive effects on the experience of an aversive event and on anticipatory and post-event effects. An acknowledged difficulty is the form and variety of cognitive strategies: "some are more effective than others (p. 95)."

"Information" is suggested by Thompson to be less reliable in ameliorating effects. Although she argues that information will not necessarily reduce the self-reports of pain, there is other evidence that self-reports and tolerance are influenced by the kind of information provided (e.g. see Staub and Kellett, 1972; Sternbach, 1968).

"Retrospective control" (equated with attributional decisions about the cause of events) is argued to be a factor determining the reaction to misfortune. A useful illustration is the reaction of accident victims to the event (Bulman & Wortman, 1977). Those victims who blamed themselves were more likely to cope successfully. One reason might be that they retained control over whether or not the accident happened again.

The above typologies are based on analysis of paradigms used in experiments measuring the effects of controllability of some form on the response to noxious stimulation. The differences in typology provide some indications of how difficult adequate conceptualisation of control is; its form may vary according to time and circumstance as well as with the nature of the subjects—human or animal. The evidence is not conclusive as to whether control always attenuates the effects of stress. Miller (1979) concludes that individuals prefer instrumental control over an aversive event, prefer self-administration, and that when control is possible are less hurt by the aversive event and less aroused when waiting for it. On most operational definitions this supports a hypothesis of stress reduction with control. However, there is little evidence of lowered arousal at the time of occurrence of the noxious event, which is against the stress-reduction view.

B. Explanations of Stress Reduction with Control

One question of interest is how the presence of control could have any ameliorating effects on the response to stress. There are a number of possible theoretical explanations and it is conceivable that no explanation will be sufficient for the varied benefits obtained from the provision of different forms of control.

i. Control as Predictability

An explanation that takes into account the personal preference for self-administration of noxious stimulation and the preference for predictable stimulation in the majority of subjects, is that control *guarantees* predictability. If a person self-administers shock, he knows exactly when it will occur. The *safety signal hypothesis* proposed by Seligman, Maier, and Solomon (1971) assumes that a person can fit in periods of relaxation when he knows that no noxious event is likely to occur. Therefore, he gains periods of respite from anxiety when noxious events are predictable. A similar explanation is that overload is reduced because a person does not have to keep searching for cues which anticipate the noxious event. The explanation begs the question a little, by assuming that the individual searches for cues which signal the occurrence of a noxious event. Perhaps the benefit of predictability implies that there are strategies for enduring the event and that these must be mobilised. Such explanations will also account for the finding that subjects prefer immediate to delayed onset of noxious stimulation (see Maltzman & Wolff, 1970) because delay introduces loss of predictability.

There are other reasons why predictability should be advantageous. A predictable event requires less attention, and less arousal is likely to be associated (see Berlyne, 1960; Sokolov, 1963). This may mean that the effect of a painful event is not augmented by its surprise and alarm value when it is predictable and therefore that overall, response levels are more moderate. The provision of a facility for instrumental control and for self-administration would both be assumed to provide reduction in alarm value because of predictability. However, as described earlier in the chapter, not all subjects choose self-administration and some may even incur a double shock in order not to self-administer shock. The "predictability" explanation of the effects of control is simplistic in this respect (see Ball & Vogler, 1971).

On the hypothesis that the effect of control is nothing more than the influence of predictability as a factor in performance once predictability is provided as a facility for the group without control, there should be no difference. There is evidence from animal studies to suggest that predictability alone may be a very powerful factor in mediating the effects of stress. Weiss (1970) examined the effects of the predictability of electric shock on a variety of stress responses such as stomach ulceration, body temperature, corticosteroid levels, and body weight changes. Rats that received unpredictable shock showed greater somatic stress reactions and more stress-induced pathology than those who received the same shocks heralded by a warning signal. Unpredictable shock resulted in more severe stomach ulceration, a greater rise in body temperature, higher plasma corticosterone concentration, more body weight loss, and greater depression of food and water intake. Weiss considers two explanations: (1) that the warning may serve to inform the animal of exact time of occurrence; (2) that the warning may inform the animal of the period of safety (Seligman's safety signal hypothesis). The two signal conditions do not permit comparison of the effects of earlier choice, but since one of the warning signal conditions involved a single tone whereas the other involved a succession of tones lasting for 30 seconds built up in pitch and intensity, it could be argued that there was less time for safety to occur and thus a test of the safety signal hypothesis was provided. Results supported the hypothesis in that the latter group were found to have greater ulceration. However, as Weiss acknowledges, the group with the succession of signals were better informed. A point not made by Weiss but which might be important is that the rise in signal intensity and pitch might well have proved stressful per se.

In human subjects an attempt was made by Geer and Maisel (1972) to separate the effects of prediction and control as factors determining autonomic responsiveness to the presentation of aversive photographs of dead bodies. Subjects in the group with control could terminate the aversive photographs; subjects with prediction were informed about time relationships but could not terminate the photographs. A third group had no control and no information about timing. Both control and predictability groups in turn were yoked to the third group so that the same exposure durations experienced by the group with control were received. Subjects with control exhibited lower GSR reactivity to the stimulus and the warning signal than subjects with predictability alone. The authors admitted that button pressing might have been a confounding factor because only the control group pressed the button. However, they point out that the effect of a button press is to *yield* a GSR (galvanic skin response) rather than inhibit one. The authors also argue against the idea that the button press could be a distraction. "The fact that the warning signal came on 10 seconds before the photographs were viewed for an average of 21.8 seconds made it unlikely that the subjects were so intently concentrating on the response that stimulus impact was reduced (p. 318)." The safety signal hypothesis was not supported at all by the results because spontaneous skin resistance response was lowest for the third group and the prediction and control groups did not differ.

Knowing about responses which are relevant in reducing shock also has beneficial effects greater than predictability alone: Geer, Davison, and Gatchel (1970) presented shock during a reaction-time task. Subjects were told that shock duration could be reduced from 6 to 3 seconds by maintaining fast reaction-time response levels. The predictability group was given information that the duration of the shock to be experienced was 3 seconds. Those subjects who could influence the duration of the shock produced fewer overall non-specific skin conductance responses and showed reduced skin conductance to shock compared with the no-control group. However, pain ratings made about the impact of shock did not differ between the two conditions.

Taken collectively, both sets of results for this particular paradigm suggest that being able to change a quality associated with noxious stimulation is more important than merely knowing about it. It could be argued that not only is control greater than some aspects of predictability, but also that having knowledge in advance about the properties of painful stimulation (in this case duration) is less important than having instrumental control over the same properties. One important feature of the two studies quoted is that the effects are not the same. In one case skin conductance is affected; in the other it is not, but the perception of pain is affected and post-experience performance is improved. Therefore the dependent variable that is sensitive to the effects of different conditions of predictability and control may change as a function of different experimental settings. Glass et al. (1973) claim that the subjects in their replication of the study by Geer et al. were more anxious to begin with.

The studies by Glass and Singer and associates involving the experience of loud noise also contribute important information concerning the predictability/controllability issue. The studies described earlier emphasise that merely having the means to switch off the noise is sufficient to ameliorate the effects on performance of tasks after the noise exposure. The important feature is that providing the switch, even though it was actually not used by subjects, was sufficient to benefit performance subsequently (Glass et al., 1969). Even when subjects were only able to operate the switch by asking another person to do it for them, the effect was apparent (Glass et al., 1971). Therefore the *belief that there is control* is a sufficient condition for ameliorating effects in conditions where predictability is not changed. It could be argued that in such a design the belief that there is the potential for predictability is as important as the belief that there is control, but predictability could only take the form of being able to terminate the event rather than determine any features of its occurrence. Perhaps of equal importance in these studies, is that the researchers found no evidence that potential control changed arousal during the task; neither was there any evidence of improved performance during the task. All the main results concerned post-impact performance although there was some evidence of reduced pain ratings (Glass et al., 1969). Glass and Singer (1972) propose that uncontrollability creates *feelings* of helplessness. This suggests a need to understand awareness of the particular aspects of instrumentality in circumstances surrounding noxious events and for a more detailed understanding of the influence of awareness of the state of controllability.

In summary, reducing controllability to predictability as an explanation of reduction in the response to noxious stimulation, may provide some basis for understanding reduced anticipatory anxiety. From Weiss's results, even in animals predictability of shock does itself have ameliorating properties. However, the predictability explanation does not provide an adequate explanation of why *potential* control is a sufficient condition for ameliorating effects. Nor does it predict that the effect of controllability is greater than temporal predictability alone, in circumstances where the experimental paradigm enables the two variables to be distinguished.

The following conclusions are justified: (1) predictability ameliorates the stressful effects of painful stimulation; (2) this is only true for some people and is manifest more in terms of self-assessment than physiological measures; (3) controllability has effects which are greater than predictability alone and are also manifest more in terms of self-assessments than in terms of physiological measures.

ii. Controllability as an Expectancy About Outcomes

The suggestion that uncontrollability creates "feelings" of helplessness (Glass & Singer, 1972), or that an individual seeks a "feeling of efficacy" or competence with respect to his environment (White, 1959), implies that awareness of the circumstances present is a critical factor that determines response in advance, at the time, or in the post-event period. Such ideas emphasise the need to find out more about what is meant by control and particularly by the *perception* that control is possible. The point of importance from evidence reviewed in this chapter is that if controllability is argued to be better able to account for ameliorating effects than predictability alone, the method whereby control can have such properties must be made more explicit.

The distinction mentioned above needs developing further before the issue can be considered. There are good grounds for supposing that individuals are motivated to seek control or mastery of the environment for its own sake, that it is biologically adaptive, and that failure to establish control may itself have unpleasant implications. This assumes that the establishment of control is desired in its own right. When the environment is already stressful because it provides noxious stimulation, the establishment of control takes on a new significance because it is the means by which the individual can restore equilibrium. The gaining of control could be seen both as a fundamental motive in its own right and a means for gaining homeostasis or equilibrium. There are two identifiable elements of control: (1) control for its own sake; (2) control as a means for maintaining homeostasis which may be reduced in stress situations.

Hendrick (1942) proposed that a major instinct was the development of the ability to master the environment. The instinct was argued to be so fundamental that it formed an inborn drive "to do" and "learn how to do." In terms reminiscent of Freudian concepts, Hendrick (1943) proposed that the instinct to master is a primary pleasure. A variant on Hendrick's proposals was developed by Fernichel (1945), who proposed that the reason mastery of the environment was sought is that it was anxiety-reducing. Not being able to control the environment creates anxiety. When the situation is mastered the ensuing anxiety reduction is actually pleasurable. White (1959) argued against Fernichel's view that the only reason for exploration and manipulation of the environment is fear of the environment. He proposed that competence is sought for its own sake. He thus comes close to Hendrick's views in suggesting that seeking competence is the major drive.

Diamond (1939) considers the sensori-neural system as the means by which higher animals maintain their relationships with the environment, and explores the notion that a higher organism responds in such a way as to *force the environment to stimulate it*. Schactel (1954) links focal attention to the fundamental aim of mastery of the environment. Sustained acts of focal attention are motivated by the need to obtain "mental grasp" on external events. Infants' attempts to inspect and manipulate objects are seen in terms of an autonomous capacity for object interest. It could be argued that control of the psychosocial environment is central to Piaget's theory of human sensori-motor development and provides the overall purpose for the gradual maturation of conceptual skills.

The possibility that personal control may be beneficial and linked with self-image has been developed by de Charms (1968). Individuals are argued to *need* to feel a sense of mastery and personal competence. Therefore, in cases where a stressful condition occurs in conditions of reduced control, a person firstly has to put up with the condition he feels unable to change. Secondly, he may perceive his own lack of competence as a further source of threat. It remains possible that both factors interact in real-life situations in a way in which they do not in a laboratory, where the decision to relinquish control and experience stress is made in advance.

a. The Minimax Hypothesis.   Miller (1979) proposed that when individuals control aversive events, they believe that the consequence is created by their own response. A stable source of change in consequence enables them to make the prediction that there is a guarantee that maximum future danger can be minimised. This helps to unify the idea that having control is a source of motivation and is of evolutionary advantage, with the notion that the presence of control ameliorates the effects of stress in ways not accounted for by predictability alone.

An experiment by Szpiler and Epstein (1976) provides a good illustration of the anticipatory advantages of the belief that control is possible. Subjects were told that shock would be delivered following a count-down. During the count-down the subjects were asked to tap rapidly; one group believed their tapping would avert shock; the yoked group were given no information which could lead them to believe this. Skin conductance responses showed lower anticipatory arousal for the group with avoidance. There was also lower anticipatory anxiety expressed by the avoidance groups. However, against the predictions of the minimax hypothesis, a study by Houston (1972) involved measuring heart rate during a cognitive task. One group of subjects believed they had control in that if they performed the task well enough they would not be shocked, whereas a second group were told they could be shocked occasionally. Neither groups were given control in that there was no shock. Houston's results suggested that those subjects who believed they had control showed more heart rate arousal.

The minimax hypothesis is couched in general terms which allow flexibility in interpretation. For example, a strict model of personal control would find it hard to account for circumstances where control is readily relinquished to "experts" or powerful others as when people seek dental or medical treatment. The minimax hypothesis has less difficulty with this since it is the *minimising* of *adverse effects in the long term* which counts. For the same reason the minimax hypothesis also predicts that there are benefits from anticipated personal control. The main criticism of the minimax hypothesis is that it is descriptive rather than explanatory. The focus is on the long-term strategy of minimising discomfort and threat, but there is little consideration on the cognitive basis of such decisions.

b. The Discrepancy Reduction Model. Fisher (1984a) proposed that the pleasure of control for its own sake and the ameliorating effects of control on stressful conditions should be explained in cognitive terms. It was proposed that the basis of the perception of control was the resolution of the discrepancy between intention and reality. According to this model a discrepancy exists the moment a goal is created. The goal might be specified in general terms (e.g. "the tomato should be halved") or in detail ("the tomato should be halved in such a way as to avoid getting juice on the table and so that it can be grilled easily. . ."). The *goal* is then compared with *reality* and the comparison is used to generate an action with the greatest perceived likelihood of resolving the discrepancy ("cut the tomato with the serrated-edged knife"). The result of the action then creates a change in reality and the resulting change in the original discrepancy is stored as a representation of the success of the action.

Under normal conditions, discrepancy reduction is part of the daily interaction with the environment and creates satisfaction from a sense of competence and control. This implies that the reference codes of discrepancy reduction can be consulted and represented in consciousness; the individual becomes aware of "felt control." If the discrepancy does not diminish as a result of action this implies lack of skill and knowledge, or lack of competence in the exercise of the skill. Under these conditions there is no reason to suppose that there will be anxiety. The action responsible for the undesired result is corrected and a new variant tried. Thus the loop is repeated until the discrepancy is modified. Such cycling is part of the planned, organised, purposeful aspects of daily activity as envisaged by Miller, Galanter, and Pribram (1960).

However, under some conditions there may be tension associated with discrepancy changes. This will occur if there is high cost attached to failure. Cost might be in terms of threat to life, pain, biological damage, or extreme discomfort. In these cases, failure to resolve the discrepancy is contained in a reference code that triggers a higher-level system which provides a memory for implications. If the implication has a high weighting then there is input to the arousal system.

The two-stage model, incorporating discrepancy reduction plus cost-analysis weighting, enables some sense to be made of some of the main findings in this chapter. First, in conditions where noxious stimulation is to occur, the individual formulates a goal which he believes may prevent or reduce the pain. If he is given facility for escape or avoidance he will use it. If not, he may evolve techniques for lessening the pain. An analogy is with the school boy who, before a beating, puts a book down his trousers. Various ways of reducing the impact of the noxious events may be tried and repeated if successful. Predictable conditions should facilitate the operation of these techniques. Provision of information about noxious stimulation should be helpful for the same reason. Discrepancy modification which is desired, leads the individual to be able to anticipate "least possible hurt." In all cases where he can escape or attenuate the actual event, the same state of affairs would be reached. Failure to predict or control should produce an unresolved discrepancy, which is assumed to provide an input to the second-stage, higher-level appraisal system concerned with cost.

In the case of avoidance behaviour the essential feedback for discrepancy reduction is not provided precisely because behaviour if successful means that the noxious event is not encountered. In terms of the model the discrepancy remains unmodified and there is input to the high-level appraisal system which evaluates the cost of failure to resolve each discrepancy.

Post-event benefits are more difficult to explain. Encounters with threatening events which turn out to have successful (threat-reduction) outcomes are likely to be as personally satisfying as other more straightforward manipulation of the environment. If benefits are to occur post-task, the "halo effect" of previous success must encourage raised effort levels, raised attempts to find successful strategies, or to find evidence of success subsequently.

According to the discrepancy-reduction model, the control facility may not necessarily need to be operated. It is sufficient that the individual *believes* that the switch will work and could be used if needed. If the individual never tries the switch, he does not disconfirm this expectancy. Therefore he can continue to gain the benefits of "expected" discrepancy reduction in terms of internal reference codes. One may not need actually to cut a tomato in half to know that such a task is possible.

The two-stage model proposed allows for dependent variables to be differentially affected by circumstance. It is possible that failure to reduce the discrepancy across successive trials will not necessarily be stressful. Therefore personal preference for control may be expressed but there may be no sign of alarm in terms of measures of arousal increase. When noxious stimulation is involved it becomes more likely that a high weighting will be given to a failure to reduce the discrepancy across trials. There will, therefore, be increased likelihood of increased alarm as well as increased personal assessment of discomfort.

Before discussing the issue of the cognitive basis of control further, it is necessary to consider the experimental evidence that suggests that individuals assess control by noting and representing successive contingencies between action and outcome. There is now substantial evidence to suggest that although people are able to summarise action and outcome evidence they are not likely to be "ideal statisticians"; bias and preconception may dominate the subjective impression of control and "positive" associations between action and outcome may form the principal basis for impressions. Behaviour in these situations may be strategic, involving awareness of the structure of events, the context and the perception of demand. These propositions are considered in the next two chapters.

3 Acquiring the Evidence About Control

In the previous chapter "control" was defined basically in terms of *mastery, power,* or *reversibility.* The point was made that control may be a determinant of what is stressful or may be a factor which determines how stressful a noxious environment appears to be. In animal research, escape or avoidance facilities seem to reduce the risk of pathology associated with a stressful event such as electric shock. In human research, experiments show that although control and predictability are often confounded, both are sought by a greater proportion of a population and the presence of control seems to be particularly associated with lowered anticipatory arousal, better post-event performance, greater tolerance, and less perceived pain. Nevertheless, there are some subjects, generally less than a third of any population, who opt for unpredictable or uncontrollable events; their motives for doing so may indicate that the total situation is viewed from a different perspective.

It is assumed in both animal and human studies that the facilities provided are somehow perceived by the subject as being instrumental and capable of effecting change. This raises the question of how such information is acquired. An issue of importance is whether there is an appraisal that involves *awareness* of the relatedness of action and outcome, or whether the perception of control is founded on the passive bonding of contiguous associations. The same issue is evident in debates in contemporary learning theory; but this is not surprising given that the assessment of control involves learning.

One possibility is that a person behaves strategically in acquiring evidence. A person may note the circumstances prevailing in a particular environment (including stressful circumstances) and may utilise this information in deciding which of a number of contingent relationships may be important. Before discussing this further, some aspects of the debate evident in contemporary learning theory are summarised.

1.   CLASSICAL CONDITIONING AND AWARENESS

Traditionally, learning theory has always been concerned with contingent relationships of one kind or another. There are two identifiable kinds of relationships: Those between stimuli (stimulus associations), or between stimulus and response (stimulus–response associations). In the former case, the organism is typically presented with a stimulus (unconditioned stimulus, UCS) to which it produces a response (the unconditioned response, UCR) and a second signal (the conditioned stimulus, CS) is made to occur in advance in close temporal proximity. After relatively few repeated pairings, the individual begins to produce behaviour characteristic of the unconditioned response to the conditioned stimulus (conditioned response, CR). Thus, in the terminology of classical conditioning, he has learned to associate CS and UCS and responds to CS occurrence with CR which is reminiscent of UCR.

Any learning paradigm which involves two variables can be described by few possibilities ($A–B$; $\bar{A}–B$; $A–\bar{B}$; $\bar{A}–\bar{B}$; where $\bar{A}$ means not A and $\bar{B}$ means not B). In a laboratory design some of these combinations may be omitted; thus in a typical conditioning paradigm $A–B$ is repeatedly presented and the organism learns to produce the response he normally produces to B, when A occurs.

Contemporary learning theorists distinguish a cognitive model of conditioning in which awareness of contingency rules evolves, from automatic bonding of responses. In the former case the individual acquires a model of the world; in the latter case he acquires a chain of S–S associations.

Even in cases where the full range of binary combinations is possible some authors prefer to explain data in terms of automatic bonding: Rescorla (1969) provides an interpretation in which positive and negative contingencies create excitatory and inhibitory associations respectively, and provide a basis for learning that only some CS–UCS cases are correlated. The idea that an animal may learn that CS and UCS are uncorrelated is inherent in McKintosh's notion of "learned irrelevance." McKintosh (1975) reported that random pairings of CS and UCS stimuli interfere with learning of associations and he proposed that there may be attentional mediation so that the organism is learning to ignore the stimuli which do not result in reinforcement.

A. Dissociation of Cognitive and Automatic Factors in Conditioning

A substantial contribution to the understanding of a very complex literature concerned with the issue of the involvement of cognitive activity in classical conditioning, was provided by Brewer (1974). Because of space limitations only a brief synopsis is provided here; the interested student is advised to read Brewer's own very detailed review.

The cognitive model of classical conditioning depends on the role of *awareness* in learning. The cognitive hypothesis as defined by Brewer assumes that human subjects come to a conditioning experiment not knowing what to expect, and during successive CS–UCS pairings each subject develops a *conscious hypothesis* about the relationship. If *autonomic conditioning* is involved, it is assumed that the hypothesis translates into autonomic activity by means of a "built-in mechanism." If *motor behaviour* is the dependent variable, the subject is likely to develop a second hypothesis about what the experimenter expects of him and comply with or resist demands. The implication of the cognitive hypothesis is that a subject can only be conditioned if he is *aware* of the relatedness of the two CS–UCS events in time. The hypothesis does not assume that the subject's awareness of the relationship is necessarily the same as the experimenter's, but there must be enough correspondence that the experimenter thinks that the subject has been conditioned.

Conditioning theory, as defined by Brewer, makes the opposite assumptions: Awareness is not necessary for conditioning to occur. Therefore any evidence of conditioning in the absence of awareness will be against the cognitive model. With these distinctions in mind, it is useful to consider in brief some of the major designs, which have attempted to provide a test of the cognitive model.

Brewer makes a number of useful distinctions between different types of paradigm designed either to change awareness by instructions, mislead or misinform subjects, mask awareness, or confuse factors in the paradigm so as to suggest different contingent relationships.

Informed pairing techniques usually involve informing subjects about CS–UCS relatedness followed by a paradigm in which CS–UCS pairing is absent. A subject might be told to expect shock when he hears a tone but then the tone occurs without shock. In three out of four studies reviewed by Brewer, the amplitude of GSR was nevertheless greater in the verbally misled subjects.

Equally there are *misinformed pairing* techniques. A subject is exposed to a conditioning paradigm but then told that the CS will *not* follow the UCS. Brewer (1974) concludes that in such studies the drop in response is "rapid and dramatic (p. 8)." One problem is that subjects may not believe the information given and may continue to expect shock even when electrodes are removed. In an experiment quoted by Brewer, data were partitioned for those who said they believed the experimenter. There was evidence of extinction in only one trial in most of those cases. An experiment by Wilson (1968) gave strong support to the cognitive hypothesis because he established differential conditioning to positive and negative stimuli, but by means of instructions was subsequently able to reverse the effect on GSR by the second trial in the series.

Instructed conditioning techniques involve designs in which subjects are told to produce CR on the occurrence of CS. Autonomic responses are less easily influenced in this way and Brewer points out that the subject may need to use a thinking strategy (such as imagining a trip to the dentist) in order to produce raised GSR.

Brewer regards *masking designs* as providing strong support for the cognitive hypothesis. Some technique is used to reduce awareness of CS–UCS relatedness. Generally there are misleading instructions, which confuse the subjects about what CS and UCS represent. Five studies cited by Brewer involving GSR showed no conditioning when the CS–UCS pairings were masked. In particular, Brewer cites a study by Dawson (1970) in which subjects thought the point of the experiment was that it was a tone-discrimination task. Those with such a belief gave no evidence of conditioning to the CS–UCS pairings.

Backward conditioning, where subjects relate CS to UCS, proves difficult for an automatic pairing paradigm, whereas a cognitive model has less difficulty. Zeiner and Grings (1968) demonstrated that GSR is sensitive to backward conditioning but is due largely to the subjects developing hypotheses about the relatedness of CS to UCS. This again further emphasises the involvement of cognitive factors.

In summary, Brewer's detailed survey of dissociation experiments favours the notion of mediating awareness as a factor in conditioning in some cases of GSR, heart-rate conditioning, and even salivary conditioning. This is particularly important because cognitive involvement in what is essentially a biologically based reaction emphasises the *primacy of the cognitive element*, although the mechanism of translation into behaviour is not clear and may depend on the operation of a strategy.

Dissociation experiments involving behavioural responses rather than autonomic responses have greater possibility for control. Operating control implies a need to be aware of the contingency, and also to deduce what it is that the experimenter requires. The conditioned eye-blink response is a useful variable, because although under voluntary control, it can also be spontaneously evoked by specific stimuli. The issue of interest is whether in a conditioning paradigm a subject is learning to blink to the CS involuntarily or whether the eye blink response is a strategic reaction to perceived experimenter demand.

Brewer reports that eye-blink response experiments showed an effect of instructional bias. An instruction to avoid learning the CS–UCS association, however, did not lead to the complete elimination of conditioning. On some occasions the groups told not to make responses were producing as many as 40% eye blinks. A factor of importance was what the subject believed the experiment was about. Compliance or non-compliance with perceived demand is a critical factor.

An interesting experiment demonstrating that subjects' expectancies can exert a powerful influence was provided by Fishbein (1967), who demonstrated transfer of training from an eyelid-conditioning paradigm under instructional bias, to a neutral paradigm. Subjects given a non-conditioning instruction were subsequently slower to learn to condition than those given a positive conditioning instruction initially.

B. Counter-cognitive Arguments in Studies of Conditioning

There are a number of criticisms against the cognitive hypothesis and the dissociation or awareness paradigms, made by other researchers at the time of or after Brewer's summary of the research literature up to 1974. The first point is that the cognitive element may be present but may not "drive" the conditioning process. Grant (1973), reviewing her own experiments and those of other laboratories at the time, does not doubt that cognitive activity is present during conditioning experiments, but argues that the difficulty is to establish the *extent* to which such cognitive activity is the determinant of performance. Grant argues that although in eye-blink conditioning paradigms subjects can be aware of, and therefore give accurate reports of, quite complex CS–UCS contingencies, the cognitions are rarely related to subjects' conditioning performance. Grant's experimental designs involved CS's of varying kinds—illumination of different sources, colours, paintings, words, letters, numbers, verbal statements, phrases. The UCS was an airpuff delivered from 500 to 1000 milliseconds after CS. Results indicated that there was: (1) accurate reporting of UCS–CS combinations; (2) perception of increasing relaxation; (3) perception that eye-blink responses progressively diminish; (4) impressions of diminution of UCR (described as "not accurate" by Grant); (5) occasional impression of voluntary anticipatory eye-blinks or inhibited blinking (described as poorly correlated with actual performance). There was very low awareness of the anticipatory eye-blink response (CR).

Grant's findings suggest two very important conclusions. Firstly, as already stated, there is no awareness of CR. Secondly, there is a poor relationship between UCS–CS contingencies and conditioning performance. She concludes (Grant, 1973) that "eyelid CR is less susceptible to cognitive control than may be the case with instrumental responses and responses governed by the autonomic nervous system (p. 80)."

Grant differentiated the V or voluntary form of response characterised by short response latencies and eye closure of long duration, from the C or conditioned form which has longer latency with more gradual and less complete closure. When the CS is more complex those subjects who showed the V-form pattern showed superior conditioning to those who did not. Thus, the operation of "awareness strategies" seems to be an important factor in determining the level of conditioning achieved, rather than whether or not it occurs. However, this has to be considered in relation to Grant's other main finding concerning awareness of CR. "The S fails utterly in reporting awareness regarding his anticipatory eyelid CR. There is simply no correlation between what he says and what he does (p. 76)." This implies that the operation of the "voluntary strategy" is not monitored by the subject and not consciously implemented. Alternatively, if it is, it must be concluded that subjects who wish to show that they condition easily are not willing to disclose information about eyelid responses to experimenters.

The question of whether awareness is a factor in classical conditioning has been recently examined by Freka et al. (1983). They consider the hypothesis that awareness mediates all forms of human conditioning and argue that the central question in the "conditioning" versus "cognitive" debate (pairing model v. contingency model) is the *extent* to which knowledge modifies responding. They make a distinction between awareness of CS–UCS relationships and *demand awareness*, or perception of what the experimenters are trying to achieve in the experiment. Freka et al. consider compliance to be an important factor: Subjects may "comply with the Experimenter's expectations and give appropriate responses (p. 70)." Demand awareness is assumed to be an additional factor to awareness of stimulus contingencies.

The main problem with finding out about the role played by awareness is that of obtaining accurate subject reports. Dawson and Reardon (1973) investigated four types of questionnaires designed to investigate awareness in a masked GSR paradigm. Experimental manipulations of awareness by means of instructions were found to be best assessed by a short, post-trial recognition test, but the problem of eliciting awareness is emphasised. Discrimination in conditioning was found for those subjects who were "unaware," with a short recall questionnaire, but who showed awareness when a short recognition questionnaire was used instead. The authors emphasise the need to evolve methods of examining awareness during the trials and not by means of tests after the trials.

Freka et al. designed two experiments to investigate the role of awareness or active thinking in human subjects, using a classical CS–UCS paradigm but employing a masking task to influence awareness of CS–UCS relationships. A post-experimental questionnaire was used to assess awareness of both CS–UCS relationship and of the purpose of the experiment. It involved both open-ended and forced-choice questions. Subjects were informed that the purpose of the experiment was to measure reaction times (RTs) in the presence of distracting tones and airpuffs or shocks. In fact, reaction times formed part of a masking task designed to divert the subjects' attention from the conditioning procedure and involved reacting as quickly as possible to the onset of a red light 3 seconds prior to each CS–UCS trial. Results showed that most subjects were aware of UCS–CS contingency. Over 70% of subjects in both experiments gave reports that suggested they were aware of the contingency although a small number of subjects actually reported events the wrong way round, with CS preceding the UCS. The following results were obtained: (1) Analysis of demand awareness showed that 80–87% of subjects in the two experiments were unaware of the real purpose of the experiments. (2) Awareness of stimulus contingencies was found to be completely unrelated to conditioning factors. (3) Awareness of responding appeared to differ between subjects. Although some subjects reported deliberately blinking to CS onset in order to avoid the UCS, only one subject could be classified as a "voluntary responder" from the actual records.

There is an important issue raised by the authors about the role of conscious strategy. Some subjects report deliberately blinking, which implies a conscious strategy that determines response style, but the authors suggest that the order of events may be quite different and that subjects' level of CR (high or low) determines awareness. In other words, the subjects with a high level of blinking become aware of responding and attribute it to a deliberate decision to blink. Freka et al. (1983) cite as evidence that subjects who reported awareness of the association between UCS and blinking were more likely to produce CRs and claim that sensitivity to the UCS is the important factor.

With regard to the issue of awareness as the factor in conditioning, the authors suggest that it is not of causal significance and believe that conditioning represents a "phylogenetically positive mechanism independent of cognitive awareness (p. 74)." One of the problems with the experimental design used is that from the account of the paradigm provided by the authors, the signal for the reaction-time task might have acted as a warning signal for the CS. Thus, awareness of the RT signal and CS relationship might also have occurred and the awareness of other relationships might have been changed as a result. The RT data are not reported, but it is possible that those who perceive the RT task as the main task might be different in many crucial respects from those who do not. Therefore, the relationship between RT, conditioning proficiency, and various levels of awareness needs to be made clear.

Dulany (1974) responds directly to Brewer's detailed review of the dissociation experiments by presenting a number of philosophical or design points which argue against a cognitive model. Again, the reader is advised to read the article in order to appraise the detail supporting the arguments. The first point made by Dulany is that if it is assumed that individuals bring their cognitive structures to an experimental situation, there is no reason to assume that they could not also bring their "conditioning history·" Awareness as defined by Dulany is "an epiphenomenon of some kind of neural process and not causally active upon response selection in any way dependent on that neural process (p. 47)." The main argument advanced is that awareness is coincidental with, but not causally related to conditioning processes.

In terms of the details of experiments described by Brewer, Dulany provides alternative interpretations largely in terms of the use of the individual's previous conditioning history. Instructional bias conditions are assumed to back up, or be pitted against, the presumed perseveration of the conditioning process. Awareness of contingency designs are argued to involve *assessment* rather than just awareness. Masking designs, when effective, are argued to operate by diverting attention (orientation) from the elements of conditioning. The presentation of instructions by means of verbal utterances may itself be providing selective reinforcement for the occurrence or inhibition of CRs in the paradigm. Equally, instructional bias may influence orientation towards (or away from) specified elements of the paradigm.

Thus, the role played by cognitive factors in driving conditioning is totally challenged by Dulany. He reiterates that, for a cognitive model, *awareness* of contingency and of experimenter expectations, plus dispositions to be compliant, are all distinguishable elements which are confused in the various paradigms. Moreover, all treatment paradigms designed to dissociate awareness involve conditions that could lead to changes in what is seen as reinforcing. Therefore, the UCS–CS relationship may be inadvertently confounded with other reinforced behaviour. Reporting of awareness could itself be manipulated by reinforcement. Dulany argues that for strong support there must be a theory that: (1) specifies a rich and precise network of cognitive variables together with interrelating cognitive operations; (2) introduces designs in which a precise network of relations can be examined. In reply, Brewer does not deny that network analysis would be useful, but he emphasises situations where Dulany has himself used cognitive explanations such as "diverting the subject's attention." He maintains his initial position that conditioning is impossible without cognitive mediation by means of "awareness."

What does seem clear is that in cases where cognitive factors are assumed to mediate the conditioning process, the response is likely to be *strategic*. A subject notes one or more of many possible relationships and responds with voluntary responses which are influenced by a perception of what it is that the experimenter wants. In the case of autonomic conditioning an added strategic approach may be required to enable autonomic responses to occur.

Before considering "strategic involvement" in more detail, a second fundamental paradigm involved in learning must be considered. Instrumental learning and learning about level of control involve paradigms which differ only in emphasis. Learning theory emphasises the S–R elements of the paradigm; learning about control is based on R–S elements.

2.   INSTRUMENTAL LEARNING AND AWARENESS: "PREPAREDNESS" OR "SUSPICIOUSNESS"?

Instrumental learning involves the acquisition of stimulus–response associations and could be argued to form the basis of most animal and human skills. Either a response is elicited by a situation in that unless it occurs there will be no reinforcement, or a randomly occurring response may be selected for reward which has no particular appropriateness for a response.

The concept of "preparedness" was developed by Seligman (1971) and defined in terms of the relative ease of learning and the relative resistance to unlearning. Evolutionary pressures are argued by Seligman to favour the learning of certain S–R pairs and to discourage the learning of others. This might be taken to suggest that there is some "functional pre-wiring" as far as associative learning is required. Seligman proposes a continuum from "prepared" to "contraprepared." At one end there is great speed of association; somatic withdrawal responses may be prepared in relation to painful stimuli. At the other extreme (contraprepared) responses generally associated with relaxation may be very difficult to learn in the presence of pain.

The explanation favoured by Seligman is that of prearranged or prepared associations. The implication is that there is an underlying phylogenetically primitive mechanism which is independent of cognitive awareness. Learning facility might be argued to depend on the features of the mechanism so that some associations rather than others are favoured. However, a different implication might be drawn if the role played by awareness, even at a primitive level in animals, is considered. Before this view is developed, an experiment by Garcia and Keolling is described because it illustrates the effects of preparedness very well.

Garcia and Koelling (1966) investigated the prepared–contraprepared distinction in terms of the acquisition of learned aversions. Rats were submitted to one of two conditions while drinking saccharine-flavoured water in a bright, noisy environment. In one condition the animals were given electric shock. In another condition they were X-irradiated at levels designed to make them sick within an hour. In the former condition rats associated shock with the bright, noisy environment and would not drink the water in such an environment. In the latter condition, the taste of the water was associated with sickness and therefore water with saccharine in it was avoided. The animals can be argued to be more likely to associate bright, noisy environments with shock and more likely to associate the taste in the water with sickness. This fits with the preparedness concept in that some S–S combinations were associated and not others. Animals did not learn to associate shock with saccharine, or sickness with bright, noisy environments. One problem is that vomiting water tasting of saccharine may have underlined the association between saccharine and sickness.

An awareness explanation need not depend on anthropomorphising about animals if it is assumed that as animals learn to master the environment, a repertoire of possible relationships is built up based on frequency and potency. An abstract representation of this enables an animal or person to have "suspicions." Food and drink types relate to sickness or no-sickness in predictable ways, so food and drink tastes form the basis of "suspicions" when sickness occurs. Brightness and noisy environments are alarming and might be associated with danger and pain. The animal extracts this relationship and it becomes the basis for suspicions about the likely cause of perceived pain. It would be biologically adaptive for both animals and human beings to develop "suspicions." Suspicions need be no more than abstractions from the properties of encountered relationships evident in memory. The concept of suspicion is linked with the concept of appropriateness. Some punishments or rewards seem appropriate for a particular behaviour; others do not. If suspicions evolve from abstractions based on experiences, then they will be of evolutionary advantage and make sense in these terms.

For human beings there may be an added source of suspicion due to the conveyance of "rules" about relationships in language and writing. People may acquire the concept "never trust a man who cannot look you in the eye" (which may be difficult to obtain on a personal basis because such encounters are not that frequent), and make use of it subsequently in quite new encounters.

The cognitive explanation assumes that awareness mediates to result in strategic responses. Certain associations are favoured and certain are not. The behaviourist explanation assumes that conditioning and learning in life history influence responses. The cognitive approach allows for the possibility that circumstances may influence the perception of contingencies and that therefore the individual may behave strategically. The circumstances and paradigm are assessed and demand is appraised. The individual then attends to some but not all aspects of the situation and produces or inhibits responses depending on personal attitude (compliance or defiance).

Experiments by Ohman (1979) involved varying CS content in a human, classical fear-conditioning experiment. Two different types of CS content were used. One was described as "fear-relevant" and involved spiders and snakes. One was described as "fear-irrelevant" and involved flowers and mushrooms. In both cases the material was presented in the form of slides preceding the UCS (shock). Results suggested that in the case of fear-relevant CS content, conditioned responses were acquired more rapidly and were more resistant to estimation. In a second design, comparable results were reported for exposure to "angry," as compared with "happy" faces. Those slides that were negative and threatening in character were more easily associated with fear and therefore formed faster, more resistant conditioning of fear responses.

The results fit with the preparedness hypothesis: Unpleasant events are more likely to be associated with negative feelings and to facilitate avoidance or fear learning. However, the results also fit an "awareness" model. Human beings face a number of sources of information that lead them to suppose that certain creatures have "evil connections." Rats are associated with disease; snakes with poisonous bites and concealment in dark places and crevices. Thus, even without exposure to such creatures, a person may develop expectancies. Moreover, part of the creation of an atmosphere of evil, darkness, and neglect in films, books, and plays, is the prevalence of creatures such as rats and spiders. The irrational expectancy of evil can be seen as an extraction from other forms of knowledge and need not depend on encounters. Awareness of circumstance could create what Freka et al. (1983) describe as "demand characteristics." Subjects may perceive the total reason for the experiment in various ways. The outcome in terms of response pattern reflects the suspicion plus perceived demand characteristics. For example the presentation of slides of snakes may arouse the suspicion that the experiment might involve something unpleasant. The presentation of the UCS confirms this hypothesis.

These considerations are important because of the implications for the perception of control and hence the association with perceived stress. Even in simple learning paradigms there may be a strong effect of awareness on the acquisition of responses. In fact the evidence taken collectively suggests that the individual will behave strategically in assessing the evidence, and strategically in integrating this information with circumstantial evidence to decide on the demand characteristics.

3.   A TWO-STAGE MODEL OF THE PERCEPTION OF CONTROL

In summary, the traditional "preparedness" explanation of learning assumes that there is "functional pre-writing" of certain combinations which have evolved because of the experiences of pre-technological man. Our "suspicions" model assumes that there is a stored set of likely relationships based on experience or social learning that form the basis of suspicions. These suspicions are the main directives for early strategies on which control depends.

It is proposed that in a broad range of experimental and real-life situations a two-stage model provides a basis for understanding the representation of evidence about the outside world and its utilisation in decision.

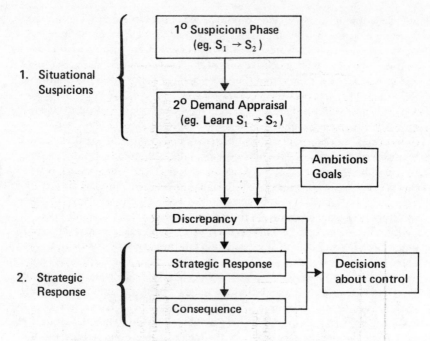

FIG. 3.1   Representation of the processes in the assessment of control.

As shown in Fig. 3.1, the first stage involves the formation of suspicions based on the cognitive store of likely relationships (S–S; S–R; R–S). Second stage suspicions are formed on assessment of demand characteristics. Both aspects provide the data that enable a person to assess reality and decide what is going on. These two stages will not be independent, in that information provided in the first phase about the characteristics of a particular situation will influence the subsequent perception of demand characteristics.

If a person becomes aware that CS is generally followed by UCS (CS–UCS), he must then decipher the demands of the experiment in those terms. The resulting suspicion is more likely to be that the experimenter is looking to see how *well* CS–UCS can be learned, or how *quickly* the association is noted. Experimenters typically reduce the availability of cues other than those they are examining in experiment contexts and therefore may quite unwittingly provide strong leads as to what is required. Figure 3.2 illustrates the possible suspicions a person may form during a conditioning experiment and provides an indication of likely demand characteristics perceived as a result.

The second part of Fig. 3.1 illustrates that the suspicions formed provide the elements that help to dictate the form planned activity takes. Both intentions and suspicions provide the ingredients which determine the size

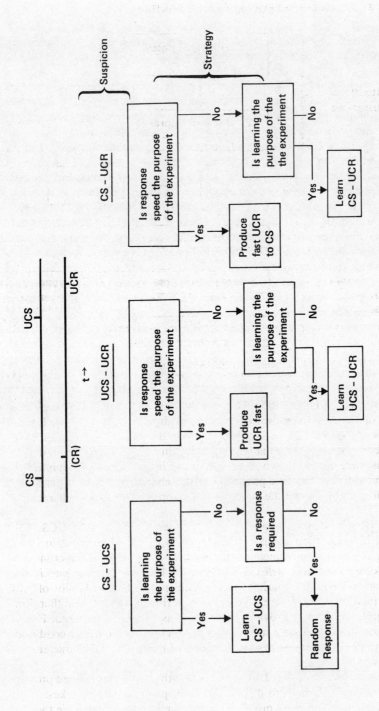

FIG. 3.2 Schematic representation of possible suspicions and perceived task demands in a conditioning paradigm.

51

and form of the discrepancy. As argued in the previous chapter, achieving control is about reducing the discrepancy between intentions and reality, and knowing that this reduction is possible.

Some indication of how complex the assessments of what is happening in a simple conditioning experiment can be is provided by a study involving 50 female subjects between the ages of 30 and 50 employed as secretarial staff. Subjects were given written instructions asking them to *imagine* attending an experiment as a subject (Table 3.1). An account was given of the details of an eye-blink conditioning paradigm and was so arranged that for one group of subjects ("contingency aware") the relationship between CS and UCS was emphasised. For a second group of subjects ("response aware") the relationship between UCS and UCR was emphasised ("every time an airpuff occurs you notice that you blink"). There were 25 subjects in the contingency-aware condition and 25 subjects in the response-aware condition. In the response-aware condition 89.4% of the subjects indicated that their response would be to speed up or slow down response speed (blink faster; blink as soon as possible). By comparison, of those contingency aware, 98.2% suggested that learning the CS–UCS relationship was what was required by the experiment.

Obviously, providing an account of an experience which is never encountered by subjects, is very different from the real experience and could even be argued to introduce very definite instructional bias. However, it does at least provide an indication of the ways in which subjects might assess situations like this. The protocols obtained from subjects are particularly interesting and illustrate the role of individual differences in this respect.

TABLE 3.1
Experimental Survey (Instructions to Respondents)

Please imagine the following situation:

You are asked to take part as a subject in an experiment with no prior information. You are asked to wear earphones so that you can hear a tone. A small gadget situated in front of you has tubes which deliver a short puff of air to both eyes.

You then take part in the experiment with no further information. You wait for a while then you hear a short tone. This is followed by the delivery of a puff of air to your eye. (*This makes you blink.*)*

You then wait again and there is after a while another short tone followed by another puff of air to your eye. (*This makes you blink again. After about six of these trials you notice that you blink when the tone comes on.*)*

When the experiment is over, you are asked to say what the experimenter was trying to find out. Please write some statements about what you would say.

---

*Added for response-aware condition.

TABLE 3.2
Illustrative Protocols from Subjects Presented with Information on a
Conditioning Procedure

A. Contingency Aware (CS–UCS)

	Subject 3
Suspicions	1. Are you trying to find out reaction to shock or attack?
	2. Eyes are vulnerable and precious, I would not enjoy the first attack, I should think.
Demand Appraisal	1. Sitting in front of a machine with headphones on doesn't give much scope for "doing" anything but my mind would be speculating madly.
	2. I would obviously jump if the puff of air was unexpected.
	3. I would try to close my eyes in case.

	Subject 5
Suspicions	1. To show that an event can trigger off a reaction to another stimulus before it has happened.
Demand Appraisal	1. To close eyes after tone to avoid air being blown into the eyes.

	Subject 6
Suspicions	1. To see if I can learn that the puff of air occurs after the tone.
	2. To see if I can learn to protect my eyes.
Demand Appraisal	1. I would show that I had learned the association by blinking to the tone.
	2. I would try to keep my eyes shut when the puff occurred to show that I know how to protect my eyes.

B. Response Aware

	Subject 8 (non-compliant)
Suspicions	1. Are you trying to see whether I can blink rapidly?
	2. Are you trying to see if I can prevent myself blinking?
Demand Appraisal	1. Shut my eyes after the tone to avoid a blink.
	2. Resist being forced to blink.

	Subject 15 (non-compliant)
Suspicions	1. To find out if you get adapted to the puff of air and stop blinking.
	2. To find out if tone and blinking have any connections.
Demand Appraisal	1. Try to stop blinking when the puff of air was delivered.

(Continued)

TABLE 3.2
(Continued)

	Subject 21 (non-compliant)
Suspicions	1. Conditioning reflex. Whether stress can be controlled by the power of suggestion, i.e. having a word or action to signal stressful situations and then try to deal with such situations on the basis of what you can do.
Demand Appraisal	1. I would have tried not to blink when the tone comes on, to prove you couldn't make me.
	2. I would have tried to be in control of my own actions and not conditioned by the tone to blink.

A sample of the statements obtained is shown in Table 3.2. As was evident from some of the studies reported in the previous chapter, individual reactions are varied; some subjects typically comply with demand but others are resistant to whatever they consider the experiment is about.

To summarise, awareness may frequently be a determinant of responding even in simple learning and especially when responses under voluntary control are required. In both life and laboratory conditions individuals may extract representations of data as a basis for suspicions. From similar extractions of circumstantial evidence, such as how another person behaves, suspicions of demand characteristics are formed. The two sets of suspicions combine to determine the input to the cognitive system concerned with formulating the discrepancy. To use the example of hammering nails into wood; a person may form suspicions about the nail and its status with respect to the wood and a second set of suspicions about what it is that is required of him in hammering the nail. It is on the basis of these suspicions that the ingredients for planned operations depend and hence it is similarly on these suspicions that the assessment of control depends.

A useful distinction is between "identification" strategies developed to find out what is going on (identify and represent the evidence) and "response organisation" strategies designed to achieve a particular consequence. Both aspects may shape the cognitive data base which later determines coping activity in stress.

4 Contingency Assessment and Control

In the previous chapter, the main concern was with the role of suspicions and response strategies in learning. Although the assessment of control is a form of learning in which response–outcome (R–S) contiguities are involved, an accurate assessment of control requires a more complex statistical operation. If we are to understand the relationship between stress and the perception of control, particularly in real-life contexts, it is necessary to consider some of the available evidence on contingency assessments in greater detail.

In real-life situations, critical occurrences may be embedded in a context of other events. The individual may be required to accumulate the evidence of relatedness over a period of time. For example, he may be exposed to a series of happenings such as $A \wedge B$; $A \wedge \overline{B}$; $\overline{A} \wedge B$; $\overline{A} \wedge \overline{B}$[1] and be required to decide about the relationship between A and B. It could be argued that as far as a complete causal relationship is concerned, one case of the lack of a relationship will destroy the notion of contingency. For example, one case of a flame not causing paper to burn, leads to revision of the notion "fire burns paper," or to a search for a qualifying fact "but not if the paper is wet." Thus, in some cases the perception of an event which violates the hypothesis is sufficient for a revision of the law on which the hypothesis is derived.

However, there are many happenings in life where an individual is required to note probabilistic relationships. "Folklore" and "old wives' tales" may be based on such observations pooled across populations and genera-

---

[1] $\overline{A}$ = not A; $\wedge$ = 'and'.

tions. A good example is the old saying that sunsets in the evening cause fine weather the next day: "Sunset at night; shepherds delight." To extract such a rule, ideally an assessment of the frequency of four relationships is required: sunset $\longrightarrow$ fine weather; sunset $\longrightarrow$ rain; no sunset $\longrightarrow$ fine weather; no sunset $\longrightarrow$ rain. These four combinations characterise the association between binary variables.

The same is true of situations which involve action and consequence. For each case where there is binary choice, action (A) can be compared with outcome (O) to determine the contingency between action and outcome. The same four possibilities remain: $A \longrightarrow O$; $\overline{A} \longrightarrow O$; $A \longrightarrow \overline{O}$; $\overline{A} \longrightarrow \overline{O}$. In laboratory situations designed to study learning processes, the four exemplars of the contingency rule are often reduced to one. This may be one of the reasons why laboratory conditions are unrepresentative of learning in life. Laboratory studies which have concentrated on trying to understand the way in which contingency data are assessed have indicated that the evidence is often too difficult to assess adequately and that preconception and data distortion are evident.

1. STUDIES ON CONTINGENCY LEARNING

Contingency learning might be a factor in either of the two learning-theory paradigms, as long as there are occasions when the temporal pairing of the target events (S–S or S–R) does not occur. The critical difference is that in most learning paradigms the focus is on the relationship between UCS and CS (in classical conditioning) and S–R (in instrumental learning). On the other hand, in the case of contingency learning the emphasis is on the balance of relatedness as against unrelatedness; what is important is the number of occasions the UCS is followed by CS (relatedness) as compared with the number of occasions it is not (unrelatedness). It could be the case that some experimental designs favour missing the occurrence of CS occasionally because of masking or distraction, so that the organism perceives a sequence such as: UCS–CS; UCS–CS; UCS–$\overline{CS}$; UCS–$\overline{CS}$; UCS–CS; etc. There may equally be cases where UCS is missed. Therefore, there may be sequences where the organism learns that nothing precedes CS (or that an unintended stimulus precedes CS) and receives data of the form: UCS–CS; $\overline{UCS}$–CS; UCS–CS; UCS–CS; $\overline{UCS}$–CS; etc.

If the two sequences described are combined, so that sometimes CS is missed and sometimes UCS is missed, there are the usual four possibilities: (UCS–CS; $\overline{UCS}$–$\overline{CS}$; $\overline{UCS}$–CS; UCS–$\overline{CS}$). Circumstances such as the masking design used by Freka et al. (1983), where an RT signal was made to occur in advance of the onset of UCS in order to reduce awareness, may actually have had the effect of creating perceived changes in contingency structure. Approximately 30% of the subjects reported being unaware of the UCS–CS contingency.

In accordance with the contingency-learning model, classical conditioning should be weakened by paradigms in which the UCS occurs more often without being followed by the CS. The organism could be argued to be engaged in a process of active unlearning or inhibitory learning in cases where UCS–$\overline{CS}$ occurs. MacKintosh's concept of "learned irrelevance" (MacKintosh, 1975) makes this assumption. The association between UCS and CS is actively weakened by UCS–$\overline{CS}$ occurrences. However, when there is no UCS–CS contingency, the association is strengthened when the probability of CS occurring is high. This is true even for animal conditioning (Kremer, 1971; Rescorla, 1972).

In instrumental learning paradigms, two response-outcome contingencies may be identified. There is the probability of an outcome given the probability of a response $P(O/R)$ and the probability of an outcome given the non-occurrence of a response $P(O/\overline{R})$. Seligman et al. (1971) argue that organisms are generally sensitive to conjoint variations in response–outcome probabilities and are particularly sensitive to response–outcome independence. This assertion is the basis of the learned helplessness model: The perception of response–outcome independence is the basis for the perception of no control and is assumed by Seligman (1975) to carry over to new situations resulting in cognitive and motivational as well as emotional impairment.

Table 4.1 provides the basis of a statistical model of binary choice. Action A could result in outcome A or outcome B. Action X could result in outcome X or outcome Y. Combinations of AA and XX are assumed to indicate that control is possible (although such combinations could occur fortuitously). Combinations AB and XY imply no control. On the basis of such a matrix it is possible to specify contingency in terms of conditional probabilities: The probability of outcome A given action A and the probability of outcome X given action X.

However, evidence suggests that human judgements are less than ideal and are likely to depend heavily on the *frequency of positive instances*. In other words, the frequency of the critical event A/A or X/X is more significant than A/B or A/X. Smedslund (1963) required student nurses to assess the relationships between symptoms and disease, and showed that judge-

TABLE 4.1
A Contingency Matrix for the Perception of Control in a
Binary Variable Condition

		Outcome	
Action	A	A (Control)	B (No Control)
Action	X	X (Control)	Y (No Control)

ments were based on the frequency of joint occurrence of symptom and disease. The three other possibilities were not influential. Judgements, therefore, had a precarious relationship to contingency data, suggesting how poor people might be as statistical scientists.

According to Smedslund there are two main indications sufficient for the existence of the concept of correlation. The first is the use of a *selective strategy* to order data into four categories for binary variable conditions. The second is the *estimation of the frequency of data* in each cell. The person with a concept of correlation will base his final estimate on the ratio of the sum of two diagonal cell frequencies and the sum of the other diagonal cell frequencies.

In a sorting experiment (Smedslund, 1963) involving packs of cards (100 cards in each pack), each card represented the details of symptoms and diagnosis for a patient. On top of each card was typed "Patient No." and a value from 1 to 100 was attached. The cards were ordered according to the numbers. The upper part of each card was headed "Symptoms" and there were four letters, B, C, D, and E, assigned to four positions at random. On 50 of the cards, A (representing a target symptom), was present instead of one of the other letters. The lower part of the card was headed "Diagnosis" and beneath it there were four different capital letters, G, H, I, and J, in randomised sequence. When a target diagnosis F was present it replaced one of the letters. This was the case for 50 of the cards.

Sixty-seven student nurses were asked to sort through one of five packs which varied according to frequency distributions of A's and F's and were told that the cards represented excerpts of files from 100 patients. The purpose of the task was to see if it was possible to form an opinion about the practical usefulness of a symptom in diagnosis. Each subject was required to decide whether A was a useful symptom in the diagnosis of F. Afterwards subjects were asked about the relationship between A and F. They were additionally asked:

1. How many cards do you think there are with both A and F?
2. How many cards to you think there are without A but with F?
3. How many cards to you think there are with A but without F?
4. How many cards do you think there are without A and without F?

Results showed that judgements and explanations differed between subjects and accuracy scores were ambiguously related to event category. *A particularistic concept* was identified; its use meant that subjects thought there was a relationship in AF cases and no relationship in all others.

The *statistical particularistic* concept involved the *frequency* of counting the positive instances (AF) ("counted after card 27 and found 11 with A and F. Think it is a fairly strong relation.") A more sophisticated version was to express AF frequencies as a percentage of the number of trials. More than half the student nurses used a frequency concept of AF occurrences. Significantly, not a single subject gave any indication of understanding the notion of a correlational relationship based on the ratio of A/F and $\overline{A}/\overline{F}$ and the sum of $\overline{A}/F$ and $A/\overline{F}$.

A second experiment was designed to reduce the strain on information processing and storing capacity. The subjects could arrange and sort the cards rather than just passively viewing them and were provided with pencil and paper for notes. Also the cards were simplified and only $+A$, $-A$, $+F$, or $-F$ were present.

Results showed that subjects again found the task hard; just over half of the subjects placed the cards in one pile. One subject sorted $+A$'s and $+F$'s into one pile and the rest in another; five subjects sorted the cards in four categories; one subject sorted them in five piles (two piles of $-A$'s and $-F$'s); and one sorted the cards in seven unsystematic piles.

The explanations were categorised by the experimenters on the basis of whether frequency was mentioned or not. Of subjects who thought there was a relationship, 75% said that this was because the number of $+A$ $+F$'s was large. One subject said there was a relationship because there were more $+F$'s than $-A$'s, and another subject said there was no relationship because the $-A$ $+F$'s were most frequent. Only two subjects referred to both $+A$ $+A$ and $-A$ $-F$ categories and the authors regarded this as some evidence of the "dawning of correlation."

A conclusion comparable to that of Smedslund was drawn by Jenkins and Ward (1965), who found that favourable outcomes biased the assessment of contingency. In a binary matrix, subjects were required to make a target event appear as often as possible. Control was assessed in terms of the frequency with which this happened. The explanation for the bias in favour of target frequency was that subjects reason that if contingency is present, favourable events occur. Favourable events are then found to occur and so it is concluded that there is contingency. Subjects do not apparently give much weight to the possibility that favourable events occur by chance.

In an experiment by Ward and Jenkins (1965), subjects were asked to judge how much seeding clouds controlled the occurrence of rain. If A_1 = clouds seeded; B_1 = rain; A_2 = clouds not seeded; B_2 = no rain, it would be assumed that the subjects would consider $A_1 B_1$ (seed–rain) and $A_2 B_2$ (no seed–no rain) as favourable. The probability of a favourable event in the absence of contingency is $P(A_1)P(B_1) + P(A_2)P(B_2)$. The expected number of favourable events varies with $P(A_1)$ and $P(B_1)$. The authors hypothesised that subjects might allow for chance factors and make judgements based on conditional probabilities, comparing the probability of rain after seeding and the probability of rain after no seeding.

Results showed that different subjects adopt different bases of judgement; thus group data was not much use. A number of different rules were therefore identified by the authors and the actual judgements of the subjects were correlated with with values generated by different rules. The rules identified were:

1. *Delta cases*; the important data would be the probability of rain when clouds are seeded subtracted from the probability of rain when clouds are not seeded.
2. *Confirming cases*; the number of seed–rain days plus the number of no seed–no rain days.
3. *Success*; the frequency of the joint occurrence of seeding and rain.
4. *Percent success*; the probability of rain when clouds are seeded.
5. *Absolute difference*; the seed–rain frequency minus the no seed–rain frequency.
6. *Ratio*; the seed–rain frequency.

Results showed that the "delta" rule was followed by 31 out of 72 subjects; the "confirming cases" rule was followed by 27; "percent success" was followed by 8. No other rule was employed by more than 2 subjects.

Further analysis involving correlations between the data predicted by the rule and the data produced by the subjects in each rule category, suggested that the rules best predicting judgements were: delta .857; confirming cases .951; percent success .848. On further statistical analysis (Duncan's new multiple range test), correlations for "confirming cases" were higher than for any other rule ($p < .01$).

Analysis also suggested that the mode of presentation of the contingency information had an important influence on the rule adopted; $\chi^2 = 20.84$, $p < .01$). The adoption of rules was unaffected by summarised information when it was given after the task, but for conditions when *only* summarised information was given subjects were more likely to adopt the delta rule and were thus more likely to make sound judgements of the contingency relationship. Overall, the authors conclude that only 17% of those receiving trial-by-trial information followed a logically defensible rule, whereas when only summarised information was provided 75% of subjects did so.

These results suggest that given a free choice from summarised information people are capable of evolving logical rules, but may find it more difficult to do so when being required to sum information over a series of trials. The authors contest the idea that the effect could be due to inability to sum information because their own pilot studies suggest that subjects could reproduce 2 × 2 contingency table of events with considerable accuracy, although their judgements of relatedness did not accurately represent contingency. Also, summary information provided after the trial did not increase the likelihood of use of a logical rule in deducing contingency. The authors suggest that the important factor may be the imposing of *organisation* on the information and that this is best done when subjects first begin to assimilate the evidence.

The results of these studies provide information that suggests that people are unlikely to obtain accurate statistical estimates of contingency levels in real-life situations. Hence their concept of control is likely to contain some important features arising from bias. Put quite simply, people may be very bad at summarising what is going on in situations. Most subjects find it difficult to evolve adequate rules and even when the information is provided in summarised form, not everyone deduces the same logical rule.

In these circumstances, it would be expected that judgemental errors are likely to occur and that bias about the nature of events would be highly influential. Jenkins and Ward (1965) suggested that a source of judgemental error was the tendency to seek *evidence of success*. There may be a starting bias towards the assumption that if a response leads to success, the *absence* of that response would have led to *no success*. This is an example of syllogistic reasoning of the form "A is followed by B, $\bar{A}$ is followed by $\bar{B}$." Wason and Johnson-Laird (1972) showed that this is a strong disposition in adult propositional reasoning.

A study by Allan and Jenkins (1980) involved presentation of slides of the presence or absence of the head of the Loch Ness Monster above the surface of the Loch (M or $\bar{M}$). An interesting aspect of their design was that there was the possibility of either an active or passive response (moving a joystick; not moving the joystick), or of two active responses (moving the joystick to the left; moving the joystick to the right). They found that the response condition markedly influenced the judgements of contingency. An active–passive alternative produced better agreement with actual contingency data, than did two active responses. In the former condition the judgements of 75% of the subjects were associated with a rule based on conditional probabilities, whereas in the latter condition only about 25% of subjects effected the conditional probability rule. In this latter situation subjects were more likely to report that their response influenced the outcome when there was no contingency present. The frequency of a positive outcome exerted a bias towards over-reporting contingency in both groups, but the effect was more pronounced in the case of the active response condition, where 44% of judgements of subjects were correlated with rules based on positive outcomes (as compared with only 5% in the active–passive case).

Overall, the results could be said to support the rule that with a fixed probability [$P(O/A)$] of an outcome (O) given an action occurrence (A), frequency of positive outcome is a critical factor which causes an increase in judgements of control when there is no contingency [$P(O/A) = P(O/\bar{A})$]. The authors argue that the "denial of antecedent" fallacy observed by Wason and Johnson-Laird (1972) provides a likely explanation because subjects assume [$(A \rightarrow B) \rightarrow (\bar{A} \rightarrow \bar{B})$].

The general finding of the study by Allan and Jenkins is that in spite of individual differences in the "rules" used to assess contingency, the greater proportion of subjects produced judgements consistent with the relation between two binary variables $P(O/A) - P(O/\bar{A})$. The operation of this rule implies that a statistical counting procedure is required to obtain:

(1) an estimate of the probability of outcome following action; and (2) an estimate of the probability of outcome in the absence of action. The rule then requires a subtraction process so that in effect subjects are deducting an estimate of the number of times the outcome follows action from the number of times the outcome occurs spontaneously.

Dickinson (1980) and Dickinson et al. (1984) have considered the possibility that an account of contingency assessment may be provided by basic features in the conditioning process. The degree of excitatory conditioning in a classical paradigm can be shown to decrease as a function of $P(\mathrm{UC}/\overline{\mathrm{CS}})$ for a fixed probability of (UC/CS). Moreover, in the absence of CS–UCS contingency, animals show greater excitatory conditioning as the frequency of UCS increases. Thus the phenomena established in human learning are demonstrated in animal conditioning paradigms and do not appear to be dependent on more sophisticated counting processes or the operation of conditional probability rules.

Dickinson et al. (1984) developed a task based on a video-game in which "tanks" progressed across the display and could be destroyed by "shells" resulting from the subject's action or "land mines" independent of the subject's action. For each set of trials $P(O/A)$ and $P(O/\overline{A})$ were fixed. At the end of a set of trials subjects were required to rate the effectiveness of the shells. A comparison of a number of contingency conditions (75–25, 75–50, 75–75) provided a test of the hypothesis that for a fixed $P(O/A)$, judgements of contingency would decrease with increments in $P(O/\overline{A})$. A comparison of (75–75) and (25–25) sets of trials provided a test of the hypothesis that high outcome frequency would be associated with judgements of control.

Finally, a negative contingency arrangement was introduced so that $P(O/A)$ was less than $P(O/\overline{A})$. In conditioning studies, a negative CS–UCS contingency results in a different form of conditioning which is inhibitory and related to the strength of the negative contingency. The "negative contingency" design used involved informing the subjects that the shell might be ineffective but may also alert the tank driver to drive more carefully through the minefield and *avoid* enemy mines. Therefore the subjects' positive action could reduce the probability of a tank exploding.

Judgements of contingency were systematically affected by the probability that the tank would explode in the absence of a hit; described by $P(O/\overline{A})$. Thus the lead variable seemed to be *instances of outcome in the absence of action*. Overall, outcome frequency levels were determinants of the assessment of non-contingent relationships; the 75–75 set produced more judgements of positive contingency than the 25–25 set. Finally, subjects were found to be sensitive to non-contingency in that when $P(O/\overline{A})$ increased to levels above $P(O/A)$, there were more negative judgements. The pattern of judgements found, supports the idea of a general rule of the form: $P(O/A) - P(O/\overline{A})$ for most subjects.

2. BIAS IN THE REPRESENTATION OF EVIDENCE ABOUT CONTROL

From what has been said so far it appears that:

1. A person is sometimes capable of using a conditional probability rule for assessing the relatedness of action and outcome.
2. He does not always use this rule and may resort to very suspect rules.
3. The form of evidence may be a very important determinant of the rule operated; summary information encourages the operation of a sophisticated rule (implying that one of the problems may be difficulties in acquiring and representing the evidence on a trial-by-trial basis).
4. Characteristics of evidence may produce systematic bias; highly frequent or positive outcome trials may lead to overestimation.

In assessing contingency levels from data across a series of trials, a person is coping with frequency data; that is, some statistical representation of events over time must be made. If we imagine that events and happenings in life history provide the raw data on which an assessment of control is made, then it is important to consider not only factors in the representation of contingency but also possible sources of bias in the representation of evidence accrued over time. It is the "episodic data" that will form the model on which a subject may generate future predictions about his future potential for control. If bias occurs and leads to a non-valid memory base then we might expect distortions to occur in the judgement of current events. Thus, the origins of pessimism and optimism in thinking may arise because of bias introduced in episodic memory for life encounters.

There are also sources of bias that arise because a person behaves more like an intuitive statistician and may create bias at the point where a global estimate is made. Moreover, there may be a failure to understand how a personally experienced sample of events and outcomes may relate to a general population of experiences. A person may tend to generalise from the particular, too readily. These issues are very important if we are to begin to understand, for example, the origins of depressed thinking. For this reason it is worth considering the findings from general cognitive research about how people make global representations of evidence.

A. Conservative Bias

A wider literature on how information is extracted from samples of data provides the basis for understanding the origins of bias. Research evidence suggests that in uncertain environments the normative statistical model provides a good first-order approximation for the psychological theory of inference. In investigations of inferences about proportions, there is evidence to suggest that a person is likely to give a more *conservative* estimate than that which is obtained from application of a statistical model.

Peterson and Beach (1967) provide an extensive review of research on the concept of man as an intuitive statistician. Examples of the concept of conservative bias are apparent in the research covered. An example of conservatism in the estimate of proportions is given by the following example: There are two urns filled with poker chips. The first urn contains 70% red chips and 30% blue chips. The second urn has the reverse proportions (30/70 respectively). The experimenter flips a coin to select one of the urns at random and then draws out a sequence of chips. For a sample of, for example, 8 red and 4 blue chips subjects must decide whether the urn contains predominantly red or blue chips. Most subjects assess the probability as about 0.75, but a statistical model predicts 0.97. (See Edwards et al., 1965.)

Peterson and Beach (1967) point out that conservatism is suboptimal but is so systematic that researchers have looked for reasons. For example, boundary effects might operate; that is, subjects fear to go too near boundaries. Phillips and Edwards (1966) compared probability estimates with unbounded-odds estimates and found the latter only slightly conservative. Conservatism can be influenced by a number of variables such as incentives, sample size, and the sequential ordering of data, but is never eliminated. This suggests to Peterson and Beach that "it has roots in fundamental aspects of subjects' understanding and use of information (p. 33)." There are two possible explanations: The first is that subjects do not understand the relationship of samples and populations. The second is that subjects are bad at aggregating evidence over trials. Neither explanation accounts for the direction of the estimations being conservative rather than risky, but it could be argued that a useful heuristic in the face of inadequate evidence for whatever reason is to err on the side of caution. It is perhaps pertinent to note at this stage that stressful conditions have been found to increase the tendency to make stronger statements based on weaker evidence (Broadbent & Gregory, 1965; Fisher, 1983b).

The tendency to give rather less weight to deviant events in estimating the central tendency of a population could also be argued to be a form of conservative bias which should lead subjects to give estimates closer to the median than the mean for positively skewed distributions. The biasing of inferences towards the median is characteristic for estimates of a J-shaped frequency distribution (Peterson & Miller, 1964).

In understanding the basis of inituitive statistical inference, the failure of subjects to extract information from the task and the lack of optimal sensitivity to relevant variables cause the judgements to deviate from the predictions given on a statistical model. Peterson and Beach (1967) argue that the assumptions made by people may be at least partly responsible for discrepant predictions.

B. The Illusion of Representativeness

If people assume that a sample of data is usually representative of the parent population, then the tendency to assume that the sample will reflect the norms of the parent population will produce bias. In effect, the sample will not be judged on its own attributes but in accordance with the features of the population it supposedly represents.

This may provide the basis of a very important potential source of error. Knowledge that suggests females differ in response characteristics from males, for example, might drive bias in the estimates provided by a given sample of data. The representativeness notion may provide the basis of bias.

Tversky and Kahneman (1971) demonstrated the illusion of representativeness by asking people to imagine an experiment run on 20 subjects with a significant result supporting the theory ($Z = 2.23, p < .05$ two-tailed). For a further one-tailed test on 10 subjects, the "judges" were asked to assess the probability of a confirming result. Although the realistic assessment should be .48, only 9 out of 48 respondents gave averages between .40 and .60. The majority gave estimates in the region of .85. The exaggerated belief in the likelihood of successful replication of a finding is based on the representativeness fallacy.

A second demonstration of the same phenomenon reported by Tversky and Kahneman involved asking subjects to generate sequences of the likely result of tossing an unbiased coin. They typically produce short sequences producing a result of 50/50 when the laws of chance would be against this happening for such a short sequence.

The same bias could be argued to underlie the well-demonstrated "gamblers' fallacy"; because of the belief of the fairness of the laws of chance plus a belief in the representativeness of small samples, a person predicts that a result in one direction (lose) will be followed by a result in the other (win). Equally, fallacies such as "errors cancel each other out" may be founded on similar faulty reasoning.

The belief that different samples have similar properties and that there will be self-correcting properties operating due to the laws of chance, should lead people to transmit preconceptions from knowledge to specific situations. Rules evident in folklore could provide a source of such preconceptions. "Never trust a man with shifty eyes" may lead to the faulty interpretation of evidence from encounters with such people. Social learning from films, books, word of mouth, and art, creates sources of bias which could determine how small samples of data encountered in life are treated. A point made by Tversky and Kahneman (1971) is that experience is unlikely to help because sampling variation is always explained. They argue that a person: "rarely attributes a deviation of results from expectations to sampling variability, because he finds a causal explanation for any discrepancy (p. 109)." This failure will secure the fallacy of the belief in conformity of small-sample probabilities to chance (resulting in phenomena such as the gamblers' fallacy).

Although much of what Tversky and Kahneman argue is aimed at scientific investigations involving small samples, the general principles are arguably true of treatment of evidence from life events. A person is rarely in a position to be exposed to a sample of even 20 subjects in a short period. Impressions may be obtained from sequential experiences widely spaced in time. How do people know how others react to bereavement for example, or whether women have different or similar attitudes to men regarding leisure pursuits? One way is from information available in literature, the arts, television; the other is from occasional experience. The possibility exists that generalisations will be unrepresentative.

C. The Availability Bias

Results provided in a review of how people are likely to judge the frequency of events led Tversky and Kahneman (1973) to propose *availability* as a judgemental characteristic. "Availability" has a simple definition in terms of "the ease with which relevant instances come to mind (p. 207)." The authors propose that availability is correlated with ecological frequency but may also be influenced by other factors and will provide a source of bias in frequency estimation.

There is clear association between the concept of availability and the concept of dominance in semantic memory. Availability as defined by Tversky and Kahneman seems to be a function of the speed and ease with which items can be generated or answers constructed. A typical availability test consisted of a 3×3 matrix containing nine letters from which words of three or more letters are to be constructed. Subjects were given 7 seconds to estimate the number of words which they could produce in 2 minutes and then were given 2 minutes to write down the words. The mean number of words produced varied from 1.3 (for XUZIBLCJM) to 22.4 (for TAPCERHOB). The product moment correlation between estimation and production showed remarkable accuracy: .96 over the 16 problems. A similar result was obtained for a different task involving item generation from categories such as flowers or Russian novelists. The mean number estimated was 6.7 to 18.7 and the product moment correlation was .93.

An interesting but different area for the exploration of availability is in terms of word-frequency judgements. The example given by Tversky and Kahneman is of the frequency of words in the English alphabet which have K as first letter or third letter. Typically, instances where K is the *third* letter of a word outnumber instances where it is the *first* letter. However, the authors argue that *availability* of first-letter examples is greater and therefore on the availability hypothesis subjects should estimate more first-letter examples. The authors obtained examples of five consonants where the frequency of the letter was greater in the third position than in the first.

Subjects where asked to produce a ratio for the balance of likelihood of first or third position. Out of 152 subjects, 105 judged the first position to be more likely for the majority of letters and the remainder gave (accurate) judgements in terms of the third position. Overall, the median estimated ratio was 2 : 1 for each of the five selected consonants.

It seems that "availability" may not be explained as a function of a straightforward concept of accumulated frequency in this case because subjects presumably had perceived more words with the consonants in the third letter position. It is necessary to assume that awareness was an added factor and that letters at the beginning of words are more easily noticed, resulting in better availability.

A direct test of the role of availability in frequency judgements was made by presenting a pre-recorded list of names of famous personalities of both sexes. Since famous names would be expected to be easier to recall, on the availability hypothesis this should lead to a systematic bias in recall when subjects are asked to judge whether the list contains more names of males than females. Each list was of 39 names recorded at the rate of one name every two seconds. Two lists included names of 19 famous women and 20 less famous men. Two other lists consisted of the names with reversed fame and frequency. After listening to the four lists one group was asked to write down all the names. The other group was asked to judge whether the list contained more names of women or men. Of the 99 subjects who made the frequency comparison, 80 erroneously judged the class consisting of the famous names to be more frequent. Thus, fame or availability in memory was a determinant of frequency estimation.

Of equal importance in demonstrating the importance of availability in determining perceived frequency is a replication by Tversky and Kahneman (1973) of an experiment by Chapman (1967), on cued recall of highly related and unrelated word pairs. Highly related word pairs such as *knife–fork* were better recalled than unrelated pairs. A group of 68 subjects were asked to judge whether each of the pairs had appeared twice or three times in a message which included pairs. Highly related pairs were better recalled, and in the frequency-estimation condition they were judged as being more frequent. Thus there is further support for availability as a determinant of frequency estimation.

Tversky and Kahneman argue that availability may be an important determinant of how people deduce the likelihood of events in life. For example, contact with divorce or premature death may influence the perceived likelihood of such events. Equally, in assessing how a patient with certain symptoms may react, a clinician may recall an instance of a similar case in the past and judge the current patient accordingly. If dramatic, salient events are better recalled, this should increase the likelihood that they will increase the perceived frequency of similar events in the future.

It is not always clear from Tversky and Kahneman to what extent sensitivity may be the factor producing the effect. Subjects may become sensitised to pairings which make sense; they would distinguish them from non-relevant pairs, thus finding a cue for the organisation of frequency data.

D. Generator Bias

An important contribution to the understanding of the assessment of frequency has been provided by Howell and Burnett (1978). They hypothesise that in the case of the generation of a stationary series of events, knowledge of the *generator*, or *source* of the events will determine the assessment made. The representation of frequency will be a function of both *task structure* and *prior beliefs*. For example, people living in wet-weather districts may be likely to overestimate the number of wet days. Marques and Howell (1979) propose that the amount of processing required on a task can be reduced by prior knowledge. Beliefs about frequency structure will act by influencing the allocation of attentional resources. This raises the possibility that beliefs acquired about a source of events, bias appraisal. A person who constantly informs his friends that he is incompetent may well set the bias for representing his occasional error frequencies: The prophesy may be self-fulfilling.

3. STRATEGIES IN THE ASSESSMENT OF CONTINGENCY

A. Problems in the Perception of Contingency Data

The conclusion that could be drawn from the accounts of research provided in this chapter is that human beings are not normally likely to obtain optimal summaries of contingency data. The conditions for contingency assessment are likely to influence the summaries obtained. Positive outcomes are likely to bias the summary; although when responses are actively produced, or the information is presented in summarised form, there are improvements.

Different studies produce different conclusions. For example, Smedslund's (1963) data from student nurses suggested that adult subjects have *no concept of correlational evidence* and when allowed to sort cards (of diagnosis and symptom) into piles, do not even evolve a sorting rule that would be effective as an aid to decision. Smedslund concludes that they do not know what the concept of contingency would depend on. By contrast the presentation of information in *summarised* form by Ward and Jenkins (1965) favoured a statistical approach to assessment of correlational evidence.

In general, people are not good estimators of contingency data. If we assume that the perception of contingency is the basis of the perception of control, it would follow that the perception and assessment of control levels are likely to be subject to bias and distortion. This is very important because if a person is inaccurate in these assessments, stressful conditions may be distorted. In particular, pessimistic assessments of control level in situations should: (1) increase the likelihood of giving up; (2) increase the threat levels a person perceives; (3) increase the possibility of depression due to failure.

B. Implications for a Model of Strategic Processes in Stress

Figure 3.1 shows a basic conceptualisation of processes hypothesised to be involved in the perception of control. Initially, "reality" has to be perceived and represented in such a way as to be compared with "intended reality" or ambition. It was envisaged that people are aware of features of situations confronting them and form "suspicions" about relationships and then about demand characteristics (or what is expected of them).

A hierarchical model of decisions in the perception of control was developed by Fisher (1984a), in which it was assumed that successive life experiences provide inputs to a system which is a "working memory" for control potential. A person confronted with a new situation is assumed to make a number of assessments about the degree of threat present and the capacity to influence a stressful situation. These assessments are assumed to be dependent on the outcome of previous encounters and a person assesses whether there are physical facilities for exerting control (instrumentality), and whether he/she has the skills available. Fisher distinguished "intrinsic risk," the risk of adverse reaction dictated by features of the particular stressful scenario, from "extrinsic risk," which is the sum total of outcomes concerning control, accrued and summarised from previous non-stressful and stressful life encounters. Extrinsic risk in effect is a representation in memory of vulnerability. It was assumed that previous experience suggesting that control is possible may lower the extrinsic risk of an adverse outcome in an encounter resulting in perceived loss of control and personal crisis. Thus, factors represented in "extrinsic risk memory" may lead to a particular stressful situation as being perceived as positive and challenging, or negative and distressing.

The research reviewed in this chapter is of relevance for understanding not only how a person perceives the facts about the potential for control in a particular situation, but how he/she represents the data acquired in temporal succession throughout life. Basically, knowledge of the potential depends on the summarising and storage of frequency data provided by the "streams" of action/outcome data presented from various sources. The person may try and succeed on some occasions, or try but fail on other occasions. He/she may persist after failure and perceive that "if at first you do not succeed, try, try again." The results of persistence may provide information to suggest that even periods of failure may later be rectified by continued effort. Alternatively, he/she may learn to give up and accept the inevitabilities of failure. During such formative encounters, we assume that a person is acquiring temporally spaced evidence and learning to formulate "rules." In other words, there is some distillation of "life event" data over a period of time. A natural cognitive efficiency would be to extract the main features of these distillations and to begin to form the "if–then" rules that characterise strategies.

Seen in this light, it could be argued that understanding the origins of bias in the assessment of contingency and in the representation of successive information is of great importance. A cognitive model of depression (Beck, 1967, 1970) gives central importance to pessimistic themes in thinking: self-blame, low esteem, and a profound sense of futility about the future are seen as causal factors. The question is how do such themes evolve? In terms of the synthesis presented above, we might ask how a person comes to develop a pessimistic bias in the way he perceives the world around him.

One answer may lie with the learning experiences in life history. It is possible that particular encounters "tune" a person to develop bias and to become increasingly unrealistic in judgements or to use unrealistic strategic approaches. If research on the representation of contingency and frequency data had suggested that a person could behave as an ideal statistical computer, then the answer to why bias develops would have to concentrate on unfortunate encounters (i.e. "life is a bad deal and our person is correctly reflecting this"). However, it is clear from the evidence that even in quite simple encounters which generate a binary matrix, people are unlikely to store accurate assessments. Moreover, the temporal series of outcomes may be biased in line with a person's preconceptions. These distortions may both reflect and maintain a developing bias. For example, a person who after only a few trials with negative outcomes, perceives that he cannot cope, is demonstrating the illusion of representativeness. Since stressful experiences could be argued to provide intense learning experiences, this may help to develop an "availability bias" for the treatment of later data; a person who has perceived failure has "failure" as an outcome readily accessible in memory. An important mediating process then lies with behaviour; lack of persistence or avoidance of a challenging situation also provide streams of life event data which may confirm both the cognitive model and the rules which characterise it: "if at first you don't succeed . . . give up."

In later chapters it is suggested that some individuals resist depression by techniques which involve distortions of evidence. Thus, extrinsic risk of bad outcome and personal crisis may be low for some people and may be held artificially low by the operation of strategies based on non-valid premises which preserve adequate strategies for coping with the world. Rosenbaum (1983) has developed the notion of learned resourcefulness; the individual is assumed to acquire skills which facilitate regulation of internal states of emotion and distress. These skills acquired throughout life history may depend on the micro-structure of the representation of life event data.

5

Alternative Models of the Perception of Control

On the assumption that the perception that control is possible is an important mediating factor determining the short-term and long-term response to stress, an aspect of interest is how decisions concerning control are made. In particular, it is necessary to understand how facts relating to control are distilled and represented in cognition and how bias in decision making about control might evolve.

In the previous chapter the emphasis was on consideration of an ideal statistical model for the assessment of control. In fact the evidence suggests that people are unlikely to use ideal statistical rules. Assessments are more likely to be influenced by *positive outcomes*, or by knowledge of the alleged *source* of a series of events. For example, in trying to decide whether a sunset at night predicts fine weather the next day, we might expect a person to be more swayed by occasions when this was the case (positive examples), but also to be influenced by knowledge of weather patterns. For example, a belief that it always rains might lead to an underestimation of the relationship between sunsets and fine weather.

Perhaps the same kind of fallacious reasoning underlies the thinking of a person who has to decide whether he can cope with an impending crisis. On the assumption that there are, represented in knowledge, facts about attempts to cope with previous happenings, together with beliefs about likely outcomes, arising from other sources (confidants, experts, books), there is a basis for making predictions about the future.

In this chapter, consideration is given to alternative ways of assessing control. There may be shorthand routes, which are less complex and perhaps less easily distorted by bias and which may be used to arrive at implicit

71

conclusions about control. The first basis for implicit decision might be the presence of stored representations of actions and consequences. If a person can consult a set of cognitive facts which tell him which actions are needed for which consequences, then the "if–then" data bank should provide him a basis for assessing control. A person needs only to select the desired consequence and find the desired action. A model developed by Fisher (1984a) based on ideomotor theory provides a basis for understanding the implicit deduction that control is possible. Basically, all a person needs to know is that *an effective course of action is available*.

An implicit decision even less dependent on information processing may be made on the basis of *ideology*. Belief that control is rarely possible may circumvent all the detailed aspects of decision making described previously.

In some cases there may be readily *accessible knowledge* which also circumvents detailed decision making. For example, knowledge that untrained people cannot fly aircraft may lead to the immediate and implicit perception that there is no control in circumstances where the only solution to a problem involves flying an aircraft and the individual concerned is inexperienced.

This chapter is concerned with alternative models of the perception of control. We begin by developing an organisational framework for the cognitive basis of control assessment. It perhaps helps to ask the question: What elements of a program for a computer would need to be written in order that it can decide whether or not it has got control over a situation? A simple answer might be that it needs to know that feedback from the consequences of action matches with what it was originally expected to be.

1.   THE ORGANISATIONAL BASIS OF CONTROL

A. TOTE Units

The proposal that skills are organised with respect to consequences and based on hierarchies of component decisions, was first established by Miller, Galanter, and Pribram (1960). The basic unit of planned behaviour was the TOTE unit; the letters symbolising successive stages of decision and action loops: TEST, OPERATE, TEST, EXIST.

Miller, Galanter, and Pribram illustrate the features of TOTE units with the aid of an example of a person hitting a nail into wood. As illustrated by Fig. 5.1, in the TEST phase, the discrepancy between the head of the nail and the surface of the wood is detected. As a result of perceiving that the nail is not flush with the wood an OPERATE phase is instigated; the nail is hit to make it flush with the wood. Finally, the discrepancy between the head of the nail and the surface of the wood is tested again (TEST) and if the discrepancy is reduced to zero, there is exit from the loop,

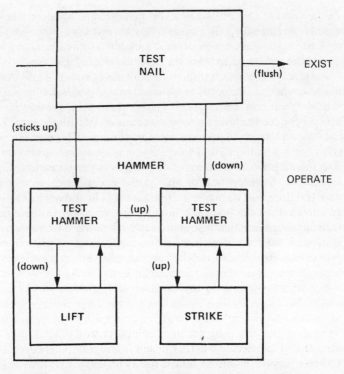

FIG. 5.1   The hierarchical plan for hammering nails. (Redrawn from Miller, Galanter, & Pribram, 1960, with the permission of the authors.)

described as the EXIST phase. Thus, TEST–OPERATE–TEST–EXIST provides a basic blueprint or program for skilled behaviour. As shown in figure 5.1, imbedded loops develop in even very simple situations; in order to OPERATE on the nail, the person must note the availability or position of a hammer and then bring the hammer down to the head of the nail to strike it. This series of operations can also be described in terms of TEST, OPERATE, TEST, EXIST. The branching complexity of these imbedded units can be easily illustrated by means of a real-life example. A person wishing to hit a nail into wood must find a hammer, which in turn may involve finding the key to the shed, finding the light switch, opening the tool box, etc. Each one of these specifiable component actions could be described in terms of a TOTE unit. Each component is an essential prerequisite for the overall aim of striking the nail and each stage is an essential prerequisite for the next stage. Thus, a whole series of dependencies may build up. A failure at any one stage has implications for the overall goal: A person may fail to strike the nail into the wood because he cannot find the key to unlock the chest in which he keeps the hammer. The TOTE unit will loop endlessly at this stage unless he invents a new way to strike the nail. Strategies may evolve as new means to desired ends and are bonded by realism, efficacy, and the limits of creative imagination.

A model which assumes that behaviour is purposeful and that activity is planned and hierarchically organised, provides a basis for understanding action as being linked to *specified* consequence. In these circumstances the action produced defines the essential features of consequence. Thus, it may not be necessary for a person to note the four possible contingency relationships for a situation. The *chosen action specifies the consequences* and all else should provide evidence of no control. A person expects that when he moves the steering wheel of his car, the car will behave in a predictable way. If it does not, he may conclude that : (1) he did not produce the action as intended; or (2) there is a fault in the car. It might therefore be more realistic to assume that a strategy for discovering how much control there is over an unknown vehicle would involve trying a variety of actions with predicted consequences and then checking the extent to which the *predicted* consequence and the *actual* consequence match. A mismatch means a fault in behaviour or a fault in the machine.

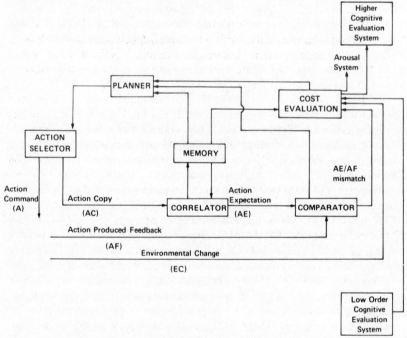

FIG. 5.2 Schematic representation of the ideomotor basis of perceived control (First produced in Fisher, 1984a).

B. An Ideomotor Model of the Perception of Control

Fisher (1984a) outlined a model which should provide a basis for understanding the perception of control in terms of variations in the predicted consequences of action. The model has been described briefly in earlier chapters and will now be examined as an alternative to contingency assessment as a basis for decisions about control.

Figure 5.2 illustrates a model based on the principles of *reafference* established by Von Holst (1954) in visual perception, or *ideomotor theory* (Greenwald, 1970). The model assumes that a command to the motor system has a neural copy. This copy is referred to as an "action copy" (AC) and contains a reference to a location in memory where similar previous copies are stored. Each copy is stored associated with an expectation (AE) of what will happen as a consequence of action. Thus, there are now two mental codes that define the action and the predicted consequences. The model allows for these codes to be evoked in advance of any real action. Part of the process of planning activity may be to rehearse *likely courses of action* against *likely consequences*. The desirability of the consequences can then be assessed and the result used to modify the action selected. For example, in considering cutting a tomato, a person may predict the consequences of using different kinds of knives and different cutting actions. The combination most likely to achieve the desired consequence will be selected. Stored (AC–AE) combinations will provide a basis for implicit planning in advance. Fisher (1984a) proposed that "implicit plan running" is the basis of "worry work." It is an important feature of behaviour in stress and the selection of strategic responses to stressful encounters.

The codes assumed to be available for predicting consequences from action are capable of describing and predicting real events in advance or in retrospect, can evoke imagery, and become a focus for consciousness. It is the manipulation of these mental reference codes which provides the basis for the perception that control is possible, and hence the perception of stress.

The main relevance for the perception of control in real-life situations is the possibility of built-in economy in information processing: By use of these codes a person may not need to represent contingency data. It may be sufficient that two relevant codes exist which predict action and desired consequences. Perceived control is reduced when a person has no action copy stored against a consequence which is in keeping with desired state, or when he perceives that his capacity to produce or sustain the action is lowered: A person may know how to add up a column of figures but predict poor ability to do so.

If a person acts exclusively on these two reference codes, he will not take into account information available in the permutations that contingency data afford. For example, he will not be evaluating the probability of outcome in the absence of action $P(O/\overline{A})$. Neither will he be representing his likely failure rates. With regard to the first point it could be argued that in many categories of situations for which action is required, the possibility of $P(O/\overline{A})$ can be discounted. A person estimating his control over a type-writer would not expect the keys to produce a result unless they were depressed. This situation is perhaps best described as "inert," in that if a person takes no action there will be no outcome. Many classes of skill should fall into this category. In inert situations the concern should be with the kind of result which can be produced.

With regard to failure rates, there is little experimental evidence about how people detect or represent their failures. An ideal system would represent failure, in the reference codes that specify control. Overall control in terms of the number of times a person obtains the desired outcome should be modified by the error term.

C. A Progress Model of the Perception of Control

A more general method of ascertaining level of control might be to monitor *progress* in terms of changes in reality as a consequence of action. In this model, it is an *implicit* assumption that if reality has changed in the desired direction, control is possible. Reverting to the previously used example of a man hitting a nail into wood, on the ideomotor model a person is assumed

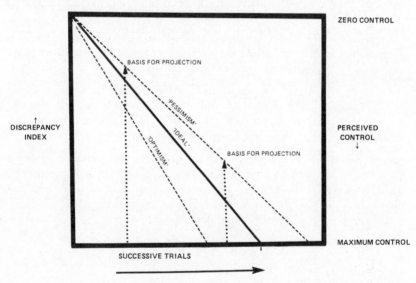

FIG. 5.3   The progress model of perceived control. (First produced in Fisher, 1984a.)

to accrue coded representations of action (hit nail) and expected consequence (nail sinks into wood). The perception that control is possible is assumed to occur if the action selected leads to expected consequences. By comparison, the progress model assumes that evidence of changes in the state of reality in line with intention is sufficient evidence for the perception of control. Both models do not require a full statistical description of evidence. In both cases, the evidence $P(O/A)$ is of greater interest and $P(O/\overline{A})$ is not highly weighted. The progress model requires that the person took some action and that there was a change considered desirable (I hit the nail; the nail is further in the wood).

The progress model is based on very basic data concerning whether it has been possible to create changes in the desired direction. Contained in the basic unit of planned activity are the two ingredients: *reality* (or state of the world) and the *intention* (or desired state of reality). The *discrepancy* produced by a comparison of the two representations is assumed to have energising properties. If a stored representation of the discrepancy is available, progress in reducing the discrepancy can be represented by means of a subtractive process. Thus, as shown in Fig. 5.3, gradual progress means an increasingly small discrepancy value. The discrepancy index at any one moment provides an estimate of current control. It is also assumed that judgemental bias may operate to influence the value of the discrepancy index. A pessimistic or optimistic judgemental bias will increasingly distort the discrepancy index if it is assumed to be the result of a succession of subtractions. However, external feedback such as is provided by knowledge of results (KOR) might provide a source of additional information. This may complement or challenge the impression provided by the discrepancy index: A person may have accrued trial-by-trial evidence to suggest that he is doing badly but may be forced to change his impressions if external feedback leads him to believe he is doing well.

D. Cognitive Processes in Control Assessment

The progress model and the ideomotor model both have the advantages of reducing the complexity of data that needs to be assimilated. The ideomotor model assumes that a person can predict outcome as a result of action and therefore assess control levels in terms of the confirmation of an expectancy. The progress model will depend on outcomes which create progress (i.e. change in reality in the desired direction) and occasions when this does not occur ($A/\overline{O}$ or $\overline{A}/O$) will not be of interest; a man may miss hitting a nail or hit it and find that it does not enter the wood properly, without revising his view of the level of control.

Both models depend on noting and representing discrepancies. The ideomotor model assumes that control assessment depends on comparing *expectancies* about the consequences of action with *actual* consequences. A mismatch creates a precondition for stress and will exacerbate an already existing stress. The progress model assumes that successive changes in the discrepancy between intention and reality can be represented and stored. Contingency is implicit in the modification of the discrepancy across successive trials and the individual does not necessarily need to check that his action actually achieves the result. She/he could be more easily fooled by circumstance into believing that there is control.

Both models have dependence on difference detection. In the case of the ideomotor model, a subject must detect the difference between what is expected and what happens as a result of action. The progress model depends on detecting differences in the discrepancy between the real and desired state of affairs. In both cases, the gist of whether or not control is possible is achieved by a process of subtraction and storage across successive trials. The relative judgement model proposed by Link (1978) in the context of reaction-time studies, provides a useful basis for understanding the essential cognitive elements involved. According to Link's model each successive stimulus is compared with a standard by a subtractive process. A discrepancy value is generated; if it is smaller than a threshold, one kind of response occurs; if it is larger a different response occurs. This basic process could determine how information about control is stored. The threshold may be determined by experience: Some individuals may tolerate a large discrepancy before deciding that control is impossible; others may be intolerant of even a small discrepancy.

The ideomotor and progress models described above are not assumed to be mutually exclusive; thus a person may note general progress or read feedback given in this respect, but at the same time note the response of the environment to action. It would be unrealistic to presume that a person faced with the task of hitting a nail into wood would assume that he had control if, irrespective of whether he took action or not, the nail mysteriously lowered itself into the wood.

In some life situations a person may be aware that his chosen action produces results but may need to note more complex feedback to know if the discrepancy between intention and reality is being resolved: A person writing a novel may know there is control in the sense that thoughts are transmitted into action and appear in print on the typing paper, but may need the feedback from readers and critics to decide whether there is ultimate control over the task and that the intention to create the definitive novel is fulfilled. Some readers may think there there is not an appropriate area of skill for the concept of control to be discussed. This raises the issue of how limited the concept should be: Is the concept of control to be limited to personal skills where action and consequence provide trial-by-trial data, or should we be thinking of a wider psychosocial environment?

2. A TYPOLOGY OF DECISIONS FOR CONTROL ASSESSMENT

A. Control Ideology

The concept of "locus of control" evolved from a background of social learning theory and the extensive literature is summarised by Lefcourt (1976) and Phares (1976). A more recent summary has been provided in the form of edited readings (Lefcourt, 1981).

Locus of control is a concept evolved from social psychology research, based on the use of scales which assess a person's causal beliefs. The most widely used scale is the internality–externality (I–E) scale devised by Rotter (1966). This had its origins in scales developed by Phares (1955) and James (1957). The scales are concerned with expectancies about control and attempt to discriminate those who believe that they have personal control over goals (internalisers) from those who do not (externalisers). The problem with most of the scales is that they assess a single factor and imply that locus of control could be used as a bipolar personality trait or typology. "Internals" are generally seen as potent, assertive, and effective, whereas "externals" are the opposite on these attributes.

One step that needs careful justification is whether the location of differences in abstract belief tendencies can be assumed to be part of a single personality trait. The I–E scale developed by Rotter is a single 23-item scale and assumes that what is being assessed is a unidimensional factor. However, application of factor-analytic techniques have indicated that there is more than one factor. Mirels (1970) provides a case for the inclusion of at least two factors: *personal control* and *social system control*. Reid and Ware (1974) lengthened the subscales and defined inner space (*self control*), psychological interaction space (*personal control*), and person–system transactions (*social system control*). Levenson (1973) developed scale profiles in terms of *internal*, *chance*, and *powerful others* dimensions. One result of the publication of results from the use of such subscales was a published defence by Rotter (1975) in which he argued that he had not intended the I–E scale to be used as such a narrowly predictive variable.

The Crandall intellectual achievement responsibility (IAR) developed by Crandall et al. (1965), concentrated on children but incorporated the notion of *responsibility* for success or failure. Thus the attribution of causation was linked to control ideology and was assessed by means of +1 (success) and −1 (failure) subscales. The authors reported low correlations between the subscales. The idiosyncratic nature of responses to situations is emphasised and the use of combined subscores is less easily justified.

Gregory (1981) assumed that since the Rotter I–E scale had been the subject of much research, there would be evidence that the attitude to positive and negative outcome situations would be equally well predicted. Gregory listed a number of studies where differences in internality–external-ity were apparent for situations with negative outcome, but was less success-ful in finding similar evidence for situations with positive outcome. For example, Seeman and Evans (1962) reported that on a version of the I–E scale, tuberculosis patients high on internality were more knowledgeable about their condition than those high on externality. Seeman (1963) found that with a group of reformatory prisoners, those with high internality knew more about how the prison was run. Gore and Rotter (1963) found that black students who scored high on internality were more likely to take part in a civil-rights demonstration. It could be argued that all three of these situations involve reaction to *adverse* conditions. The individual who is high on internality is more likely to attempt to change or attenuate the adverse circumstances.

A study by Houston (1972) concerning shock avoidance is perhaps more clearly addressed to unambiguous negative outcome. Houston's design in-volved either avoidable, unavoidable, or no-shock conditions. In the avoi-dance condition subjects were led to believe that errorless task performance would lead to shock avoidance. The results showed superior performance in this condition for those who scored high in internality.

Taken collectively, these studies could all be argued to suggest that I–E differences in adults occur when there is an encounter with a situation which has negative qualities and which is to be avoided. Put quite simply, the I groups appear to collect information together, find out what is going on, then engage the problem. The E groups are less likely to behave this way. In terms of the issues about stress and strategy developed in this book, it could be argued that the generalised belief that control is always possible leads some people to implement "finding out" and "operating" strategies, whereas others never really engage the problem.

Gregory (1978) provided a direct test of the hypothesis of whether such differences would occur for a situation characterised by positive outcome as well as one which involved negative outcome. The design used was based on a design by Rotter and Mulry (1965) using an angle-matching task. Subjects who were high on internality were found to take more time to reach a decision when they believed that the result could be influenced by skill rather than chance. Gregory introduced *response cost* by informing students that they would lose credit for a mistake, and *reward* by informing students that they would be rewarded for each angle matched correctly. The results showed that those subjects who scored high on internality spent longer than those scoring high on externality at the angle-matching task when there was negative cost attached to failure, but there was no difference when reward was the outcome. However, one qualification is that Gregory did not use the Rotter I–E scale but used the malevolent–benevolent scale. The correlation of the malevolent subscale and the I–E scale is reported as .40 and suggests that malevolent expectancies are associated with exter-

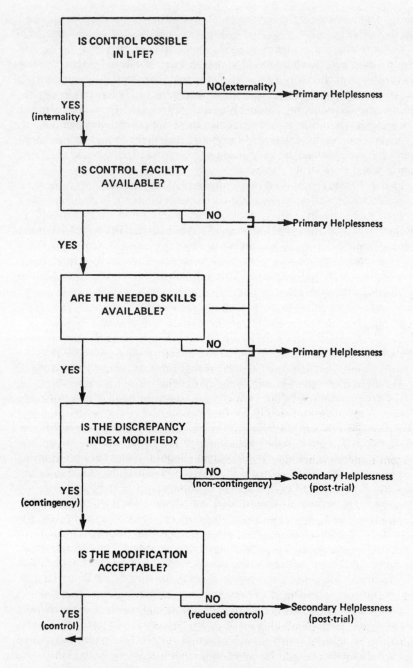

FIG. 5.4 Hierarchically ordered decisions in the perception of control in specific situations. (First produced in Fisher, 1984a.)

nality. There was no significant correlation for the "benevolent" scores and the I–E scale.

Collectively, the evidence suggests that a person may believe he has control over negative outcomes but may not necessarily believe that he has control over positive outcomes. If this is true, then beliefs about control, far from representing an ideology that determines all behaviour in all situations, may actually involve highly specific appraisals. However, as far as stressful situations are concerned, since these are potentially negative-outcome encounters, the existence of a polarised ideology should be influential and as argued previously could lead to quick, superficially based decisions about whether control is possible.

Fisher (1984a) proposed that any situation, stressful or otherwise, afforded a hierarchically organised series of decisions about control. Fisher argued that logically, strong ideologies in beliefs about control should be at the top of a decision-making hierarchy. As illustrated in Fig. 5.4, a person who strongly believes he has no possibility for control would not need to consider further processing with a view to assessing the situation, and would behave in a way that suggested little effort had been made to tackle the problem (primary helplessness).

B. Control Facility

Assuming a person decides to engage a problem, a main decision concerns the availability and reliability of *control facility*. In Fig. 5.4, this is depicted at the stage of decision following the first, ideological decision.

Different situations will be expected to have different implications for decisions about control facility. In some cases a person may know implicitly that there is low control because *the means for operating control* is not identifiable. A person could not control a car if the steering wheel was missing. She/he could not control personal pain if there were no drugs or the outcome for a sick relative if there was no medication to influence the disease. Perception of no means for operating control (whether correctly or incorrectly perceived) should render a person effectively helpless.

In some cases, especially where there is previous experience which is relevant, a person may implicitly identify the control facility directly from memory. In other cases a person may need to consult the memory store of action and consequence and then deduce what control facility is needed. For example, imagine a person who sees the bursting of a dam half a mile away and sees a wall of water coming towards him. Use of a car would give him a speed advantage. He locates a car and concludes that there is control facility. He then finds that the key is missing; he must break in and connect the ignition leads in order to make use of the potential control facility. However, if the key is not in the car and speed of the advancing wall of water is fast then he will not be able to start the car in time; the facility is useless. Throughout this "if–then" decision making, there is the implicit assumption that if only the key were available driving the car would be no problem. A novice driver might be in quite a different decision-making situation and might decide at an early stage that escape is impossible.

In laboratory conditions any switch or lever that can be operated to produce a change provides a subject with potential control facility. Most straightforward experimental paradigms involve use of control facilities of some kind or another and a subject is usually scored on his ability to make use of the facilities. Reaction time is a score of speed in indicating a choice by means of a response on a switch. Errors represent occasions of misuse of control facility in some way or another. However, in laboratory or real-life conditions involving threat, a person may need to *identify the means of control* over the threatening condition.

These points draw attention to the need to analyse situations with regard to *what the perceived threat is, what the goal is*, and *what control facility is available*. Control facility may involve simple or complex decision making. In the most complex cases, control is achieved by routes which are not straightforward. For example, in the case of a person whose mother is dying the identification of control facility may depend on a complex mapping of subgoals:

> Overall goal ⟶ make mother better; Subgoal 1 ⟶ obtain better treatment; Subgoal 2 ⟶ work harder to obtain more money.

The decision that control facility is available may depend on: (1) identifying a possible treatment; (2) identifying a means of implementing it (e.g. make money to buy treatment). Conflict occurs if the consequences of behaving in relation to one of the specified subgoals creates a difficulty for some aspect of the original goal. For example, the overall goal "make mother better" may be sacrificed if the person cannot look after his/her mother because she/he is working harder to obtain the money for treatment.

An important aspect of the perception of control facility might be described as "control over what?" That is, the availability of control facility is defined with respect to what a person seeks to control. In any real-life situation, this in itself may be complex and involve personal cost attached differentially to different perceived aspects. Imagine a person who is told she/he is terminally ill with cancer. She/he may need to sacrifice comfort and incur the distress of unpleasant symptoms attached to chemotherapy in order to survive. Therefore, the overall goal "control the illness" evokes loss of control over comfort and appearance. An alternative overall goal "control the distress in others" may mean trying to appear healthy and refusing to tell anyone about the illness. This may evoke reduced control over obtaining help when it is needed. A third alternative might be "control

84

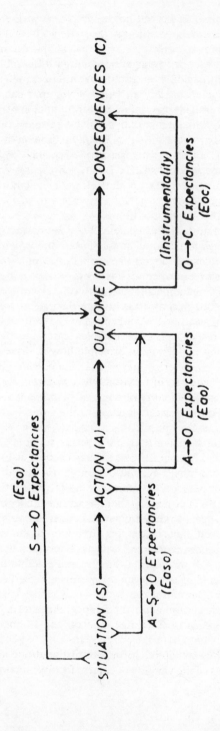

FIG. 5.5 Representation of four stages of expectations that determine the probability of action. (Reproduced from Heckhausen, 1977, with the permission of the author and the American Psychological Association.)

the feelings": A person might turn to palliatives such as drink and drugs to damp down fear and distress resulting in loss of control over personal image as perceived by others.

This example illustrates that any situation may be associated with a network of potential control facilities. A strategy could be defined as the process of locating *the most appropriate facility with the least cost attached*. Thus a person identifies what is possible for his life circumstance and weighs up the cost of the consequence of operating it against its long-term benefits. The exploration of a likely facility for control involves consideration of *personal skill and capacity*. This was located as the third decision level in the model proposed by Fisher.

C. Personal Skills and Ability

An intrinsic aspect of assessment of control is *perceived ability*. In simple encounters a person may implicitly assume that she/he has the resources necessary. In the case of operating a switch, a person may have sufficient knowledge about its operating characteristics to recognise its potential; for most people skill and capacity for operating a switch is hardly disputed. The question is whether the switch can be operated to achieve a desired result (speed or accuracy). A person may have doubts about personal abilities in this respect. In more complex cases the basic skill could be doubted. A person may know in principle how to drive a car but not feel able to drive one for a variety of reasons. The *potential* for control is there but the personal assessment may imply low control.

Perception of personal competence may be critical; if a person believes she/he is unskilled or lacks capacity (even if this belief is unfounded), subjective assessment of the situation suggests low control. If factors such as stressful circumstance, or prevailing moods, influence these judgements, then the basis for assessment of control may become distorted. The question of interest is how a person consults stored knowledge in order to make an assessment about personal potential for effective action.

Heckhausen (1977) proposed a framework for conceptualising the prediction of behaviour in terms of a four-stage sequence of events from situation to consequence. The first stage is the perception of the initial situation; the second stage is personal action; the third stage is the outcome of the action. The fourth stage, anticipated outcome, is the essential aspect of the basis of expectancies and relates to the other stages in the sequence. As shown in Fig. 5.5, there are thus four types of expectancy: situation–outcome expectancies (Eso); action–outcome expectancies (Eao); action by situation–outcome expectancies (Easo); and outcome–consequence expectancies (Eoc).

In terms of this descriptive formulation it could be argued that central to the assessment of the viability of control facility is action–outcome expectancy (Eao) and outcome–consequence expectancy (Eoc). The subject must appraise control facility as a means for achieving outcome and then assess personal capability.

Two possible decisional orderings are possible. On the "consequence" model, a person projects the desired consequence (e.g. window broken). This information is used to locate action. Fisher (1984a) proposed that on the ideomotor model, a store of correlations between past actions and outcomes should provide a basis for looking up a suitable action for a specified outcome. In other words, the correlational store can be used to advantage in two directions: Either a selected action can evoke a strongly associated consequence, or a consequence can evoke a strongly associated action copy. Thus, *hitting glass with hard object* evokes the expected consequence *broken glass*. A plan to *break glass* could by means of the same store evoke the action blueprint *hit glass with hard object*.

An alternative, but arguably less efficient, strategy for deciding about the level of control, might be to search out and imagine the results of using all the objects or actions available. This strategy might be useful in a situation where a person is constrained by circumstance or as a final resort when an action cannot be found which will evoke a desired consequence. Thus a prisoner may search the room for an object which could help him escape. An unlikely object discovered may evoke strings of potential outcomes which will help progress towards the aim to escape.

Equally, a person may use this method in circumstances where he allows control to be delegated to a "local expert" such as a doctor or dentist. She/he perceives a need (remove tooth, cure pain in stomach) and consults an expert. It could be argued that control is relinquished but it could be counter-argued that the best control is achieved by considered delegation to an expert with skill. This is like using another person as an instrument—a source of action that will bring about desired change.

It is possible that storage of the necessary information about personal capabilities and control is also available at a very general level. This would remove the need for consultation at a detailed level in the ideomotor correlational matrix. A person does not need to go through a decisional procedure: Tooth must be removed; can I remove tooth?; will the pliers remove my tooth?; could I weaken it by moving it?; etc. She/he knows "dentists remove teeth painlessly." This knowledge may lead to a course of action backed up with implicit assumptions about the skill and competence of dentists.

Equally, a person may accept written knowledge, or personally acquired information about rules, without ever having had the chance to test the hypothesis or to test personal skills and ability. "Always stare a dangerous animal in the eye!"; "Never show signs of fear"; "Do not run in front of a bull." These may be "rules" that are acquired but for most people never tested until a sudden encounter.

.3. THE REVISED HIERARCHICAL DECISION MODEL

A. Spheres of Control

In addition to the problem of the non-unitary nature of Rotter's I–E scale, there is the problem of the paradoxical finding of a positive correlation between the Machiavellianism scale (Prucuik & Breen, 1976) and the externality scale. The finding seems paradoxical since those who attempt to manipulate others should be deemed unlikely to perceive themselves as externally controlled. Paulhus and Christie (1981) point out that the difficulty is overcome by the partitioning of interpersonal control. This led indirectly to a conceptualisation by these authors in terms of three behavioural domains or "theaters." The first is seen as central and is concerned with the self and personal achievement in non-social contexts. Solving puzzles, building bookcases, climbing mountains are all aspects of personal skill and achievement. Perceived control is defined in terms of *personal efficacy* in this domain. Secondly, the individual acts in a social context and may or may not acquire *interpersonal control*. Thirdly, the individual acts within a socio-political context, and may organise demonstrations, strikes, or run campaigns to achieve social or political aims. If successful the person acquires *socio-political control*.

On the basis of this conceptualisation, three scales were introduced by Paulhus and Christie with the assumption that there may be different expectancies of control in each of the three domains, although the three expectancies should show a moderate correlation. This approach provides the basis for a *control profile* measured by means of the spheres of control (SOC) battery. Paulhus and Christie point to three advantages obtained by the tripartite division: (1) it entails partitioning in terms of spheres of activity; (2) it provides a basis for separating and assessing interpersonal control; (3) it subdivides the internal core to provide a meaningful set of attributes. The Machiavellian individual is likely to try to manipulate others but could have, for example, low personal skills. Intercorrelation data provided by Paulhus and Christie support this hypothesis, and demonstrate the near independence of Machiavellianism and interpersonal skill.

From the results of a comparison of control profiles conducted by Paulhus and Christie on college athletes (footballers and tennis players) and non-athletes, it was predicted that athletic groups should have higher personal and interpersonal control scores than non-athletes. Football players were assumed to have the highest interpersonal control because of team involvement, whereas tennis players should have highest scores on personal efficacy because tennis is individualistic and competitive. Scores on the control profile were found to support these predications.

The Paulhus and Christie partitioning is greater than just a specification of spheres of influence. They present a "facet analysis" based on four critical parameters or facets: source; target; valence; and sphere of control. Their analysis provides an ANOVA design in which any item in a perceived control inventory is represented as a cell in a 3-dimensional matrix. They point out that most items have the form "X controls Y in situation Z," where X is a control source, Y is some target and Z is the behavioural sphere. They describe a fundamental statement capable of generating $3 \times 2 \times 2 \times 3 = 36$ different, main or kernel sentences.

$$
\left\{ \begin{array}{l} \text{Chance,} \\ \text{skill and/or} \\ \text{hard work} \end{array} \right\}
\begin{array}{l} \text{determines} \\ \text{any} \end{array}
\left\{ \begin{array}{l} \text{success} \\ \text{failure} \end{array} \right\}
\text{that people have in}
\left\{ \begin{array}{l} \text{personal achievement} \\ \text{interpersonal life} \\ \text{sociopolitical} \\ \text{activity.} \end{array} \right\}
$$

The authors speculate that the entire domain of perceived control may derive from a linguistic or attributional structure centred round a generator sentence such as "X controls Y in situation Z," or "X causes Y under circumstance Z." The model not only incorporates the major aspects of perceived control defined by other researchers but provides a basis for understanding control in terms of causal schema and linguistic structures.

B. Strategies for Locating Control

If we accept that externality is not one-dimensional, there are implications for decision making and strategy. The hierarchical decision model proposed by Fisher (1984a) assumes that internality–externality decisions have primacy in that a decision that no control is possible should logically lead to inertia, helplessness, and failure to engage the problem. However, the work by Paulhus and Christie suggests that a person might fail to find the means for control in one domain but find it in another. He may decide, for example, that he has no personal control over the situation but could create changes through socio-political channels.

The hierarchical decision model can take account of this if it is assumed that a person makes decisions in a number of domains. She/he may decide that control is available in one domain and then cease to sample the others. Alternatively, she/he might process the evidence in all domains and finally decide there is no means for control. It is assumed that the principles of hierarchical organisation are operative for each domain. Thus, if a person decides in principle that she/he has the potential for control in a particular domain, she/he may then need to process further to find out about control facility and skills available.

However, as suggested earlier, the superordinate decision may be influenced by the nature of the situation and the skills required. Thus, quite implicitly a person might recognise that although she/he generally does have the potential for control she/he does not have it in this particular situation. The difference is illustrated by the example of a car driver contemplating flying *Concorde* or driving a tractor. She/he may know immediately that flying *Concorde* is out of the question without training, and no in-depth analysis of control facilities and skills is necessary. In the case of the tractor, she/he may feel that it will be possible because it is similar in many respects to a car. Before deciding, more information is required about the controls and the skills needed. Decision making involves two aspects: It is necessary to choose an appropriate domain and to decide about control levels within the domain selected.

If it is assumed that the assessment of control occurs in different domains, the issue of "control over what" can be better tackled. A person may relinquish control to a skilled professional as when a dentist or doctor is consulted. Mills and Krantz (1979) investigated the effects of giving blood donors increased control over details of when and how blood was taken (timing of event, choice of arm) and found that those with more control were more distressed than those with less control. This could be argued to be because the donor recognises his lack of skills in taking blood and prefers the action to be taken by others. In terms of domains, the donor normally retains control over his health and wellbeing by transferring responsibility to a professional. The individual has relinquished personal control but has retained control over outcome by using the services of an expert.

Figure 5.6 shows the hierarchical decision model revised to take account of the above findings. According to this model a person makes decisions within domains: *personal, interpersonal*, and *socio-political*. When there is failure in one domain, another might be consulted. For example, a person who perceives a low chance of personal success might operate control by means of the skills of others (consulting doctors, dentists, or surgeons) or may find political solutions to a problem. Part of the strategic response to a threatening situation may be to try to operate control via different domains.

Within each domain a person may assess the possibilities for control and actually engage the problem on a trial-and-error basis for a while. Alternatively there may be implicit knowledge suggesting for example little chance of personal control (I cannot diffuse a bomb, or fly *Concorde*, or extract my own tooth). A person may then seek to obtain control in a more appropriate domain, seeking to acquire the skills of trained specialists or experts.

In theory, it is possible to specify an orderly, logical process in which different domains are consulted. However, specific situations may demand the involvement of a particular domain. Equally, a person may develop a cognitive style which involves seeking control in a particular domain. Strategies may evolve for locating the most effective means of control in different situations.

The order in which different domains are consulted is a major aspect of the strategy a person employs to cope with a stressful environment. A person who favours the personal domain will seek the means for direct personal intervention (e.g. in the case of a room on fire, use the urn to pour water over the flames; shut the fire doors to contain the fire). The

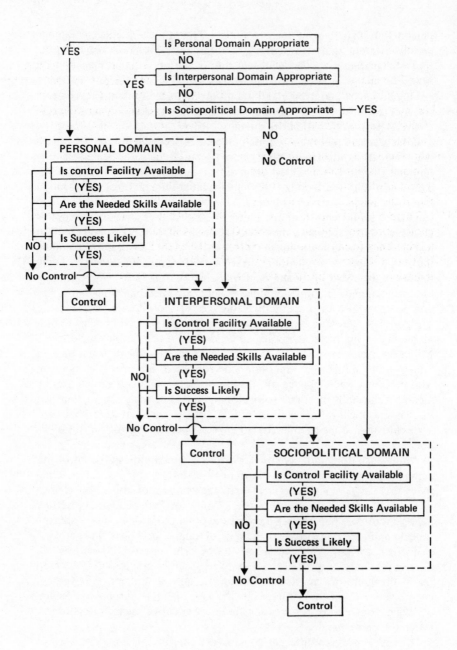

FIG. 5.6   A reformulated model of decision processes in the perception of control.

person who favours relinquishing control to an expert might have a completely different approach, characterised by seeking help (attract attention, find a telephone, etc.). In the case of a fire in a room, the political domain would be inappropriate.

This raises the point that resolution of certain environmental contingencies may be favoured by action in particular domains. *Choice of an inappropriate domain in attempting to control the situation may inevitably lead to failure.* To return to our example, a person confronted by a fire in a room who seeks to control it directly may benefit if the spread of the fire is minimal but may risk his or her life if the fire is well established. Conversely, a person who relies on help from a professional may put him or herself at risk if the telephone is inaccessible, etc.

Therefore, even in the basic decision about how to tackle a situation, choice of control domain may be critical. The vulnerable person might have a preference for an inappropriate domain. This raises the issue of compatibility of this element of strategy with the ideal for the situation. These issues are discussed again in the last two chapters of this book.

6 Stress and Competence: The Arousal Model

An important aspect of establishing control is competence. A person may *know* how to complete a series of actions but may occasionally fail to maintain accuracy. In stress, the occurrence of errors or slowness may be particularly important. If we imagine a strategy as involving a series or sequential group of behaviours, linked by the purpose of achieving a desired goal in order to obtain control, the occurrence of errors in the output can weaken the effectiveness of the strategy. A person who intends to escape from a smoke-filled room by pushing open the fire doors, will fail in overall strategy if slipping whilst climbing over the furniture.

Fisher (1984a) pointed out that the *perception* of control may depend on whether or not the error is detected. A person who fails to detect an error but notes change in reality, may attribute the change to a strategy failure. A person who notes the occurrence of his errors may be able to qualify the change in reality by attributing it to a slip of execution, and preserve the notion that action is effective.

Stresses change the probability of error and influence the speed of performance. However, what is unclear is to what extent behaviour in stress is itself strategic (as if, for example, a person decides to work faster and risk errors), or to what extent behaviour is "driven" directly by the features of the stressful condition and the impact on the nervous system. It is useful to distinguish *direct hit* or mechanical effects from *strategic* effects. The former are unavoidable effects because of changes produced on mental activity. The latter are brought about by decisions concerning all aspects of the situation.

A useful example is that of driving too close to the car in front in conditions of fog. A direct-hit model would assume that fog changes driving behaviour directly by, say, increasing arousal, and therefore produces faster driving which means that the car is too close to the car in front. The same scenario could be explained by a strategic model; the driver has the goal of getting home before the fog worsens, therefore he drives more quickly and takes more risks.

There is a substantial research literature addressed to the issue of changes in human competence in stress. What has not really been considered is whether changes in characteristics and competence of behaviour result from direct hit or from strategy. Stresses are frequently associated with behaviour designed to protect, attenuate, or avoid and so it is intuitively plausible that strategic behaviour is invoked. If the synthesis of ideas presented in this book is accepted, strategic behaviour underlies all exposures to problems in life; stressful conditions merely describe a category of vital problems. This is not to deny that mechanical changes to thinking occur in stress.

Before discussing these issues further it is useful to consider the major "direct-hit" models that provide an explanation of behaviour in stress. The shift in theoretical stance from Fisher (1984a) is that now we argue that the response to threat is two layered: Strategic response, characterised by policy and style decisions, provides the base features of all behaviour in stress; while mechanical effects directly overlay and colour these decisions.

1. STRESS AND COMPETENCE

A substantial research literature compiled over the last 30 years generally supports the idea that changes in competence are frequent in conditions of threat or stress. Inevitably the stressful conditions most studied are those which can be adapted to the laboratory, such as noise, heat, electric shock, fatigue, loss of sleep. In these circumstances, a typical laboratory design involves a subject performing a task in the presence of conditions of environmental stress. Assessment of competence changes depends on changes in the performance of the task in the stress condition, as compared with the non-stress condition. Evidence based largely on laboratory research is summarised by Broadbent (1957), Poulton (1970), Fisher (1984a) and in edited readings by Hamilton and Warburton (1979) and Hockey (1983).

The evidence concerning stress and its relationship with competence in the performance of tasks is frequently inconclusive—in some cases stressful circumstances lead to improvement, in other cases there is no change, and in some cases there are improvements in performance. Much depends on the stress, the context in which it occurs, the task, the duration of task or stress, instructions, and the criterion for acceptable performance. What the accumulated research has provided is insight into specific conditions likely to increase or decrease the risk of poor performance, and at the same time it has given theoretical insight into the rules that determine the changes.

2. THE AROUSAL MODEL

Much has been written about the concept of arousal and its relationship to performance. In spite of intuitive appeal, there are many details yet to be worked out and it remains possible that arousal change is no more than an epiphenomenon with no direct causal association with performance. First, an outline of the historical development of the concept of arousal as an explanatory tool is provided. Then some of the recognised difficulties with the concept are discussed. Finally, applications to the understanding of changes in performance competence in stress are considered.

A. The Principles of the Yerkes–Dodson Law

Research by Yerkes and Dodson (1908) on laboratory animals was oriented towards the understanding of the relationship between drive level, inferred from independent variable manipulations, and learning ability. The Yerkes–Dodson law has two fundamental aspects: First there is the hypothesis that an inverted 'U' relationship exists between drive level and performance.

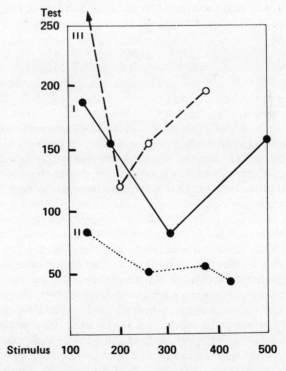

FIG. 6.1   Data from Yerkes and Dodson (1908) showing inverted U relationship between arousal and performance.

There is thus assumed to be an optimum drive/performance position. The second aspect is that there are hypothesised to be families of inverted U curves for different levels of task complexity: Complex tasks have lower inverted U optima than simple tasks. As illustrated by the data from Yerkes and Dodson in Fig. 6.1, both aspects are supported by the results of an experiment in which learning was examined as a function of shock intensity.

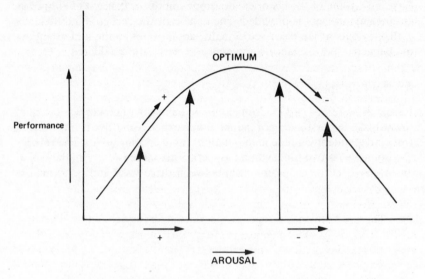

FIG. 6.2 Idealised representation of the inverted arousal–performance relationship.

Figure 6.2 illustrates the inverted U model in idealised form and illustrates the fractionating relationship between arousal and performance. As illustrated in the figure, increased arousal at low arousal levels produces performance improvement, whereas at high levels, it is likely to produce decrement. Therefore, base position is an important determinant of the result of increased arousal.

Figure 6.3 illustrates the second assumption of the Yerkes–Dodson law in idealised form. It is assumed that the level of task complexity interacts with arousal properties in determining the final form of performance. For simple tasks, increase in arousal can be tolerated before over-optimum levels of arousal are produced and performance decrement occurs. Conversely, complex tasks are vulnerable in that increase in arousal rapidly produces hyper-arousal states and performance deterioration.

Although Yerkes and Dodson were working with the concept of drive in animals, the principles of the law have come to be closely associated with the concept of arousal or activation. Thus, the term "Yerkes–Dodson law" is often retained as an alternative label for the arousal model. There are some points of difference worth emphasising. Firstly, in the Yerkes–Dodson

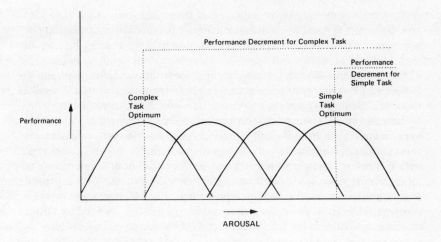

FIG. 6.3   Idealised representation of test difficulty as a determinant of optimum arousal level.

research, the concept of drive was manipulated by depriving an animal of
a basic need, or exposing it to external painful stimuli. Secondly, the Yerkes–
Dodson law was founded on empirical relationships between the level of
an independent variable such as shock, and the dependent variable. The
arousal model as developed in the 1940s and 1950s depended more on
correlating measures of existing physiological states and performance, or
on inducing states of tension.

Duffy (1962) proposed that there was a single energy dimension on which
states of motivation and emotion were distinguished only by intensity,
without discontinuity. Emotions were generally seen as more intense states
on the dimension. The implicit assumption was that there was a single
dimension and that any number of states could be specified with respect
to this dimension. Both Freeman (1948) and Hebb (1955) developed the
concept of an inverted U relationship between arousal and performance
level. Freeman provided evidence to support the concept from a single
case in which reaction-time scores were used to measure level of performance and palmar conductance was used to measure arousal.

Hebb's approach was more theoretical and involved some further clarification of the effect of a sensory event. There were two distinct functional
aspects: "Cue function" served to *guide* behaviour; the "arousal" or "vigilance function" was concerned with energy. "Without a foundation of
arousal, the cue function cannot exist (p. 249)." Hebb argued that arousal
is synonymous with drive and saw the concept as physiologically committed.
The main assumption was that cortical synaptic function is faciliated by a
"diffuse bombardment of the arousal system (p. 250)." When arousal is at
a high level, greater bombardment leads to interference with the delicate
adjustments involved in cue function. In an article proposing the utility of

the inverted U model, Hebb pointed out there was great significance for understanding risk-taking or the attraction of fear and danger, but did not work out the details of how it is that motivation to seek sources of increased arousal could occur.

There are three identifiable sets of evidence from reported studies in the 1940s and 1950s that lend support to the credibility of the inverted U model. First, Malmo (1959) cited data showing that drive level, increased by deprivation, shows an inverted U relationship with performance. He quoted experimental data from Belanger and Feldman in which water deprivation was manipulated in rats. Heart rate was found to show a progressive change with increasing hours of water deprivation. Up to 48 hours of deprivation, an increasing monotonic relationship between the number of bar presses and hours of deprivation was demonstrated; after 48 hours, the reverse was true. Thus, it would appear reasonable to infer that as need and drive increase, response rates first increase and then decrease. The problem is, of course, that deprivation of a vital need such as water may induce a state of need in which energetic behaviour cannot be sustained. Malmo's own research on loss of sleep, provided support for the idea that deprivation can have activating properties. He pointed out, however, that the drive state will still be in part determined by environmental stimulation—in the absence of stimulation a person may feel drowsy. Thus, deprivation and environmental conditions together dictate the level of arousal.

The second set of evidence involves studies in which arousal is induced in a subject and a measure is taken of physiological arousal and performance. As shown in Fig. 6.4, studies by Courts (1942) showed that increased dynamometer tension exerted by subjects produced at first an improvement and then deterioration in score in a memory task. Malmo (1959) argues that although it would be tempting to conclude that tension induction is simply one of many ways of increasing arousal level, it is possible that squeezing the dynamometer produces generalised activation changes. A specific criticism of this kind of design was provided by Näätänen (1973). In summarising the results of a number of comparable U curve results, Näätänen pointed out that the force required to push a lever or squeeze a

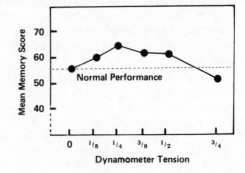

FIG. 6.4   Data from Courts (1942) showing the relationship between dynamometer tension and memory proficiency.

bulb is calculated in relation to a subject's strength. The decrement in performance occurs "only when heavy physical efforts have been performed simultaneously (p. 161)." Näätänen argues that the increasing demands of the "induced tension" task may be the factor that induces performance deficit. He also found evidence of cases where no U curve exists (e.g. Duffy, 1962; Hokanson, 1969). Therefore, presumably even the supposition that induced tension produces decrement because of raised demand, needs further qualification.

Näätänen provided evidence that levels of arousal previously induced by a bicycle ergometer with different gear settings, resulted in no connection between heart rate and reaction time. However, the same reaction-time task performed while still cycling showed a deterioration of reaction time with increased heart rate level as a direct result of the gear setting on the ergometer. Comparable results were obtained for a task in which speed of arm movement rather than reaction time was involved: heart rate bore no relationship to movement speed when arousal levels were induced prior to performance, but when the task of cycling occurred at the same time as the arm-movement task, deterioration occurred as a function of arousal level indexed by heart rate.

A third set of evidence about the relationship between arousal and performance concerns situations where physical effort is not manipulated, but incentive or anxiety variables are involved. Stennett (1957) manipulated incentive during an auditory tracking task. He obtained recordings from four different muscle groups as well as palmar conductance recordings, as measures of arousal level. The incentive conditions are described as varying from one in which the subject was not aware that his scores were being recorded, to high-incentive conditions in which the score was used to determine whether or not he avoided a 100–150 V shock or earned bonus money of two to five dollars. The inverted U relationship between arousal and performance was found to hold regardless of whether muscular or palmar conductance recordings were used as the criterion of arousal.

This design could be argued to qualify for Näätänen's criticisms since the extra incentive conditions could create a dual task environment where considerations about high incentive detract from resources required for the task. However, the design is different from the "effort paradigm" described previously where the subject is required to produce more physical effort; therefore, the finding that the inverted U relationship held is of some importance.

A design involving the partitioning of subjects on the basis of anxiety levels was used by Matarazzo et al. (1955). Figure 6.5 shows that anxiety level as measured by the Taylor manifest anxiety scale was related to the time required to learn to criterion in the form of an inverted U curve. However, results from a similar study by Matarazzo and Matarazzo (1956) with a tracking task gave no evidence of a relationship with anxiety. The

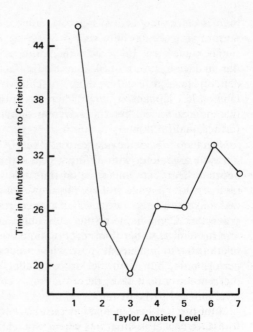

FIG. 6.5   Data from Matarazzo et al. (1955) showing learning proficiency as a function of anxiety level. (With the permission of Matarazzo and the American Psychological Association.)

conditions under which U relationships are and are not obtained need further investigation. At least one factor may be the nature of the task.

The design in which anxiety levels are linked with performance could at least be said to be free of the major point of criticism raised by Näätänen (namely that the inverted U arousal– performance relationship arises because of dual task demands), because "anxiety" is indexed but not created by subjects. In spite of the analysis difficulties, Matarazzo's results give some support to the assumption that levels of arousal directly influence performance.

B. Biological Arousal Systems

Much of the impetus for the notion of arousal as a factor determining performance came from studies in electroencephalography (EEG). Research demonstrated a progression of rhythms from deep sleep to highly alert states. In deep sleep, large low-frequency waves are predominant. In light sleep, the frequency of the waves increases and is further increased in waking states. In relaxed wakefulness, 8–12 cps alpha rhythm predominates, and beta frequences of 18–30 cps are more common when there is increased alertness. In conditions of heightened alertness there is a change from regular, synchronised activity to desynchronised rhythm, where amplitude of the waveform is reduced. Desynchronisation is found to be associated with increased states of alertness in a variety of animal and human experiments. Thus, the notion of some progression in levels of arousal along a single dimension of arousal is given physiological support.

The underlying mechanism controlling cortical arousal has been located in the diffuse system of fibres ascending in the hind and mid-brain region. The mechanism is termed the "reticular activating system" (RAS) or in anatomical terms, the "internal capsule." Useful accounts of the RAS and its relationship with electrical activity on the cortex can be found in Magoun (1958), on the alerting function of the RAS. Cortical desynchronisation, or beta activity, increases when subjects are surprised, embarrassed, or apprehensive. The RAS is assumed to receive collateral input from incoming afferent or sensory systems. The overall effect of RAS involvement is increased excitation on the cortex, although the RAS is complex and there are inhibitory components. Additionally, the cortex is hypothesised to exert inhibitory control of lower centres including the RAS. Experiments by Bard and Mountcastle (1947) demonstrated that when cortical connections were severed, a state of "sham rage," characterised by heightened activity, was obtained. This provided strong evidence for the "damping-down" influence of the cortex. Thus, there is a major feedback loop in cortico-reticular activating system association. The cortex has some control over the excitation of the RAS but is itself alerted by it.

More recent research has explored the role of cholinergic pathways in the RAS. The hippocampal system may have an important function in helping to regulate activity in these pathways. A prime function of the system may be to regulate activity in accordance with stimulus properties so that redundant or expected stimuli do not cause increased cortical arousal, whereas novel stimuli are more likely to do so. This means that cortical desynchronisation reflects uncertainty and novelty and is evidence of the complexity of relationships within the arousal systems (see Warburton, 1975). An important point is that the degree of arousal exhibited in terms of cortical excitation may reflect the discrepancy between expectancies and reality. This is one of the proposed bases of the perception of control, as outlined in the early chapters of this book.

A system of arousal which is stress-linked and which has a longer history of research is that of autonomic arousal. The autonomic arousal system, sometimes referred to as *body* as opposed to *brain* arousal, involves neural and hormonal components. The principal form of neural control is by the autonomic nervous system, a system of neurones situated down the length of the spinal cord with connections into the central nervous system. There are *sympathetic* and *parasympathetic* components. The former is more centrally situated with respect to the innervation of bodily organs and is primarily activating in its mode of response. The latter is more rostrally situated and is moderating rather than activating. Sympathetic neural pathways stimulate the adrenal medulla to secrete the *catecholamines* adrenaline and noradrenaline; sympathin is a chemical released locally at nerve endings.

The sympathetico-adrenal route was examined in detail by Cannon (1932), who proposed that the secretion of the catecholamines was part of the alerting response of the body to stress. The main function was to release and mobilise blood sugar and increase the intake of oxygen to produce raised energy potential. Thus, Cannon made sense of the bodily changes accompanying autonomic arousal in terms of the *principle of homeostasis*. Raised heart rate, blood pressure, and changes in respiration rate were central to the mobilisation of energy resources. Symptoms such as vaso-constriction and reduced salivary secretion, could be argued to be an economic aid in the concentration of resources. Other changes such as changes in gastric motility, could be argued to be byproducts of the arousal process or to represent changes in internal control resulting from the need to concentrate resources.

Adrenaline and noradrenaline have many properties in common although there are some known points of difference. Since the work of Cannon, adrenaline has been thought of as the *emergency hormone* which increases the likelihood of effective physical effort involved in fight or flight because of the mobilisation of energy resources. Noradrenaline has general vaso-constrictor action with the exception of coronary vessels and generally leads to increase in systolic and diastolic pressure. Catecholamine excretion levels are low during resting for healthy individuals. During normal activities twice the level is produced, and during mild stress the level is between three and five times the resting level. At greater levels of stress a further increase is likely (see Frankenhaeuser, 1971).

Continuous infusion techniques have shown that the presence of adrenaline causes perceived feelings of excitement, restlessness, tension, or apprehension and is accompanied by dryness of mouth, palpitations and tremor (see Frankenhaeuser, 1971). However, important research by Schac-ter and Singer (1962) emphasised that the final emotional experience in cases of adrenaline injection is likely to be situationally determined. Sub-jects given injections of adrenaline (believing that they were receiving vitamin injections) and then exposed to either "happy" or "irritable" social environments, reported emotional experiences appropriate to the experi-ence. The evidence suggests that adrenaline-induced arousal produces only an "as-if" experience and that it is a *necessary* but *not a sufficient* condition for emotion. Continuous infusion of noradrenaline does not appear to produce qualitatively different emotions. The effects are generally of a less intense nature (Frankenhaeuser, 1971).

The pathways resulting in release of corticosteroids are also relatively complex. The hypothalamus and pituitary are responsible for the release of adrenocorticotrophic hormone (ACTH). The locus of action of ACTH is on the adrenal cortex, resulting in the release of corticosteroids. Discovery of and research on the corticosteroid hormone route is commonly attributed to the work of Selye (1956). One of the problems is that research has been directed towards either the release of catecholamines or the release of corticoid hormone, but rarely both together. Even when they are, the results may be published as separate papers (e.g. Mason et al., 1968a, b).

Shannon and Isbell (1963) provided evidence that anticipatory features of situations where there is little control result in corticosteroid secretion. Their design involved measurement of hydrocortisone following various forms of dental injection. In one form, hydrochloric acid was used at 2% strength. In another this was combined with adrenaline. On a third occasion sodium chloride was involved. There were two dummy runs in which nothing was injected. Under all five conditions there was a rise in hydrocortisone in the blood and it persisted up to 15 minutes after treatment. The dummy and non-dummy runs were not distinguished, suggesting perhaps that perception of threat is the critical factor.

Studies of the exposure of rats to extremes of low temperature by Selye (1956) indicated the existence of changing hormone levels as a function of period of exposure. Stress was assumed to be a state manifest by a syndrome: the general adaptation syndrome (GAS). The sum of non-specific changes that occur as part of the syndrome were described in three phases: the alarm reaction; the stage of resistance; and the stage of exhaustion. Only the most severe stress leads to exhaustion and death. In the stage of alarm created by initial exposure to low temperature the adrenal cortex discharges fat granules containing corticol hormones and the animal is vulnerable to a further drop in temperature. In the stage of resistance unusually large fat granules develop. During this stage, animals can generally survive even colder temperatures. In the exhaustion phase there is increased corticoid activity, loss of fat droplets, and the animal cannot even survive the original low temperatures to which it was exposed.

C. Patterning of Arousal States

The view of a single energy state which varied only in intensity was proposed for what is sometimes now seen as a different aspect of arousal, namely autonomic arousal. "Autonomic arousal" is the term used to describe the multitude of changes that occur leading to and resulting from the release of adrenal hormones. It may now seem surprising that with such high potential for richness in pattern, the system could ever have been seen as a bland, unidimensional state. This assumption partially arose because of Selye's observations of changes due to increased autonomic activity common to all illness conditions (see Selye, 1956). The belief that there was very little directional information contained in autonomic arousal prevailed. Thus, Hebb (1955) distinguished between cue function and energy associated with intense stimulation: "the drive is an energiser, but not a guide; an engine but not a steering gear (p. 249)." However, Hebb did also point out that "it may reasonably be anticipated that arousal will be found to vary qualitatively as well as quantitatively (p. 249)."

In fact, some evidence for such a proposition was already in existence at the time of Hebb's review paper but remained unquoted. Ax (1953) studied anger- and fear-producing situations in terms of autonomic measures. Induced anger was accompanied by a rise in diastolic pressure, an increase in muscle tension and skin response, together with a drop in heart rate. By comparison, induced fear was accompanied by increased respiration rate, skin conductance, and the number of peaks in muscle tension. Ax believed that the anger profile might be linked to adrenaline and noradrenaline combined, whereas the fear profile is similar to the effect of injected adrenaline alone.

Later, Averill (1969) used exposure to films of various kinds and made distinctions between sadness and mirth. Both mood states appeared to be associated with increased activation, but cardiovascular changes were more characteristic of anger, whereas respiratory changes appeared to distinguish mirth.

Idiosyncrasies in the response to stressful events had been noted by the end of the 1940s. Malmo and Shagass (1949) reported that in response to painful stimuli, those neurotic patients who had high somatic muscle tension reacted with increased muscle tension, whereas those characterised by cardiac changes reacted to pain predominantly with heart-rate changes. In other words, there appeared to be prevailing response modes. The arousal response, far from being bland, featureless, and represented on a single energy dimension, was characterised by changes in "lead" variables that differed for different individuals (response specificity).

In a careful test of the response specificity hypothesis, Lacey et al. (1953) used exposure to four different types of stress: mental arithmetic, hyperventilation, letter association, and a cold pressure test, and reported differentiation of physiological responses between individuals. For two measures, autonomic tension (maximum level reached during stress) and autonomic lability scores (maximum displacement scores), the evidence favoured a constant pattern across stress conditons: "Maximal activation occurs in the same physiological function whatever the stress (p. 19)." A source of between-subject variation was the degree to which responses were stereotyped.

The existence of evidence for stimulus specificity or response specificity is difficult to interpret. This is illustrated by the study by Funkenstein et al. (1957) in which Harvard students were exposed, after a series of normal tests, to a rigged test incorporating an unsolvable problem. One group was found to adopt a self-blaming style ("anger-in"). A second group was found to adopt an outward blaming style ("anger-out"). The cognitive style could be predicted with great accuracy by friends of each subject and appeared linked to physiological patterns indicative of the presence of either epinephrine[1] (for the anger-in group) or norepinephrine[1] (for the anger-out group). Findings such as this raise the causal issue of whether the cognitive style

---

[1] Epinephrine is the equivalent of adrenaline. Norepinephrine is the equivalent of noradrenaline.

creates the hormone balance with accompanying physiological pattern, whether the reverse is the case, or whether there is a third factor which creates both.

There is now increasing research evidence to suggest that a number of factors might influence adrenaline/noradrenaline balance (see Frankenhaeuser, 1971; Frankenhaeuser & Gardell, 1976; Fisher, 1984a). For example, studies of working conditions by Frankenhaeuser and Gardell (1976) showed that factors such as the duration of work cycle are reflected in adrenaline levels; durations as low as .5 seconds per cycle were found to be associated with high adrenaline levels and decreased subjective well-being. By contrast, restriction of work posture and machine-paced work conditions were more likely to be associated with increased noradrenaline and increased feelings of irritation.

Mason et al. (1968b), using monkeys, confirmed that novelty and uncertainty were more likely to be associated with raised adrenaline, whereas steratyped situations or situations deemed unpleasant were more likely to be associated with raised noradrenaline.

The influence of the perception of control is also indicated. Mandler (1975) suggested that response availability may be the critical factor; if there is no control available, adrenaline secretion increases, whereas if it is available, noradrenaline secretion is raised. Equally, experiments by Frankenhaeuser and Rissler (1970) showed that increasing situational control was accompanied by preponderance of noradrenaline to adrenaline. Weiss (1968) showed that noradrenaline levels were raised in the brains of rats able to avoid shock, but not in yoked controls. Collectively, all these studies support the view that there is a close association between cognitive appraisal of situations and the pattern of autonomic arousal which results.

More recently, Frankenhaeuser and Johansson (1982) have pointed to the possibility that conditons may create different balances of catecholamines and corticosteroids. Basically *effort*, when control is possible, is more likely to be associated with raised catecholamine. *Effort and distress*, when control is not possible, are more likely to be associated with raised catecholamines *and* raised corticosteroids. In a low-control situation in the laboratory, subjects performed a 1-hour vigilance task involving pressing a key to detect a weak light. In a high-control situation, the subjects performed a choice reaction task with high personal control because there was an opportunity to modify the stimulus rate so as to maintain optimal pace during the 1-hour session. Results showed that the high-control task induced subjective effort but no distress and was associated with high catecholamines, whereas the low-control task induced subjective effort and distress and was associated with raised catecholamines and raised cortisol levels.

Summarising the development of the concept of arousal in historical perspective, it seems that arousal was first seen as more closely associated with drive but then became linked physiologically with cortical arousal level. The association with stress and autonomic arousal provided a basis for the assumption that the two states were part of an overall state of arousal. In spite of growing evidence suggesting that even within the autonomic arousal system there was evidence of patterning in different stimulus situations, and evidence of idiosyncratic response profiles, these facts were not given weight in conceptualising the arousal–performance relationship.

The relationship between the more gross systems of autonomic, cortical, and behavioural arousal have been considered in detail by Lacey (1967). Lacey reviews evidence indicative of fractionating relationships between behavioural and cortical arousal, as well as between autonomic and cortical studies. Lacey points out that it is possible to produce cortical somnolence with a behaviourally agitated animal. Equally, behavioural somnolence in the presence of desynchronised cortical rhythms can be engineered. To Lacey this suggests that cortical and behavioural arousal coexist in *temporal parallelism* but are not necessarily to be seen as part of the same overall arousal system. Reviews of the relationship between autonomic and cortical arousal have indicated that there are feedback systems that can act to cause fractionation. Thus, Bonvallet et al. (1954) showed that in cats, distension of the carotid sinus produced a reduction of the frequency of electrical activity on the cortex to as low as three to five per second. Nakao et al. (1956) further confirmed the effect. Bonvallet and Allen (1963) hypothesised that there is an ascending bulbar inhibitory mechanism, separate from the classical ventro-medial inhibitory reticular system. The function of the mechanism appears to be to control the episode of activation associated with a particular event. The overall effect would be to cause diminution of arousal. Bonvallet and Allen (1963) also pointed out that discharges in the area of the ascending mechanism are synchronous with cardiac activity.

Thus, there is strong evidence of a built-in device for fractionating the relationship of autonomic and cortical arousal. Putting it another way, cardiac control over the high centres of the brain is possible. The inhibitory effects can be produced by changes in heart rate or by increased blood pressure, although the evidence is that the effect is clearer for the latter than for the former. In addition, the stiffness of the wall of the carotid sinus, which is under physiological control, can attenuate or augment the effect.

The existence of fractionations either within or between located systems which mediate arousal, raise great problems for the inverted U model of arousal which is based on a concept of a single dimension of arousal from sleep to wakefulness. Fisher (1984a) has suggested that *compatibility* of the arousal system must be taken into account in determining the change in performance. It is normally assumed that there is a base arousal position, which represents the existing level of arousal. The new arousal influence interacts or adds to this base position in determining the new position ($A_F = A_B + A_N$) where A_F = the final state of arousal, A_B is the base position,

A_N is the new arousal influence. In fact the compatibility of A_B and A_N may be the factor of importance. Stimulus and response circumstance may be influential. For example, if a person has just been aroused by anger, base position on the relevant dimension of arousal appropriate for a new input may be different from the base position created by fear. The new potential influence on arousal may be appropriate for the former and not the latter or vice versa. Thus A_F when $(A_{B(a)} + A_N)$, is true, is different from A_F when $(A_{B(f)} + A_N)$ is true (where (f) = prior fear and (a) = prior anger).

D. The Directional Influence of Stress on Arousal

A further difficulty for the arousal model is that although intuitively it might at first be supposed that all stressful conditions cause increased arousal because stressful stimuli instigate autonomic arousal as part of the homeostatic response to disturbed equilibrium (Cannon, 1932), the influence of stresses on cortical arousal presents a different picture. Tiredness and fatigue, for example, are more likely to be associated with diminished arousal. In drowsy states there are more low-frequency waves evidenced in the cortical rhythm, than in wakeful states.

In the case of sleep deprivation, Malmo (1959) pointed to the difficulty of interpreting the evidence in terms of changes in arousal. Firstly, he pointed out that after 60 hours deprivation the activation level was likely to be *higher* than before sleep loss. "Physiological indicants reveal an upward shift in activation that is gradual and progressive throughout the vigil (Malmo, 1959, p. 373)." Secondly, however, Malmo noted that the assumption that 60 hours of deprivation would invariably produce a state of heightened arousal could not be made because a sleep-deprived person requires constant stimulation to stay awake. When working at a task, the stimulation produced by the task is sufficient to produce increased activation. When the subject is not working, lack of stimulation results in drowsiness and sleep. Paradoxically therefore, the subject in sleep loss could be argued to be simultaneously under- and over-aroused. The hypothesis that loss of sleep is de-arousing is not easily substantiated. In a review paper, Wilkinson (1965) attempts to reconcile these findings by arguing that the sleep-deprived subject makes great effort to sustain arousal. Therefore, when the task is highly stimulating, over-arousal might be the expected result. When the task is dull and boring or the subject merely waits to be monitored, under-arousal is more likely. The problem with the "dual motivation" approach is that it has to be assumed that in the absence of a high level of arousal it is possible for an individual to find the motivational resources to increase arousal level.

Difficulties in predicting, a priori, the directional effect of different stresses have been partly reduced by experiments on the interaction of stresses. By combining a stress with a drug of known effects, the presence or absence of an interaction provides information about whether a common mechanism is involved. The nature of the combined change provides information about whether the variables are acting in the same or in opposing ways. It is also possible to build up logically the evidence of the likely direction of influence of a particular stress from the information provided by combining the particular stress successively with other stresses or drugs.

There are a number of good accounts of research on stress/drug pairs and their interactions (see Broadbent, 1963, 1971; Poulton, 1970). Some of the principal findings and the conclusions are the following: A reported interaction between incentives and tranquilisers (Steinberg, 1959) gives weight to the intuitively plausible view that incentives are activators. A reported interaction between the effects of sleep loss and incentives (Wilkinson, 1961) provides support for the view that sleep loss is a de-activating agent. The reported interaction between sleep loss and noise (Corcoran, 1962) confirms noise as an activating agent, whereas a priori it might be argued that noise by masking stimulation could be de-activating.

The "interaction experiments" also indicate stresses which when paired do not appear to act on a common mechanism. Thus, high temperature does not interact with other environmental stresses. The results suggest either that a different mechanism is required to explain the effects of heat, or that a different arousal mechanism is involved.

E. Further Difficulties with the Arousal Model

The causal association between arousal level and performance competence has considerable backing, and is to some extent supported by anecdotal observations. It also provides a basis for explaining within-group differences in reaction to stressful circumstances in terms of different base positions. However, in addition to the criticisms already listed, there is a growing number of major dissatisfactions with the arousal model as an explanation of performance changes in stress. Some of these points have been neatly summarised by Schönpflug (1983). First, there is the problem that arousal may occur in situations of threat to life but may not be so easily produced in the laboratory. Schönpflug points out that techniques to induce over-arousal (extra stimulation, air deprivation, incentive) may merely divert the subjects' attention. This is comparable with the Näätänen argument discussed previously. Schönpflug further points out that if direct physiological measures of activation were taken, the assumption that arousal level rises as a function of stressful conditions would be in question. Schönpflug and Schafer (1962) used six groups of subjects and presented them with a learning task with sound levels of varying intensity using skin conductance as a measure. The results showed a Z *function* relating skin conductance to sound intensity level (inverted U for 45–85 dB, then a higher peak at 95 dB). There was a monotonic relationship between skin conductance and performance but the function relating the two to sound intensity was cubic. "Apparently the variation of sound intensity had effects which cannot be described unidimensionally (Schönpflug, 1983, p. 311)."The authors argued that three dimensions could be distinguished: (1) an *arousing effect* which facilitated performance; (2) an *interference effect* to which subjects reacted by trying not to listen; (3) *compensatory effort* in which subjects tried to put extra effort into the learning task. These distinctions were based on self-reports provided at interview. An interesting result is the relationship to sound level: at 55 dB, the arousing effect was predominant; whereas at 95 dB, compensatory effort and tolerance were prevalent.

In this chapter, we have attempted to provide the student with an account of some of the empirical findings and theoretical issues concerned with the effects of stress on arousal level. It is implicit in the research reviewed that stimulation and stress cause direct changes in function consistent with raised arousal and that behaviour directly reflects this change. The fact that the systems may fractionate and that arousal is probably not best described on a unitary dimension, does not mean that it will not provide a basis for an account of behavioural changes in stress. It does imply that the inverted U model in current form is less than adequate.

Before these ideas are discussed further it is necessary to consider some of the other "direct hit" models that provide a potential explanation of changes in behaviour in stress.

7

Stress and Competence: Mental Load and Strategic Rules

1. THE MENTAL LOAD MODEL

The arousal model provides one example of a "direct hit" or mechanical model in that changes in performance competence are assumed to occur as a direct result of changes in internal energy level. An alternative is what might be described as the "mental load" model; the main assumption is that as mental work load or demand increases, errors will occur on a secondary or non-salient aspect of a task as capacity is exceeded. The mental load model has been traditionally reserved for the relationship between workload and task performance. However there is evidence to suggest that stress increases mental demand. Explanations of stress effects in terms of increased workload provide a viable alternative to the arousal model.

A. Stress and Worry

There has been relatively little research on the likely effects of mental demands created by stress. The lack of research in this area seems even more surprising given that "worry" is a frequently mentioned aspect of the effects of stressful circumstance in lay articles. Fisher (1984a) attempted to draw together logical, psychological, and "circumstantial" evidence in concluding that in stressful circumstances, people were likely to be under considerable mental demand, and that there should be implications for changes in performance competence. Before exploring this argument, it is useful to introduce some of what has been written on the topic of "worry."

A dictionary definition of worry generally includes the two notions of being very active, aggressive, and persistent with a situation (e.g. "to persist"; "to pester"; "to harass"; "to devour ravenously"; "to tear with the teeth") – and of being in a mental state of anguish or anxiety ("trouble"; "perplexity"; "anxiety"; "to be unduly anxious"; "to fret" – *Chambers Twentieth Century Dictionary*).

Carnegie (1948), writing from a lay perspective, reported that a search of the New York Libraries produced little by way of books on the topic of "worry," which he regarded as the plague of businessmen and the reason for lack of success, incompetence, and ill health. He found a total of 22 books listed under the title "worry" and 189 books under the title "worms." He comments: "Almost nine times as many books about worms as about worry! Astounding isn't it? Since worry is one of the biggest problems facing mankind, you would think wouldn't you that every high school and college in the land would give a course on 'How to stop worrying'? (p. 3)." Methods of reducing or preventing worry listed by Carnegie in his book include:

1. Operating the strategy of crowding worry out of the mind by taking on other activities and becoming busy.
2. Operating the strategy of thinking only about each day as it arrives and not thinking too much about the happenings of the past or events in the future.
3. Operating the strategy of always imagining the worst that could happen in a situation, coming to terms with it, and then working out ways in which to make the worst situation seems a little better.
4. Operating a strategy of a "stop loss order" on worries. This borrows from a strategy used on the Stock Exchange by an acquaintance of Carnegie, Burton Castles, who was very successful. His strategy was to establish a loss point for the value of purchased shares; if the value fell below this point he would sell automatically. Carnegie emphasises "The cost of a thing is the amount of what I call life, which is required to be exchanged for it immediately or in the long run (p. 88)." He points out that by putting a "stop loss order" on resentments, anguish can be prevented.
5. Operating the "no use crying over spilt milk" strategy in that past mistakes are analysed and stored but not allowed to provide a constant source of distressing thoughts.

Contained in Carnegie's book is the message that worries are counterproductive and that strategies should be designed to diminish the time spent worrying. There is no suggestion that worry may be in any way productive. In fact, part of the early section of the book is devoted to considering the adverse effects of worrying by means of anecdotally acquired material on the reported worries of businessmen and the consequences in terms of business failure and physical illness.

At least one of the themes developed both in the present book and Fisher (1984a), is that worrying may be a highly productive process, that thinking of all future outcomes is likely to increase the likelihood of competent responses when the event happens, and that sifting through the events of the past may be a prerequisite for successful behaviour in the future.

An approach that emphasised the possible productive aspects of "worry work" was developed by Janis (1958) in the context of the effect of impending surgical operations on patients. A small sample of hospitalised patients was studied intensively before and after surgery on the basis of intensive pre-operative and post-operative interviews and behavioural records. Observations of specific cases reported by Janis indicated that "mental rehearsal" and accompanying anticipatory fear may be a prerequisite for successful adjustment to surgery and its consequences. Janis argued that if a person is given appropriate preparatory communications before being exposed to the trauma, the chances of reacting positively are increased. Incomplete or misleading information may have the reverse effect. In a study of 77 surgical cases, 26 were informed about the effects of surgery. Those who were informed reported less disturbance when recalling the operation, recalled less anger on the day of the operation and greater confidence in the surgeon at the present time. All difficulties were significant at the 5% level. The cost of this advantage is greater pre-operative fear in the informed group. This raises the fundamental issue that the cost of worry work in advance may be preoccupation and trepidation. The benefits in the long term may be greater ability to accept and adjust to the results of trauma. Janis (1958) argues that there is a strong tendency in most people to deny dangers and to "bolster their sense of personal invulnerability by developing blanket immunity expectations and thus almost completely ward off anticipatory fear (p. 360)." The stimulation of anticipatory fear by provision of information about the forthcoming event breaks into the denial process and forces patients to think about what is to happen. "Informed worrying" seems according to Janis's studies to be beneficial in the long term.

Another area of research in which there is some implication that worry may be productive in influencing the impact of an impending event, concerns parachute jumping. In studies investigating the psychological and physiological responses to parachute jumping, Epstein (1962, 1967) and Fenz (1964, 1969, 1975) have shown that in terms of physiological parameters such as respiration rate and heart rate, arousal levels increase relative to base during the sequence of events beginning from the moment the potential jumper arrives at the airport until the moment just prior to the jump from the aircraft. Fenz (1975) reports that prior to the jump there is a difference between good and poor performers. As shown in Fig. 7.1(a) when the aircraft is advancing to the height for the jump, for novice performers, those who subsequently make good jumps have begun to show a slight decrease in arousal (as measured by respiration rate and heart rate; only respiration rate shown in the figure). This alone is not convincing

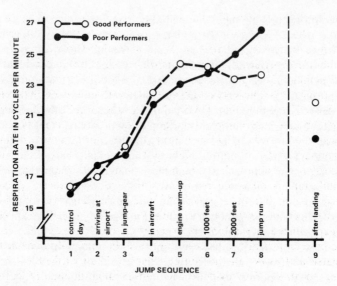

FIG. 7.1a   Respiration rate as a function of jump sequence for "good" and "poor" *novice* parachutists. (Redrawn from Fenz, 1975, with the permission of the Canadian Psychological Association.)

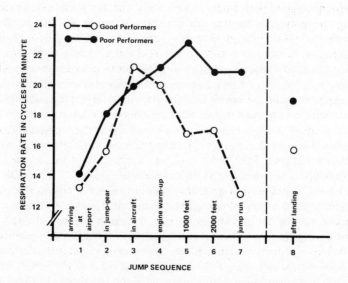

FIG. 7.1b   Respiration rate as a function of jump sequence for "good" and "poor" *experienced* parachutists. (Redrawn from Fenz, 1975, with the permission of the Canadian Psychological Association.)

114

evidence for intervening mental activity because it may simply be the case that those who have slightly lowered arousal jump better; an assumption which would be in keeping with the arousal model. However, Fig. 7.1(b) shows that for experienced jumpers the difference between good and poor jumpers is much more pronounced in terms of the pre-jump arousal level. This is stronger evidence because the experienced jumpers only have previous knowledge of the jump. This might suggest that the change in arousal is brought about by utilisation of this knowledge. Epstein (1962, 1967, 1972) and Fenz (1964, 1969, 1975) have elaborated on the approach-avoidance conflict model as described originally by Lewin (1935) and Miller (1944). Positive valence or approach to the jump is equated with anxiety; avoidance with inhibition. A proposed parachute jump produces these conflicting tendencies. Reduction in arousal at the time of the jump is assumed to be the result of a change in thinking about the impending jump. The superiority of the experienced, good jumpers in terms of the ability to lower arousal prior to base, comes about because they have the material to enable them to rehearse and work out the consequences of likely difficulties and the response to them. The evidence for intervening mental processes is strengthened by the fact that after an accident, the V curve in arousal prior to the jump is lost (Fenz et al., 1969).

Taking the work collectively, a drop in arousal could be seen to represent increased inhibition (decision against jumping), in which case the tendency of experienced good performers to behave in this way is not explained; or a change in thinking consistent with mastery, in which case the tendency of experienced good performers to show this effect is more easily explained. An alternative explanation is that the decision to jump represents the outcome of cognitive activity concerning whether or not control is possible. Novices are less equipped mentally for making the decision because there is no prior information. Experienced jumpers have information about what to expect and may consult this in deciding how much control is likely. The evidence hints at the involvement of productive worry work in the experienced jumpers with the appropriate cognitive codes.

A study by Epstein and Clarke (1970) was concerned with manipulation of information concerning heart rate and skin conductance levels preceding and following a brief burst of noise at 107 decibels. The information provided was found to have a very influential effect, in that those subjects who were led to expect that the noise would have a negative effect, showed the greatest anticipatory arousal preceding the event. This perhaps provides a more convincing demonstration of the importance of intervening mental activity in anticipatory stress.

Wherry and Curran (1965) provided one of the few demonstrations that anticipatory mental activity can affect performance at the time. In a study of the advance effects of anticipated electric shock, they showed that disruption of performance reflected a number of factors associated with the shock such as its proximity, probability of occurrence, and perceived degree of unpleasantness.

Credit for early exploration of the notion that "worry" activity is influential in determining performance competence is due to Sarason (1972, 1973), Doris and Sarason (1955), Liebert and Morris (1967), and Wine (1971), who worked with test anxiety, and Hamilton (1974, 1983), who worked on socialisation anxiety in children arising from doubts about competence and self-esteem.

The research on test anxiety has utilised self-report data in showing that those who suffer from test anxiety, experience intrusive thoughts about the consequence of failure. These thoughts are defined by Sarason and by Wine as "task irrelevant" in that they are not oriented towards the task in hand. Sarason's studies have shown that instructions before a test designed to be reassuring, improve the performance of those high on test anxiety but do not influence those low on test anxiety. Thus, the interference produced by task-irrelevant cognitive activities may be diminished if appropriate information is provided. Equally, information about how the problem might be tackled helps to reduce test anxiety (Sarason, 1973). The debilitating effects of task-irrelevant thoughts were found by Doris and Sarason (1955) to centre on self-blaming responses. Low test-anxiety subjects were more likely to blame the situation and conditions of the test; high test-anxiety subjects centred on their own personal difficulties. In this respect, the results provide interesting comparisons with the results of anger-in and anger-out as responses to simulated failure as reported by Funkenstein et al. (1957) (discussed in previous chapters). Those who blame the test situation for any failures are not debilitated by preoccupation with the consequences of failure in the way that those who blame themselves are. This might suggest that feelings of personal reponsibility (control) are responsible for preoccupations.

Test anxiety theory was originally proposed by Mandler and Sarason (1952) in an article which introduced the test anxiety questionnaire (TAQ). The TAQ was designed as a measure of anxiety proneness in specific stressful circumstances and test situations. It was assumed that in testing situations there are two kinds of drive. One is "learned task drive" reduced by reponses which lead to the completion of the task. The other is "learned anxiety drive" which can elicit responses related to task completion *or* those which interfere. The TAQ was designed to measure the latter. It is a 37-item questionnaire in rating scale format, directly aimed at indexing self-oriented interfering responses.

Both the TAQ and a later 21-item version, the test anxiety scale (TAS), are highly correlated and indicate that those subjects scoring high on test anxiety tend to do so because of their tendency to generate internal self-oriented responses. Subsequent experimental comparisons, in which high and low test-anxious subjects were required to describe themselves orally, suggested that highly test-anxious subjects describe themselves in more negative terms, are responsive to reinforcement, and do not condition or learn well when positive self-references are encouraged.

Conditions where there is an audience present, or where instructions are present that specify the task as a means of evaluation, influence high test-anxious subjects negatively (see Wine, 1971). One of the main problems is that on the arousal model, highly anxious subjects would be more debilitated by highly motivating conditions or instructions. It is difficult to be confident that task-irrelevant cognitions alone account for the changes, in spite of the evidence from self-report (quoted previously).

A promising approach is provided by Liebert and Morris (1967), who presented an analysis of test anxiety, in accordance with which worry and emotionality scores were separated on the TAQ scale. Scores on the worry (W) component were found to be constant across time whereas scores on emotionality (E) reached a peak immediately before a test. The results showed that E scores remain independent of performance expectancy whereas W scores are correlated negatively with rated performance expectancy. Worry was defined in terms of cognitive expression of concern about one's own performance. Emotionality was defined in terms of autonomic reactions.

An approach developed by Hamilton (1974) is more concerned with the long-term debilitating effects of anxiety brought about by faulty socialisation processes. Hamilton argues that anxiety provides "a source of internally presented stimuli or signals containing information (p. 16)." The state of being overloaded exists and provides a source of information which is presented in competition with daily task information. Hamilton provides a formal description of the way in which performance impairment may come about in these circumstances. Hamilton's extension of the worry model from work on socialisation in children is useful but the formulation lacks the direct evidence to show that changes are due to worry and not to arousal due to loss of control. Hamilton links faulty socialisation to feelings of emotional rejection, rigidity, criticism, lack of empathy, and coldness. The memory store codes this information as part of anxiety. Hamilton (1983) argues that anxiety is information in permanent memory about negative outcomes.

Implicit in the preceding paragraphs is the idea that worry work is largely anticipatory, yet it is intuitively reasonable that preoccupations may also be reflective, involving retrospective analysis of past events. A person may rethink previous arguments or events carrying the impact of the event long after it has occurred. Fisher (1984a) argued that the sifting through of courses of action taken, courses of action that might have been taken, and likely associated consequences, could be highly productive. Bridge or chess players frequently like to analyse the moves in the game after it is over in order to explore relationships between decisions and outcomes. Reflective worry may be of the same use eventually. This is the way a person learns the rules of the stressful encounter game and may provide the basis for future strategy.

Case studies provided by Parkes (1978) from investigations of the effects of bereavement, reveal that preoccupation with the past and the deceased is a recurring feature prevalent in the immediate post-bereavement period. Yet little is made of this behaviour, which could seem on first analysis strange. Why continue to think about past events? They are finished and never to be encountered again. The person is dead, and yet reflective thoughts concerning him or her govern the life of the bereaved for a while. Perhaps these reflective thoughts are unavoidable—the material is so intrusive because of its emotional content, that a person cannot stop thinking about it. Perhaps, however, such reflective activity is built into the design of the mind because it is highly functional and permits old plans and attitudes to be revised and discarded in preparation for new ones. It is not unreasonable to argue that reflective activity of all kinds, whether of negative emotional content or not, is of strategic value.

The notion that interruption of ongoing activity is likely to produce activated, even emotional, behaviour is inherent in the idea of interruption theory as proposed by Mandler (1962, 1975) and Mandler and Watson (1966). A general proposition on the effects of interruption as stated by Mandler (1975) is that the interruption of an integrated response sequence produces a state of arousal followed by emotional behaviour. Mandler and Watson specify the likely consequences as: (1) persistence towards completion of the interrupted sequence; (2) increased vigour with which the sequence is pursued; and (3) substitution of alternative elements in the sequence. The theory supported by Mandler is that interruption frees the energy contained in plans and that the "tendency to completion" remains for a while. It is at least possible that reflective thinking is also determined in a similar way. Old plans and activities thwarted by interruption continue to "grab" at thinking processes. They become highly dominant, emotionally loaded sources of intrusive material.

Fisher, Frazer, and Murray (1984) investigated the effects of a relocation to boarding school, in terms of the problems and worries spontaneously reported by a sample of 50 male and female school children aged 11–16. Of particular interest was whether the new school would provide the main source of problems or whether the major source would still be the home. The method of obtaining data was by means of diary-style recording. A distinction was made between problems and worries. A "problem" was the description of the content. A "worry unit" was the occasion of considering the problem, i.e. worrying about it. Therefore, for any particular problem, there would be at least one unit of worry. This gave two dependent variables. The diary record across the first two weeks of attendance at the new school showed that more reported problems concerned school rather than home: There was an average of between 5 and 6.5 school problems per person across the two weeks of the study but only between .8 and 2.2 home-oriented problems. However, there were proportionately more worry units attached to home-oriented problems than to school-oriented ones. In addition, a ratio of problem/worry units (P/W) was calculated on an individual subject basis and it was found that the ratio was .59 for school problems but .26 for home problems. Thus, although more problems concern the new school environment, there is proportinately more worry activity concerned with home problems. It is hoped that further research with the P/W ratio will provide insights into the mental demand across time of a number of different stressful conditions.

B. The Concept of Spare Capacity

The assumption that preoccupation and worry are likely accompaniments of stressful encounters and that there is a causal association with change in levels of competence, is dependent on the notion of a limitation in processing resources. As originally formulated, the concept of *spare capacity* was based on the notion of a fixed central resource that was utilised by all demands made on mental activity. Thus the degradation on one task could be used to index the difficulty level of a main task when two tasks were presented simultaneously.

The spare capacity concept and the dual-task technique for indexing it were given very clear exposition by Brown (1964). He defined spare or reserve capacity as the difference between capacity and the perceptual load imposed by some imaginary task. Reserve capacity and perceptual load cannot be measured directly from performance on any task performed singly, because performance should be error-free. In fact this assumption is questionnable since error rates for continuous single-task performance vary between 1 and 7 (see Rabbitt, 1966; Fisher 1984a). There seems to be an irreducible minimum in human skilled performance as far as perfect performance is concerned. Although it is normal to treat error production as the result of a change in speed/accuracy adjustment, it remains possible that the error represents a moment of transient overload of resource.

Figure 7.2 shows Brown's conceptualisation of the technique for measuring reserve capacity using a second task. The demands made by tasks A and B on resources cannot be assessed if performance is virtually errorless, but the provision of a second task common to both enables the differences in resource demand to be indexed. Thus, as shown in the figure, the difference between the two tasks which cannot be directly assessed, is estimated by means of decrement on the secondary task. The secondary task can be used to act as a loading task so that subjects capable of 100% proficiency on a main task then perform the task in the presence of a loading task constant for all main task situations. The proportion of maximum performance on the primary task is then measured when subjects are performing at different levels of difficulty on the loading task. A slightly different use for the secondary task is as a subsidiary task; the main task is performed

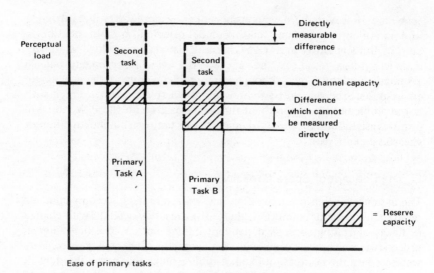

Ease of primary tasks

FIG. 7.2   Model of the use of the secondary task technique to index level of mental load. (Redrawn from Brown, 1964, with the permission of the author and the Royal College of Surgeons.)

as well as possible all the time while the person performs as well as he can on the subsidiary task. In this situation there will be "overspill" errors on the subsidiary task as the primary task increases in difficulty or is performed under difficult circumstances. The overspill errors will index the relative demands made by different primary tasks.

There were problems discussed by Brown initially when providing an account of the secondary task technique. More problems have since been recognised. In spite of this, secondary task design and the assumption of a fixed, limited resource or pool from which all incoming inputs must draw remains central to the main formulation of the relationship between worry and incompetence.

Brown listed six major problems with the use of the model:

1. Capacity may not be fixed; it may be changed by the demands of the task. In other words, a person may increase his effort when confronted with two tasks. Pope (1962) is quoted by Brown, since he showed that the addition of a tracking task resulted in better monitoring performance on a vigilance task, than when it was performed singly.
2. Performance on the secondary task may not be linearly related to perceptual load on the main task.
3. There is no evidence to support the fact that response bias on the two tasks remains constant; correct responses on one task may reflect a change in response bias.
4. Individual differences in ability will introduce variance unless each man acts as his own control.

5. A high score on the secondary task may not indicate a large reserve capacity; the person may be leaving unprepared responses to less probable stimuli on the primary task.
6. The method is not sufficiently objective since performance on the two tasks depends to a great extent on subjective assessment of ability to divide attention and perform effectively.

In a subsequent paper, Brown (1978) listed a number of points of difficulty with the model. One of the important points made in the article is that in general, deterioration on the secondary task is gradual in character rather than involving a step-function change or sudden implosion of errors. The term used by Norman and Bobrow (1975), "the principle of graceful degradation," is used to describe the effect. The implication is that a person will not suddenly become incompetent but may cope for a while, gradually showing incompetence as demands increase.

An important difficulty for the spare capacity model is that research evidence was provided showing that tasks which demanded the same output modality were most vulnerable when paired. For example, McCleod (1977) showed that the probability of response production on a main continuous task was affected by the concurrent production of manual responses, but the interference was reduced when a verbal response was required instead. Therefore, the idea that all competing sources draw from a single source is too simplistic as in some cases it appears that two response streams can be independently controlled. One possible explanation is that a verbal response requires less of the common resource than a manual response. Therefore, the apparent reduction in interference when a verbal response is involved could be the result of a change in demand.

Neisser and Becklen (1975) showed that when a subject is attempting to process information over time the perceiver finds it difficult to process any other information stream. Brown (1978) interprets this to mean that the dual-task method is less applicable because workload is determined by overall structural complexity rather than by component parts. However, it seems reasonable to argue that the processing of structurally complex material provides a demand on resources leaving less available for other demands.

With regard to the importance of the stage of learning a task, learners are "data limited" (Norman & Bobrow, 1975), in that they are determined by naive sampling of stimulus conditions. As learning proceeds, they may become more "resource limited" because they have some but not all appropriate strategies. Once the strategies are fully available the individual is again "data limited". Brown argues that this provides an objection to the use of a dual-task design because of decreased demands as skill progresses.

The principle of the secondary task technique has been applied to provide an index of the changing demands of a main task. Thus a secondary "probe" reaction-time task is paired with a task such as a main letter-matching task. As illustrated by Fig. 7.3, the probe is introduced at varying times during

SS-E

the main task and the *delay* in response time is used to provide an index of the varying demands of main task processes. The underlying assumption is again that there is a common resource utilised by both tasks; to the extent that the main task processes demand more of the resource, the probe time is delayed. One difference with the secondary task model is that the emphasis is on delayed responses rather than errors. The method has been used to measure the attentional demands of movement (e.g., see Ells, 1973; Kerr, 1973; Posner & Keele, 1969) and the demands of letter matching (Posner & Boies, 1971; Posner et al. 1973).

Many of the difficulties itemised for the secondary task design also apply when the task is indexed by probe techniques. McCleod (1978) investigated modality-specific effects by pairing a probe reaction time (RT) task with a letter-matching task. When the response to the probe was manual, the pattern of interference was different from a condition where the probe response was verbal. The manual probe peaked at the time of the arrival of the second letter in the matching task. The verbal probe profile remained higher for the period of the warning signal and arrival of the first letter, but showed a decrease (faster RT) just prior to the second letter. McCleod points out that if a single resource was accessed by the letter task processes and the probe task processes, the pattern of probe RT should not be modality dependent. He concludes that it is not possible to use a single form of probe task as a measure of central capacity. There is little exploration of

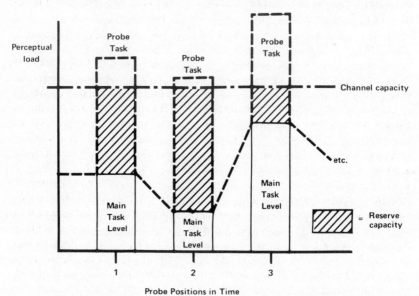

FIG. 7.3   Model of the use of the probe RT secondary task concept to reflect changes in mental demands during the performance of a task. (First produced in Fisher 1984a.)

the notion that a verbal form of a probe task might be more difficult and therefore more likely to absorb capacity. However, the verbal probe RT is not slower for all conditions of the letter-matching task, and so the most likely explanation is of differential interference.

C. Application of the Mental Load Model

There have been a number of notable attempts to develop the idea that stresses create additional demand on resources and thus result in lowered competence. In the area of socialisation anxiety, Hamilton (1974) used a formulation based on the concept of spare mental capacity. Average processing capacity (APC) and spare capacity (SPC) define the resource available. Internally generated information (I_{ist}) together with external task information (I_{ept}) are assumed to compete for the available resource. Performance impairment occurs when (I_{ept}) and (I_{ist}) exceed the available resource. Thus, successful performance occurs when:

$$[(APC + SPC) > (I_{ept} + I_{ist})] \quad \text{(Hamilton, 1974, p. 18)}$$

Hamilton further qualifies the nature of internally generated information. $I_{ist(A)}$ describes internally generated information arising as a result of anxiety. Task-irrelevent competing information, $I_{ist(C)}$, is also assumed to be internally generated and is assumed to increase as a function of increased drive or anxiety. $I_{ist(A)}$ is assumed to affect the size of internally generated information $I_{ist(C)}$. Decreased competence is expected when:

$$[I_{ist(A)} > I_{ist(C)}] , \quad \text{and} \quad [(I_{ist(A)} + I_{ist(C)} + I_{ept}) > (APC + SPC)].$$

A point emphasised by Hamilton is that the intrusion of task-irrelevant or relevant information is not under voluntary control. If the total information processing demands exceed (APC + SPC), the simplest available strategy is to "shut down" some of the task. For example, the subject might narrow his attention processes. This point is an important one because, as will be argued in the next chapter, attentional narrowing may have a number of possible explanations, one of which is the fact that it is a strategic response to increased demand.

The mental load model seems at first rather less applicable to environmental stress situations than it does to conditions of tests and examinations where fear of the possible consequence of failure is involved. However, it might be quite wrong to assume that the same preoccupations are unlikely in laboratory, or real-life encounters, with for example noise, heat, or loss of sleep. One possible result of any increased effort with performance in stress is that rather closer monitoring of performance may be required. Switching into a performance-monitoring mode might involve capacity normally required for the task. Thus if the subject is trying to work harder at the task *and* trying to make internal assessments of his likely proficiency, there would be greater demand and ultimately less effective performance.

There have been two notable attempts in the area of noise research to use subsidiary task decrement as an index of noise effects. Boggs and Simon (1968) varied the degree of stimulus–response compatibility in the display control relationship on a four-choice reaction-time task. The noise characteristics remained constant, but the introduction of noise caused a deterioration on a subsidiary task. Thus, two tasks could be monitored without loud noise, but capacity was exceeded when noise was introduced. This suggests that the effect of noise was to deplete information processing resources needed for the task. Boggs and Simon (1968) concluded: "The introduction of the noise used up some of S's reverse capacity, that is, S had to draw from his reserve so that primary task performance would not suffer as a consequence of noise (p. 152)."

Finkleman and Glass (1970) took a similar approach but assumed that by varying the noise characteristics for a constant level of main and secondary task there would be a difference in capacity requirement of the noise which would reflect in secondary task competence. Predictable noise was assumed to be less demanding than unpredictable noise and therefore to have a smaller capacity requirement. The results showed that whereas performance on the main compensatory tracking remained apparently unaffected by the difference in noise characteristic, performance on a secondary task involving delayed recall of digits was impaired in the unpredictable noise condition.

Figure 7.4 provides an illustration of the two designs used by Boggs and Simon and by Finkleman and Glass. In both cases it is assumed that noise uses up processing resources. The difficulty is to know why. It is possible to suggest a number of plausible explanations. Firstly, on the Hamilton model, anxiety or high arousal might be assumed to produce a train of connotative signals. A person cannot avoid being mentally preoccupied with loud noise. A second explanation, not necessarily exclusive, is that noise causes a challenge resulting in raised effort levels and closer need to monitor performance. This hypothesis would suggest that the extra effort a person puts into the task involves demand on mental activity because more general processing of information about performance is needed or because increasing effort is itself attentionally demanding. The latter explanation will now be familiar to the reader as similar to the one used by Näätänen (1973) to explain the decrement in task performance as a function of raised arousal produced concurrently by means of effort in, for example, increasing muscle tension.

Some evidence to suggest that in noise, the processing of information is more superficial, was provided by Weinstein (1974). He examined the detection of errors on a proof-reading task and found that in high noise subjects maintained comprehension ability but failed to detect errors which depended on reading context, whereas they remained able to detect errors not dependent on context such as letter transposition errors. Weinstein (1974) argued that arousal theory could not account for the "relatively

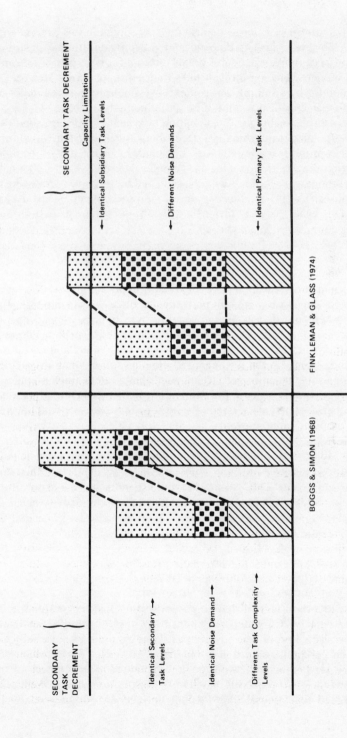

FIG. 7.4 Illustration of the concept of noise as a demand requiring processing resources and capacity. (From designs provided by Boggs & Simon, 1968, and Finkelman & Glass, 1970. First produced in Fisher, 1984a.)

125

complicated pattern of heterogeneous effects observed in this experiment (p. 552)." However, capacity demand may not provide the only realistic explanation because Weinstein also points out that for both types of errors the effect was no worse on difficult lines than on simple lines. This could be accounted for by assuming that context assessment is impaired in noise and therefore line difficulty will not be an influential variable.

Use of the probe technique of estimating task demand was provided by Millar (1980). A letter-matching task (Sternberg, 1969, 1975) provided the main task. A probe reaction-time task was made to occur at 50 msec and 250 msec after the occurrence of the test stimulus. Normally, each additional member of the target set of letters to be searched for, prolonged the search by 35–40 msec. The probe latencies were found to be lengthened further in noise. This again suggests that delays on the secondary task in noise occur, reflecting loss of spare capacity.

D. Strategic Response to Increased Demand

One important result of the increased demand imposed on a person may be a strategic attempt to maintain performance on aspects of the task. In situations where the density of information over time is stepped up, a person may respond by leaving some signals unattended by making guesses rather than considering the data, or by delaying responding and trying to "bunch" the actions. In the next chapter, the question of what a strategic response might be is considered; it is argued that strategy implies choice. An important consideration in this section is whether in increased mental demand a person really does operate a strategy for coping or whether he is simply "grabbed" by the events.

Strategic response to overload on a complex multi-source task was investigated by Miller (1962). He identified a number of strategies that might be utilised as an adjustment. The adjustments are assumed by Miller to involve an active organisational process and are not seen as inevitable or unavoidable. He lists the following techniques for coping with overload:

1. Not processing certain stimuli (omission).
2. Processing some signals incorrectly (error).
3. Delaying responses during heavy work periods (queuing).
4. Selectivity in information processing (filtering).
5. Giving approximate responses (approximation).
6. Making use of alternative channels where possible (multiple channels).
7. Escape (leaving the situation or taking steps to terminate the input).

These strategies were used by different subjects but were also situationally determined. The strategic response to overload is assumed to be implemented as a response to the need to remain competent when the increased demands of the task make incompetence more likely. This is a "cut your losses" rule – it is better to try to do some of the task well than to appear uniformly bad at all of it. Associated with this may be "cut your losses, but maximise the potential gains." This would suggest that it is better to cut down on those areas of a task least likely to pay off in terms of utility value or success. On rules such as this, an individual might "pass" on a question he cannot do, in order to gain as many "right" answers as possible overall.

However, one very important point is that the very effect of overload may make it difficult for a person to respond strategically. He perhaps lacks the resources to work out what is going on, what the priorities are, and what he should best do to cope with a situation. Therefore, we might predict that the operation of effective strategies would be weakened in stress and that the person is more "here and now"—more captured by events and more unlikely to see what is essential and what is not.

Some arguments against this as an inevitable conclusion are provided by the results of Fisher (1977). A five-choice serial reaction task (main task) was paired with an auditory–verbal simple addition task (secondary task). The load on the five-choice task was increased by making it incompatible. The combined tasks were then very demanding. However, the organisational features of time sharing between tasks were not destroyed. The organisational structure of integration was retained but there was a change in attentional priorities reflected in the integration pattern.

A more detailed study by Fisher (1984b) of the integration of a four-choice serial response task and a secondary visual monitoring task, presented on the display of an Apple microcomputer, permitted the comparison of single to dual decrements on both tasks for a group working in loud noise and a group working in quiet. Overall comparisons and comparisons involving the microstructure of performance suggested that although there was a single to dual task decrement on both main and secondary tasks, the slowness was more pronounced for the detection task in noise. Comparisons within the main task showed that in noise there was increased slowness at the time a monitoring signal arrived and had to be dealt with, but that subjects compensated for this by increased speed *between* these occasions. A number of rules that might be operated in noise were identified. The first was "always adhere to priorities indicated by instructions and shut down non-salient aspects of the task." A second was "whether there is an expectancy of or perception of slow performance, compensate afterwards by speeded response rates." These would be viable strategic responses to increased demands imposed by performing two tasks in noise.

In conditions where stress effects are mild and there is no threat to life, where competence is part of the plan, and where responses are trained, it is more likely that strategic response patterns will be characteristic. Adequate strategies may be less likely in environments where there has been no previous training. Sudden unexpected catastrophes or disasters may be just like this. A person may fall back on strategies of a general nature (e.g. "when danger is great, abort and escape") rather than attempt more elegant strategies. In armed combat conditions faced by troops, one way of terminating the threat is to kill off the enemy, but for those unused to the idea of killing or of responding with aggression, the hide or escape tendency may be more dominant, controlled only by various costs of escape (shot for dissertion, court martial and disgrace, etc.). The obvious compromise might be to find an acceptable condition of hiding or escape in which the attached costs are reduced. Feigning mental or physical illness, getting lost, even inflicting real wounds, may be obvious strategic solutions. Strategic responses which are bounded by considerations of costs and penalties or gains and advancements, are likely to be more refined and sophisticated and planned in advance.

Experienced individuals trained in response–outcome possibilities are arguably more likely to sustain strategic responding. Producing strategies and utilising existing strategies may be differentially sensitive to intense stress.

2.   COMPOSITE MODELS

There are currently two composite models purporting to explain the relationship between stress and performance. Both could be argued to be "direct hit" models in that performance is assumed to be the result of a combined identifiable influence. The first model, by Poulton, is developed with respect to noise specifically. The second, by Fisher, has different origins and is of more general relevance.

A. Poulton's Composite Model

Poulton's composite model is addressed specifically to the understanding of the effects of loud noise on performance. It evolved because of a growing conviction that noise was likely to influence performance negatively because of its effect on the processing of task data and the recall of information about the task, rather than because of any effect due to arousal. Because of the limitations of space, it is not possible to give a full coverage to the development of Poulton's ideas. The reader should follow up the progression of arguments and ideas across the series of articles (Poulton, 1976a, 1977a, 1977b, 1978a, 1978b, 1979, 1981). The reader should also be aware of counter-arguments (Broadbent, 1976, 1977, 1978; Hartley, 1981) and the existence of an account of "the masking controversy" and Poulton's composite model in Fisher (1984a). Finally, since much of the argument presupposes that the reader has some knowledge of the effects of noise, the following references are useful: Broadbent (1957, 1958, 1971); Hockey (1983).

The origin of Poulton's ideas stemmed from noting some work and comment by Stevens (see Kryter, 1950; Stevens, 1972). Poulton (1977a) observed that Stevens never found a negative effect of noise that could not be explained in terms of the masking of sounds from the task and auditory feedback from responses. The task data were likely to be slightly suppressed or even distorted by masking sound. Poulton further pointed out that there could be interference with "inner speech" and rehearsal processes on which task memory depends.

This led Poulton to re-examine a number of existing experiments purportedly demonstrating negative effects of noise and he proposed alternative explanations in terms of the masking influence of noise on task information, feedback, or memory. For example, in the case of the 20-dials test (Broadbent, 1954), Poulton suggested that there was a degree of incompatibility present because the relationship between knob and dial fractionated; the needle on the display moved up to a fixed point and down again. A correction made by moving the knob could result in the needle moving upwards or downwards as a function of base position. This, Poulton argued, would make the subject very dependent on feedback about cancellation of the switches. A reported finding by Hockey (1970a, b) involved a dual-task design in which a central tracking task had to be maintained together with monitoring of a series of six lamps arranged in a semicircle. The effect of loud noise was to produce slower detection of signals in peripheral sources than of central sources where signals occur more frequently. Hockey argued that this demonstrated selectivity of attention in noise. Poulton argued that the effect could be explained as an artefact resulting from suppression of feedback from the switches; those switches situated peripherally involved more uncertain finger responses and therefore had greater dependence on auditory feedback (Poulton, 1976b). A finding reported by Broadbent and Gregory (1965) of a shift towards use of extreme confidence levels in noise was reinterpreted by Poulton in terms of the consequences of internal masking of information (see Poulton, 1978b).

Replying to these and others of Poulton's criticisms, Broadbent (1978) outlined three criteria that could be used to demonstrate that acoustic masking is not responsible for a reported effect:

1. Conditions where the same response gives no demonstration in noise when a non-acoustic condition is unchanged.
2. When different response mechanisms give the same harmful effects in noise.
3. If acoustic manipulations leave the effects unchanged.

Broadbent argued that one or more of these checks had been applied to his own or other criticised experiments. In return, Poulton (1978b) criticised the criteria in relation to experimental detail and claimed they are not "watertight" (p. 1074).

The strongest statement of the masking hypothesis forms the major assumption of the composite model proposed by Poulton. All negative changes in performance in noise are due either to the masking of essential task and feedback information or to suppression of rehearsal in memory due to interference with internal speech. Perhaps the strongest support for this comes from the demonstration by Poulton and Edwards (1974) that reducing the frequency of high-intensity noise prevents adverse effects on a five-choice serial reaction task; the reduction of frequency is assumed to reduce the masking qualities of the noise.

Positive effects of noise on performance are attributed to increased arousal, which is more likely at the beginning of the task. Poulton does not consider that decrements in noise arise as a result of increased arousal and is thus directly opposed to Broadbent in this respect.

The composite model formulated by Poulton (1979) thus assumes that noise may cause negative effects due to masking and positive effects due to arousal increase. The two effects may combine to determine the character of performance in noise. The composite model allows for the effects to cancel each other out on occasions; final performance is the combined effect of both (positive) arousal influence and any (negative) masking influence.

B. Fisher's Composite Model

The composite model proposed by Fisher (1984a) has different origins and different characteristics. Fisher argued that there was a tendency to seek a single-factor explanation for performance changes in stressful circumstances. This may have advantages as far as the scientific testing of hypotheses is concerned, but may mean that a number of plausible sources of influence are ignored. The data provided by the activities of the subject generally do not permit the exact kind of influence to be identified; a subject who fails to remember a high proportion of items on a list when he is in stressful conditions may be argued to fail because: (1) he is under or over aroused; (2) he is mentally preoccupied with stress, the task, or the consequence of failure; (3) he is distracted by the stress; (4) the stress masks essential information. All these different kinds of influence can be plausibly linked to competence changes. Moreover, there is support for the notion that a stressful condition causes a specific change (mental load, arousal, distraction, masking) and will result in alterations in performance detail. Thus laboratory studies have shown high levels of mental load to be a sufficient condition for increased errors or increased slowness in performance (secondary task, probe reaction task).

In the case of noise, viewed in historical perspective, researchers have found evidence to support one view and then changed their minds later. Noise was first regarded as a distracting stimulus, which at sufficient intensity could create blocks or gaps in performance hypothesised to be due to attentional failure. The "perceptual failure" view of noise influence was developed in *Perception and communication* (Broadbent, 1958), and the reader who wishes to gain some idea of the development of ideas regarding perceptual failure theory and Broadbent's model of attentional filtering should read the relevant sections of the book. Long tasks, noise levels greater than 90 dB, and continuous tasks, were most likely to reveal irregularities in performance as a result of the attentional demands of noise. Broadbent argued that the effect was not one of "mental paralysis" but of distraction, since high noise intensity was most likely to cause irregularities in performance and was likely to be associated with fast response latencies when presented as the main signal. Fisher (1972) confirmed from examination of the microstructure of the effect of a noise that distraction was the most likely explanation.

By the late 1960s, the view of the effect of noise was changing towards the idea that noise caused a change in arousal level and that attentional phenomena were best understood as a result of the change. This brought noise into line with the traditional view of stresses as stimuli that created changes in arousal. The difficulty of pinpointing the likely direction of noise influence on arousal was alleviated by the experiments on stress interactions (see Chapter 6). A summary of the new approach to noise and other environmental stresses can be found in *Decision and stress* (Broadbent, 1971) where the notion is developed that changes in arousal influence decision making.

Poulton created a new twist to the explanation of the effects of noise on performance with development of his ideas about the masking effects of noise. The arousal influence was reserved for positive changes in performance; masking was assumed to account for all negative changes.

There is, in addition, the possibility explored by Boggs and Simon (1968), Finkleman and Glass (1970), Weinstein (1974), and Millar (1980), that noise acts to reduce processing capacity because it provides a source of competing demand.

Taken collectively, we are left with an account of a stimulus which at sufficient intensity may distract, activate, mask, or increase mental demands. One temptation is to build models that account for one influence in terms of the effect of another: For example, increased arousal causes increased tendency to distraction; increased mental demand causes increased arousal; increased mental demand is the result of distraction; increased arousal creates connotative signals which absorb capacity and increase mental load.

Noise research provides a useful illustration of the problems of competing explanations, perhaps bolstered by the varying evidence that has arisen because noise has been a favoured stress for experimentation. There seems no good a priori reason for neglecting evidence identifying a particular kind of influence. The composite model developed by Fisher (1984a) assumed that any *one* stress has a *number* of influences, all of which can operate simultaneously. Thus, to use the example of noise again, it may variously distract (mode 1), mask data (mode 2), arouse (mode 3), increase mental demand (mode 4). The modes of influence identified are assumed to be only *potential*. Situational factors such as the task and the instructions may determine which modes actually operate to influence performance. Thus noise may operate a *potential* masking influence but a task which has minimal dependence on acoustic cues and memory will not allow the manifestation of the masking mode. Put another way, the task and instructions provide a *gate* device that allows some influences to become operative and not others. Therefore, there may be a stress with (n) possible modes of influence, which has only one or even no modes of influence in a particular situation.

Secondly, the task itself is a potential source of stress influence. A very complex, demanding task may provide a source of arousal increase which will further interact with particular modes that are operative. Thus "noise arousal" may be added to by "task arousal" as a determinant of the final form of arousal influence. The same statement could be made for mental load.

The concurrent state of the subject in terms of arousal or information processing load is likely to be influential in determining whether a particular operative mode has positive or negative effects on performance. For example, a person already at a high level of arousal is more likely to show an adverse reaction to further arousal increase.

However, largely because of the physiological evidence concerning different types of arousal and the fractionation of arousal systems, Fisher argued that there was a need to consider *arousal compatibility*. To illustrate this using a hypothetical example, a person who reacts to a previous event with raised heart rate and then is presented with a situation that is likely to induce raised heart rate in most people, has high *compatibility* in arousal influence. A person who first reacts with raised muscle tension but then faces a situation likely to increase heart rate may have relatively lower compatibility. Fisher argued that compatibility is a factor that determines the extent of arousal influence for a given situation. If some people always react with increased heart rate whatever the stress (see Malmo & Shagass, 1949), then compatibility will be high. If situations determine the form of arousal, then compatibility will be low for those who experience a previous, different arousal influence.

Figure 7.5 represents the composite model proposed by Fisher (1984a). The main premises are as follows:

1. Any particular stress environment or threatening event has associated with it a number of *potential modes of influence*. Some are *specific*, acting to distort task data; others are *general*, acting on mental resources or arousal.
2. Not all modes of influence operate. The task, its demands and requirements as well as its features, determine which modes will become operative. The task therefore acts as a gate device.

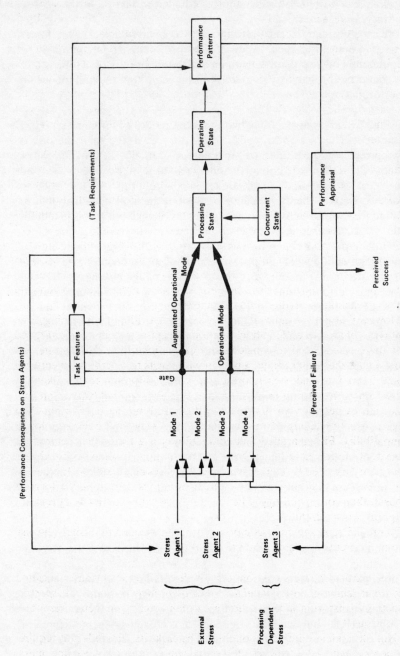

FIG. 7.5 A composite model of the relationship between stress and performance. (First produced in Fisher, 1984a.)

3. The task may also contribute to existing modes of influence. A complex task may contribute a further source of high arousal or a further source of increased mental load.
4. The existing and recent past situation (concurrent state) determines base state against which incoming influence occurs. Base state may be compatible or incompatible with incoming influence. Compatible states increase the probability of effective influence of operational modes on performance.

In Fig. 7.5, stress agent 1 has two potential modes of influence, mode 1 and mode 2. The task contributes further to mode 1 and since the task is "appropriate" for the influence of that particular mode, the mode becomes operative. It is therefore operative and *augmented*. In the case of a second mode of influence (mode 2) the task is not appropriate for the mode to become operative. Therefore, the task gates out the mode as a likely source of influence. Stress agent 2 also has mode 2 influence but this is gated out by the same task. Mode 3, however, becomes operative but is not contributed to by the task. Therefore as illustrated in the figure there are the following possibilities: (1) an operative mode (not augmented); (2) a non-operative mode; (3) an operative mode which is *augmented*.

The figure also illustrates that the *concurrent state*, the result of recent past in terms of information processing load and arousal, provides the base state against which incoming influences occur. The combined effect determines the *processing state*. The translation of the settings of the processing state into performance is assumed to be in terms of three control centres: (1) ingredients for plans; (2) speed of plan running; (3) rules of plan running. The control centres permit interactive or additive influence and are considered in the next chapter, since there are implications for the origin and instigation of strategies. The interested reader who would like to read a fuller exposition of the model and the proposed translation into the detail of performance should read Fisher (1984a, Chapters 4, 5, 6 and 7).

The composite model allows stress and task influences to create an apparent *state* of processing. Thus a digital reading across the state at any one time should provide an account of combined influences. The control centres reflect the same state in terms of the detail of performance parameters. Thus, a person may, as a result of mode 1 and mode 2 influence, be: (1) lacking critical plan ingredients (attentional dysfunction); (2) running the plan fast (running state increase); and (3) violating one of the rules of plan running.

The combined influence on the setting of parameters in control centres thus determines the degree of constraint on strategic response. This is the basis of consideration in the next chapter. The issue is an interesting one. Coping strategies imply choice, freedom, and efficiency—some degree of control. Stresses may create operating states where such coping strategies cannot be conceived of or, even if they are, cannot be operated.

The following principles were argued by Fisher to be important determinants of performance impairment in stress:

1. The greater the *number* of modes that operate, the greater the *probability of general impairment of performance*.
2. The greater the *intensity* or *magnitude* with which a mode operates, the *greater the probability of general impairment*.
3. The greater the *duration* of the operation of a particular mode or mode combination, the greater the probability general impairment of performance.

3. STATE MODELS OF STRESS AND PERFORMANCE

Hockey and Hamilton (1983) have developed the idea that the *pattern* of behaviour changes for different stress and circumstantial conditions. The concept of "state" as used by Hockey and Hamilton is defined in terms of the characteristics of a complex system at any one sample time. "The state is defined as the set of all states the system can be in and is represented by an *n* dimensional array made up of the functional ranges for each property of the system (p. 332)." Each state that can be specified is a point in the space created by all possible states. This approach conceives of the response to stress as the result of a number of changes in different parameters simultaneously. It is in keeping with a systems-oriented approach to human behaviour and is not incompatible with many of the assumptions of the composite model proposed by Fisher (where a reading of "processing state" should provide *n* specifications for final behaviour at any one time).

Hockey and Hamilton are concerned with constellations of behaviours in time. A person facing a particular stress may be, for example: (1) tense; (2) slow to remember; (3) fast to respond; (4) inaccurate; (5) feeling panicky; (6) preoccupied with thoughts of failure, etc. Knowledge of the way in which constellations of behaviours change depends on the measurements taken by scientists. If preoccupation with failure is not assessed, then in the above hypothetical example, this particular factor remains absent in the constellation specified. This is perhaps an important point, because either experimental designs or some theoretical structure are prerequisites of providing an adequate specification of a constellation. The body of research on which the composite model rests does at least provide some insights into the particular constellations that are likely.

Hockey (1983) favours a narrow-band research design in which one task, such as the serial response task, is used and a number of stressful circumstances such as drugs, heat, loss of sleep, incentives, etc., are examined in relation to the parameters of the main task. A broad-band research design involves considering one stress such as noise and examining the pattern of performance that results in different tasks. Hockey and Hamilton argue that both approaches are necessary in order to build up a picture of states created by stress and circumstance.

The authors attempt to develop a notion of the performance pattern that specifies a "map of the noise state," involving changes in selectivity of attention, changes in the speed–accuracy trade-off, and changes in memory function. The reader should follow the details as provided by Hockey and Hamilton (1983, pp. 342–345).

A useful distinction made by Hockey and Hamilton is between *strategic variables*, "effects of stressors which are peculiar to the task situation and its demand characteristics," and *structural variables*, "change in the operating parameters of the system" (p. 347). The point is that some features of performance may be changed as an act of volition as a response to stress, whereas others are structurally limited. However, Hockey and Hamilton argue that in practice the distinction is difficult to sustain, largely because human information-processing ability is interactive and flexible. This should not in itself be an argument against making the distinction, merely an argument for refining the experimental lines of inquiry to identify the differences. For example, on the assumption that speed and accuracy are partly personally controlled and partly circumstantially determined (I can *decide* to speed up; a stimulating drug would make me speed up), the interaction of instructional bias with stressful conditions of various kinds provides a basis for separating the two elements. An instruction to slow down should be less easy to operate in the presence of a stimulating drug than in the presence of a tranquilising drug.

Some of these points and the implications for understanding the origins and maintenance of strategies for the establishment of control are discussed further in the next chapter.

8

Stress and the Initiation of Strategies

1. THE INGREDIENTS OF STRATEGIES

Although there are many books and articles on the subject of coping in stressful situations, few have been concerned with explanatary models of features of coping strategies or with considering the cognitive facts on which such response profiles depend.

A number of basic distinctions can be made about strategies. Most dictionary definitions of the term imply that it is a response made to *gain an advantage* in a situation. The underlying implication is that a strategic response involves *choice*. If stresses exert a direct effect on thinking and behaviour, the voluntary elements of behaviour may be reduced. A simple illustration is provided by the following example: If a person is struck with sufficient force he or she will fall over. A strategic response might be to fall in such a way as to reduce damage, or to prevent being struck again. If the force is strong enough, a strategic response may be impossible; the individual does not have any choice about how he falls. If it is the case that stress creates a change in mental state by "direct hit" (see previous chapters), then choice is reduced, because there is in effect a temporary mental structure which restricts the freedom to act. This point was made in more general terms by Fisher (1984a). Stressful conditions were argued to demand a highly efficient mental response and yet to decrease the likelihood that such responses would be possible. This should *not* be taken to imply that lowered competence is inevitable in stressful conditions. As will be clear in the early sections of this chapter, there is experimental evidence to suggest that in some cases performance improves in stress. Constraint could be advantageous or disadvantageous depending on circumstance.

137

It is argued that strategic responses are operated to increase the probability of gaining control. In previous chapters it has been argued that the notion of *domains of influence* must be included in any analysis of the perception of control in any situation. The individual analyses the possibilities within one domain, such as the personal domain, and then explores another domain if the outcome appears negative. Thus, a person who decides he has low personal control may seek control in another domain such as the interpersonal or socio-political domains.

From what has been established in previous chapters, the development and execution of coping strategies in stress are likely to be complex with high dependence on cognitive processes. First, a person must perceive reality (including the stress). This may require strategic activity. Then some appraisal of "task demand" is required (e.g. what is the likely outcome?; what effect will the stress have?). Both appraisals require the collection and representation of the evidence. The detection and representation of evidence and the selection of action have high dependence on attention and memory. These cognitive processes are affected by stress. For this reason, we begin this chapter by considering the changes in memory and attention that are likely in stress.

2.   ATTENTIONAL DEPLOYMENT IN STRESS

A. Macro-attention Processes

One of the most interesting issues to develop in the last 20 years concerns the deployment of attention across an array of sources that are spatially separated. There are two fundamental aspects to attention deployment: how a structure for deploying attention is made available and how internal control is maintained over the structure. In the former case it is important to distinguish the use of a pre-existing structure from conditions of novelty where a structure must be simultaneously acquired.

The indications are that individuals do have a great deal of internal control over the allocation of attention but also that situations—especially stressful situations—might reduce control. The interesting question is whether there is personal control over attentional structure (strategic) or whether changes occur as a consequence of the stress ("direct hit").

One of the strongest statements suggesting that in dual-task designs people can hold and maintain a "priority structure" came from Kahneman (1973), who presented evidence suggesting that capacity may be allocated efficiently. Subjects can maintain performance on a primary task, allowing deterioration to occur on a secondary task as difficulty levels increase. Kantowitz and Knight (1974, 1976) found some contradictions; although secondary task performance declined with increasing task difficulty, the extent of the decline did not relate as clearly as might be expected to level of primary task difficulty. They assumed that the lack of interaction between primary and secondary task difficulty refuted the basic Kahneman view. Lane (1977) argues that the interaction is not essential to the Kahneman view because whether the two variables interact will depend on the shape of the function relating task difficulty and capacity to performance as well as to the difficulty of each task.

However, work on dual-task interaction has shown that although instructional bias changes the priority structure in a way which would be expected (Fisher, 1975), increased mental load also changes the priority structure (Fisher, 1977), whereas sleep deprivation preserves the existing instructional priority structure (Fisher, 1980): Either different strategies are brought about by the dictates of different circumstances, or different mental structures are directly created by stress.

Learning may be a factor that changes the way two tasks are combined. A useful idea by Gopher and North (1977) was to present subjects with a sequence of single- and dual-task trials. Tracking was one of the tasks; digit cancellation was the other. As single-task performance improved, task difficulty levels were increased. In spite of this, dual-task performance continued to improve. It could be argued that it is an illustration of an improvement in the actual time-sharing process. This might be taken to suggest that time-sharing strategies can be improved with experience. The subject is gradually learning a strategic response which will pay off, in that he will be able to accept increasing pressure and continue to produce adequate performance on both tasks. An underlying explanation may be that economies are operated. Efficient ordering of responses or the running off of automatic sequences which are not closely monitored, may provide the basis for effective strategies.

B. The Strategic Control of Attention Deployment

i. Multi-source Laboratory Tasks

An aspect of many complex tasks is the existence of a number of different elements requiring either spatial or temporal distribution of attention for adequate performance. The vulnerability of multi-source tasks to arousing conditions such as loud noise has been demonstrated (Broadbent, 1951, 1953; Jerison, 1957); the addition of more sources of information increases the probability of performance deterioration. At least one possible explanation is that it is not the increased uncertainty that is important, but the requirement to deploy attentional resources effectively under conditions where limitations are unavoidable.

However, if anything, work on multi-source monitoring tasks has indicated that the limitation in attentional resource is not some naturally occurring structural process but the result of a cognitively driven process, perhaps similar to the operation of a strategy.

The research that first drew attention to this possibility was by Hockey (1970a, b). Using a task designed originally by Bursill (1958), in which a subject was required to track a central display change and at the same time monitor a semicircular array of six lamps for the occurrence of signals, he compared performance changes on both tasks for biased and unbiased signal conditions in quiet and noise. Hockey reported an improvement on the error scores of the tracking task and on centrally placed signal sources in the biased condition, relative to peripherally situated sources. The effect of unequal detection times in the biased condition was true for quiet, but more evident in noise; thus noise had the effect of enhancing the biasing of attention.

Unfortunately, there have been a number of difficulties which have weakened the confidence that might have been attached to the result. Firstly, Poulton (1976) pointed out that the apparent channelling effect towards central sources could be explained in terms of the masking effect of noise on peripheral switches likely to produce less certain responses. Secondly, in a series of four experiments designed to replicate Hockey's main findings, Forster and Grierson (1978) failed to find any evidence to support the selectivity phenomenon. A later replication by Hartley (1981) provided some support for the selectivity hypothesis in reporting an interaction between central and peripheral locations reliable at the 5% level. Although Hartley sees his results as roughly comparable with the Hockey effect, Poulton (1981b) points out that two of the results for the tracking task are in the wrong direction, and overall tracking is reliably worse in noise.

There is other evidence that supports the notion of attentional limitation. Attentional restriction in high arousal towards perceived high-priority rather than low-priority elements of the task was observed by Bacon (1974). Priority differences imply cognitive involvement. Using a task involving the monitoring of three sources for faults, Hamilton (1967) measured observing responses to the three sources and found that when the rate at which observing responses were made was slowed by pacing, there was increased sampling of the high-probability source. This effect was subsequently found by Hockey (1973) to be augmented in noise, and the double-checking of sources was reduced.

The selectivity hypothesis has also been investigated on versions of the Stroop test (Stroop, 1935), in which the colour indicated by a word normally interferes with the naming of the colour of the ink in which it is written (see Jensen and Rohwer, 1966). Interference produced by the word-colour and the colour of the ink will be reduced if attention is more selective, and there should be less delay in naming the ink colour. Thus Callaway and his co-workers showed that amphetamine reduces the level of interference (see Callaway & Dembo, 1958; Callaway & Stone, 1960), although the effect is apparent in terms of overall speed and may not represent resistance to the confusion produced by word naming (e.g. see Jensen & Rohwer, 1966;

Venables, 1964). An investigation of the effects of noise on the level of interference on the Stroop test produced some further complexity: Hartley and Adams (1974) found that when the Stroop colour words were presented on playing cards that were required to be sorted, noise increased the time it took to sort the "Stroop effect" pack by about 3%, which would suggest interference to be greater. In a second experiment, where the material was presented in written form on sheets of paper and noise exposure was varied, subjects showed less interference in the combined condition for 10-minute noise exposure. These findings would argue against the view that increased arousal reduces interference at the central level, because the phenomenon depends on presentation conditions.

The main issue of interest is whether stresses directly change the parameters that control the attention process or whether the individual has internal control and operates a strategic response. Before this is discussed further, it is useful to consider the explanations of attentional selectivity that have been proposed. In the case of mild or laboratory-based stressful conditions, the issue of interest seems to be the explanation of limited attention and whether or not it is somehow "automatic" or cognitively driven. In other words, the main question is really whether a person under pressure cannot exert an influence on his attention processes and is a slave to stressful effects ("direct hit") or whether there are attentional manoeuvres which are strategic and which maximise the gains and minimise the costs.

In the case of intense stresses where there is threat to life, the question seems less pertinent. Behaviour at very high levels of arousal is characterised by fragmentation, disorganisation accompanied by agitation, frenzy and panic. It is poorly coordinated, fragile, and totally incompetent. Fisher (1984a) defined "personal crisis" as the state of total incompetence brought about by a number of worsening conditions in a scenario of stressful events, and envisaged this state to be one of total disorganisation. This state, also well described by Korchin (1964) and Levitt (1968), could hardly be seen as strategic. It appears almost by defintion to be the result of a failure of all strategies.

ii. Models of Attentional Selectivity

Most of the models of attentional selectivity in stressful conditions have assumed that the response is not strategic; the subject cannot control attentional processes. Control is relinquished and the subject is "stress-determined." In the models to be discussed next it is assumed that the effect is due to increased arousal or drive. The individual is assumed to be under internal tension and as a result attentional selectivity occurs. It could equally well be argued that under high mental load, there will be loss of resource and that changes in selectivity could result. The "mental load" model might, however, have more trouble in explaining the orderly nature of attentional changes since there should not be sufficient resources for maintaining control.

There are two much-quoted models that account for changes in attentional selectivity in stress. Both are based on the notion of a relationship between arousal and attentional parameters. Perhaps the best known is the hypothesis by Easterbrook (1959), which supposes that there is increased cue restriction with increased arousal. This is beneficial at first in limiting input to what is essential, but not later, in that relevant signals are missed. The restricted cue-utilisation hypothesis assumes a single monotonic relationship between arousal and attention in accounting for the inverted U relationship between arousal and performance.

The Easterbrook hypothesis does not make it clear why the monotonic relationship should exist or how restricted cue utilisation favours performance in the early stages. A model that does tackle the logic of relationships between arousal and attention deployment but seems, if anything, to increase complexity is that of Callaway and Stone (1960), based on their experiments on the effects of amphetamine in reducing the Stroop effect. These authors propose a reduction in probabilistic coding of environmental events because of high arousal. The effect of this is increased load on a person and greater need for attentional restriction. The Callaway and Stone model assumes that attentional selectivity comes about because of reduced coding of events and therefore implies that the attentional limitation is a strategic response to potential overload rather than being directly linked with arousal.

The Easterbrook model could account for the interaction of arousal influence and task difficulty because a difficult task involves more sources of information or environmental cues. The problem is that the cue-restriction model could be used to explain away any data. The Callaway and Stone model does not appear to cover the problem of task complexity but would presumably assume that a more difficult task needs more probabilistic coding, and if arousal causes this to break down, then there is no basis for ordering information; thus overload is further increased.

M. Eysenck (1983) argues that Easterbrook's hypothesis does not provide a very satisfactory account of the effects of anxiety on performance, largely for the reasons considered earlier in this chapter, namely that anxious performance is not just characterised by attentional focus on one or two elements of a task. Logically, when a person has an internal representation of task structure, increasingly restricted cue utilisation should lead to increasingly "blinkered" attention but it should remain focused on the task. Eysenck quotes two studies of anxiety which show that attention to *task-relevant* information is reduced in anxious compared with non-anxious subjects (Deffenbacher, 1978; Nottelmann & Hill, 1977).

Eysenck further emphasises difficulty with the cue-restriction hypothesis: Evidence from Fowler and Wilding (1979) suggests that incentives *enhance* incidental recall of spatial locations of learned words, whereas white noise causes *reduction*. Eysenck additionally cites studies of the effects of failure and shock on the performance of high- and low-anxiety subjects. On the

Easterbrook hypothesis the effect should be increasing attentional restriction for both failure, threat, and shock. Eysenck's results show that failure feedback impairs performance to a greater extent for high-anxiety subjects, but shock impairs performance to a greater extent for low-anxiety subjects.

A different model purporting to provide an explanation of the effects of increasing arousal (drive) on performance features is that of Broen and Storms (1961). It is based directly on the notion of response competition provided for in the learning-theory models of Hull (1943) and Spence (1956). The main point is that any situation defines a set of dominant and non-dominant responses. As drive level increases, since it is multiplicative with habit strength, the propensity for behaviour to be governed by dominant responses is increased. As drive level increases further, a limit is reached. This ceiling means that dominant responses have maximal influence, but non-dominant responses can continue to increase and dominate behaviour. In this model the limitations are response-related rather than attentional. The underlying principle is almost the reverse of "restriction" because it involves an increasing implosion of responses with an internal "ceiling" effect, which eventually inhibits dominant responses. There is no research that tests the model directly.

As mentioned previously, none of the models provide an adequate account of behaviour at very high levels of arousal. If anything, perhaps the Broen and Storms model has some advantage because non-dominant responses (of all kinds) can determine behaviour. This does at least allow for "here and now," unplanned, disorganised activity to be manifest. The Easterbrook cue-restriction model needs extra assumptions. One of them is the assumption that there is loss of control over the sampling process at high levels of arousal so that although restricted, the attention process is also unstable. Wachtel (1967) uses the analogy of a beam of light, and argues that attention at very high levels of arousal is described by a beam with narrow width and unstable scanning characteristic. As a result, the perceptual world appears fragmented and the individual is a "slave to minor variations." The inexperienced individual in this state would have an inadequate data base and poor control over sampling. Behaviour would appear energetic but be disorganised and random.

The point made by Wachtel is that there may be important differences between "broadening" and "narrowing." Two logically distinct dimensions are "scanning" (or how quickly the beam moves across the field), and "focusing" (or the width of the beam). Wachtel cites an example of an obsessive personality who, on clinical observations, appears to create great breadth of scanning but uses a "narrow beam." Thus, intellectually there is a great deal of material available, but concern is with details, and the material is poorly integrated. Wachtel criticises the view that at moderately high arousal levels, attention is narrowed, whereas at high levels there is general breakdown, because this suggests that there is a sudden point of breakdown: Two specifiable locations on the relationship between arousal and performance are required. Wachtel argues that when behaviour is disorganised and any event captures attention, width could be argued to have increased and performance should improve again. This gives a "two-humped camel curve" (Wachtel, 1967, p. 420) not actually found in practice.

Wachtel believes that the problem can be resolved on the assumption that at very high levels of arousal, although there is narrowing, the beam begins to move in a rapid and unstable way. Thus the anxious person is a slave to minor variations in the field, is unable to concentrate, and is hyperdistractable. A possibility raised by this is that a mediating speed factor is involved; at very high levels of arousal, scanning speed is raised to the point beyond which information can be properly processed. Under these circumstances control of scanning might also break down, because the data base becomes inadequate and unrepresentative.

Taken collectively, these considerations suggest two important conclusions:

1. When in stress, a person needs to sample the environment effectively in order to acquire a realistic representation of the world, which is a prerequisite for the selection of an adequate coping strategy.
2. The sampling process involved may itself be stress influenced.

All the models take account of a progression from increased efficiency at moderate arousal through restriction and inefficiency to disorganisation and loss of control over behaviour at high levels of arousal and anxiety.

iii. Attentional Strategies

There are two main ways in which the operation of attentional strategies might be identified. First, there are conditions where there is an effect of stimulus bias. Second, there are conditions where instructions seem to influence behaviour. In each case it is necessary to ensure that the observed change is strategic rather than inevitably created by the stressful condition.

Hockey (1970a, b) showed that the main effect of loud noise on attentional deployment across a spatial array of signal sources on a secondary task was dependent on probability of signals arriving at these sources. When there was bias in favour of signals occurring in central source locations, there was attentional deployment in favour of these sources in quiet conditions, but the effect was enhanced in loud noise. In other words, noise appeared to enhance the tendency of bias to salient sources. The main problem with the finding is that the detection of high-probability sources depends itself on sampling. Subjects were not told initially of the bias. Increased bias in attention depended on noting the distribution of signals across sources. Ideally, the subject must sample effectively and liberally in order to form a data base for the operation of an effective attentional strategy.

Use of instructional variables does offer some prospect of identifying strategic responding. If attentional sampling is shown to favour the directions given at the beginning of the task more strongly when a stressful condition is present, this would support the view that subjects are able to control attention and that attentional restriction is more likely to be due to the operation of a "shut down" rule for preserving effective performance in the presence of raised demand.

Performance changes in noise consistent with the operation of "shut down" and "compensatory" strategies have been identified in a dual-task design (Fisher, 1984b). A central task involving a four-choice serial response task was paired with a six-source signal-detection task. Both were presented concurrently within the confines of the space provided by a television monitor attached to an Apple microcomputer. Relative to single-task performance, performance in the dual-task condition showed deterioration for both the main task and the secondary task. However, the deterioration, manifest as increased slowness, was more pronounced on the secondary monitoring task in the presence of 100 dB noise as compared with quiet. This suggests that an attentional strategy was operated in noise so that the central task was maintained as far as possible. This view is supported by evidence of adjustments made within the central task. For example, in noise there were slower responses at dual-task moments, but *faster* responses in the intervals between such moments.

The evidence also provided a basis for arguments *against* a strategic response explanation. First, in noise relative to quiet, subjects were more likely to interrupt the central task whenever a signal occurred on a secondary task source. This would not fit well with the strategic view of priority structure. Additionally there was evidence that secondary signal sources in contralateral opposition to the location of a current central task signal, were associated with slowed response times for signal detection. This seems more like a structural limitation than an attentional deployment strategy and may indicate that attentional parameters may be narrowed with increased mental demand or increased arousal. A theoretical account would have to include mechanical or "direct hit" effects, as well as strategic changes.

3.   MEMORY IN STRESS

If we are to understand the origin and use of coping strategies in stress, it is essential to consider memory and how it is affected. Stress may so constrain memory processes as to create a temporary structure. If responses are mechanically determined, strategy is restricted. There is a second aspect, equally important: Changes in memory function are observed in stressful conditions and it remains speculative as to whether the changes occur because of changes in the parameters of memory processes or because of the operation of strategies. Memory in stress may constrain strategy and may itself be a function of learning and recall strategies.

There is now a great deal of research from different areas of experimental psychology that leads to the conclusion that memory processes are different in stress. There is evidence from different conditions of arousal to suggest that:

1. Short- and long-term recall are differentially affected by learning circumstances.
2. Recall of that information from long-term memory is differentially affected by condition of arousal.
3. Order of presentation and recall may interact with stressful conditions.

A. Short-term Recall in Stress

If a person is required to select an appropriate strategic response, it is important that he correctly represents the structure of a current situation especially if he has not encountered it before. There is some evidence to suggest that high arousal level influences ability to recall information immediately. This being the case, a person would perhaps be impoverished in his ability to represent the structure of the task adequately in stress.

A study by Kleinsmith and Kaplan (1963) involving the association of shock with certain paired associate items presented under high states of arousal (skin resistance), showed items were better recalled after a day or even a week had elapsed, whereas the same items presented in low states of arousal were better recalled within 45 minutes of presentation. Poor immediate recall of high-arousal-learned words is explained by Kleinsmith and Kaplan in terms of reverberation of the memory trace; during the early perseveration phase, the trace is assumed to be relatively unavailable; therefore immediate recall is impaired.

Berlyne et al. (1965) presented paired associates and reported that in comparison with quiet conditions, noise improved recall after 24 hours, but immediate recall was impaired. Berlyne et al. (1966) subsequently confirmed that high noise facilitated long-term recall but did not impair short-term recall.

All these findings fit roughly with the proposal developed by Walker (1958) that there is greater temporary inhibition during arousal. In the case of the Kleinsmith and Kaplan result, there is the added difficulty of possible unexplored effects of suppression, caution, or perceptual defence. In the case of experiments that have been concerned with noise, it is worth speculating that on a masking hypothesis (Poulton, 1979), suppression of rehearsal should inhibit short and long-term recall. Poulton is quite specific about the likely changes in memory function consequent on masking; he argues that noise interferes with the duration of the storage of items. More frequent rehearsal is then required and a consequence of this is capacity reduction, which will slow down the rate of additional processing and produce memory errors. Poulton later claims that the lowest level of continuous noise found to produce deterioration through masking is 72.5 dBA or 75 dB (flat) and cites in support an experiment by Frankenhaeuser and Lundberg (1977).

There is relatively little discussion of the nature of impairment. The normal characteristic of memory performance in noise is depression of recall rather than total "knockout." In addition, recall may be facilitated later. If a person were unable to complete the processes necessary for storage, we would expect loss rather than attentuation and we would not expect subsequent improvement when a person is later asked to recall. For this reason, it might be better to consider masking as depressing retrieval at the time, rather than producing total interference.

Millar (1979) attempted to suppress rehearsal by use of an articulatory task. On the masking hypothesis, quiet/noise differences should be reduced. Unfortunately, Millar's results are equivocal. Firstly, consistent with the masking hypothesis, where articulation suppresses rehearsal, on the first day noise and quiet groups have almost identical recall. On the second day, recall reliably improves in noise: Millar suggests that a factor might be reduced novelty, leading to boredom and fatigue on the second day, which causes deterioration in quiet. Acoustic confusions and omission errors were reduced in noise in all conditions, which argues against masking.

There is some evidence from Baddeley (1968) to suggest that rehearsal might involve articulatory rather than auditory processes, because 70 dB noise impairs perception but not retention of items. Broadbent (1978) has questioned involvement of auditory encoding: Deaf children produce acoustic errors in memory for letters. Folkhard and Greeman (1974) propose that high muscle tension associated with increased arousal damages subvocal processes needed for short-term rehearsal.

In summary, the short-term memory characteristic in stressed states should mean that a person is not well equipped to represent the task structure very well. If he has not encountered it before, he may fall back on old, well-tried strategies. If a person does have a store of strategies since long-term recall is facilitated, these may be readily available.

B. Long-term Recall in Stress

Research on arousal at the time of recall has generally provided confusing evidence. Pascal (1949) found that relaxation instructions prior to recall enhanced performance. In contrast, Uehling and Sprinkle (1968) reported improved recall in arousal. Both studies support the idea that arousal is a relevant factor in recall. Investigations by M. Eysenck (1974, 1975) involved personality factors, rated activation levels and white noise as means of manipulating arousal. The first finding of interest is that a retrieval U-curve was obtained; extraverts (assumed to be low-arousal) who were activated produced better retrieval levels than those who were not, but they still performed worse than introverts (assumed to be high-arousal). Equally, introverts who were low on activation did better than those who were high. The second important feature is that both arousal, as measured by introversion/extraversion, and activation—measured by Thayer's activation–deactivation check list (Thayer, 1967, 1970)—interactively determined recall latency for both category and item recall.

Both Eysenck and Millar (1980) independently confirmed that items that are dominant in semantic memory have faster retrieval in conditions of high arousal. Millar's results differed from Eysenck's not only in that recognition was affected, but there was no evidence of suppression of non-dominant items. His results therefore suggest overall heightened efficiency. Extrapolating from this, a person with a store of relevant strategic information might be assumed to be likely to recall it rapidly and efficiently to cope with a sudden crisis. However, some caution is needed. Firstly, there is no information available as to whether rules and strategic responses can be remembered as well as single-item exemplars. Remembering "sparrow" as an example of the category "bird" is very different in many respects from remembering the rule "never trust a person with shifty eyes" when encountering a stranger at the door. However, overlearning of such rules may lead to quick and easy access in the same way that single-item exemplars of categories are recalled.

C. Selective Learning in Stress

One of the interesting aspects of learning is the apparent capacity to acquire information incidentally. Levitt (1968) argues that incidental learning may be more significant in human life than formal learning. A problem for all studies of incidental learning is that what is "incidental" is defined not objectively but subjectively, in terms of the priority structure as perceived by the subject.

In the laboratory it is possible to manipulate what is objectively incidental by presenting the subject with a formal central task and later asking for recall of incidental material. Silverman (1954) showed the effects of anxiety on an incidental learning task. The main task involved making a response to a display consisting of the appearance of a line of appropriate length. At the same time, 20 two-syllable words were recited in the background at a muted level; this was not presented as part of the experimental situation. The stressed subjects, continuously threatened by electric shock during main task performance, recalled about half as much of the incidental material as the control group.

The close association of learning and attention is illustrated by these studies. It is impossible to say for certain that the effects are the result of learning rather than of the sampling process on which learning depends. A subject who does not see an event cannot be expected to have any recall of it. In terms of the attention models considered earlier, it is possible that at high levels of stress, attention limitations operate, and incidental material is not sampled. The difference between central and incidental aspects of performance increases with increasing age (e.g. see Lane, 1979), suggesting perhaps that the balance reflects capacity level.

These considerations are important because there is research evidence to suggest that the structure of material presented for learning has an important influence on the properties of recall. Strategies may have a high degree of intrinsic structure. The generation of "if–then" rules in a problem-solving situation could be argued to contain implicit structure because there is a sequential series of decisions involved. It is possible that the learning of strategic response sequences is favoured by this. Experimental findings show that high noise or incentives improve recall of ordered material when the same ordering of material is permitted (Dae & Wilding, 1977; Hamilton, Hockey, & Quinn, 1972; Hockey & Hamilton 1970; Millar,1979). Incentives and noise appear to act differently in this respect, because evidence suggests that whereas noise aids ordered recall, it does not aid recall of spatial cues; incentives appear to increase the efficiency of both (see Davis & Jones, 1975; Fowler & Wilding, 1979; Hockey & Hamilton, 1970). However, some experiments have failed to show an effect of noise on ordered recall (e.g. Davis & Jones, 1975; Haveman & Farley, 1969; D. Murray, 1965; Sloboda & Smith, 1968). Moreover, there is some evidence that suggests that recall is actually impaired (Salame & Wittersheim, 1978; Wilkinson, 1975). It is worth noting that there could be a relationship with task difficulty level; Dornic (1974) showed that category clustering in recall was reduced by the addition of a secondary task; item information was affected, but order information was not.

Bower et al. (1981) were concerned with selectivity of learning caused by affective states. Specifically they investigated the hypothesis that remembering of text is influenced by the mood of the reader at the time of reading. Two hypotheses were contrasted: The first, "mood congruence" hypothesis suggested that readers like to read about events congruent with their current mood. The second, "Pollyana" hypothesis assumed that people will seek out, enjoy reading, and will remember pleasant events. Mood states were induced by hypnosis. The results supported the "mood congruence" hypothesis in that sad readers recalled more information about sad facts. The "sad" proportion recalled was 45% for happy subjects and 80% for sad subjects. There was some asymmetry, in that recall of happy facts by happy subjects was not so pronounced but in general the results do support the view that state of mind is a critical factor determining the features of information recalled.

Taken collectively, mood induced during learning created selective learning of congruent facts but did not influence recall processes per se. Bower et al. consider a number of explanations. One is that mood-congruent material is more memorable because it elevates the intensity of subjects' feelings whereas mood-incongruent material has the reverse effect. A second is that subjects focus on mood-congruent material in order to explain and justify their hypnotically instructed emotion. This is an explanation in terms of *strategic* response. In effect this implies that the hypnotic induction procedure creates demand characteristics in the minds of the subjects. The result is an attentional bias towards the material being assimilated.

The findings raise the importance of the distinction between *structure* (the mood *creates* a change in attentional deployment towards certain aspects of text); and *strategy* (the mood-induction procedure provides an instructional bias which determines which features are attended to). There are cases where non-induced moods are found to be influential in determining the recall of events. Thus, Lloyd and Lishman (1975) showed that subjects who were depressed showed evidence of increased speed and intensity in the recall of unpleasant memories. The authors suggest that depression is associated with a "hedonic set" that directs recall towards unpleasant experiences.

D. Strategies and Memory

The issue of whether stresses create change automatically in performance or whether they encourage the selection of strategies is complex. From work with noise, Smith (1983a) disputes the idea that stresses produce changes which are mechanical and invariant because experimental studies have shown that factors such as changed level of task difficulty, changed probability of the need for action, and changes in prior experience, may reverse or abolish effects. Smith develops instead the notion of *strategy choice theory*; he proposes that noise may influence the choice of strategies used in particular situations.

For example, he reports the results of a memory experiment in which noise selection influences recall of complex stimuli. A global representation of a letter is made up of small letters which are not the same as the global letter. In quiet, subjects recall global features. In noise, subjects are more likely to recall detail and thus remember more small (component) letters, than the global letters which they compose. However, it remains unclear whether the effect is attentional or due to memory changes, and is relatively weak support for an explanation in terms of strategy.

Equally difficult to interpret is the finding by Smith et al. (1981) that noise reduced the degree of clustering in the free recall of instances of categories due to fewer words initially in the clusters and more individual words subsequently. However, the effect was reduced if the word lists contained weak instances of categories or if exhaustive categories were used. Broadbent (1983) interprets the results to imply that words are clustered less by meaning when noise is present, but the effect does not appear when the meaning groups are difficult—suggesting perhaps that the effect is the result of a strategy.

The difficulty of deciding whether an effect is strategic or due to "direct hit" is illustrated by an experiment by Smith (1983b) who investigated in detail a running memory design reported by Hamilton et al. (1972, 1977) in which subjects were asked to write down the last eight items of a sequential running series of spoken digits from the point at which the sequence was arbitrarily stopped. Hamilton et al. reported that in noise, immediate items were favoured whereas more distant items were less well recalled, suggesting that in noise the memory characteristic is different. There is more throughput of information but reduced holding capacity. Smith's experiment involved a visual version of the running memory experiment in which digits appeared on a television screen at the rate of 1 item every 2 seconds. When ***** appeared on the screen, subjects had to recall each digit in the position corresponding to its presentation position. The difference was that one group of subjects were required to recall eight items back, whereas the other group of subjects were required to recall only five items back. Thus the memory load factor was varied. A within-subject design was used for the noise and quiet conditions.

The results showed that when five items were recalled, noise improved the recall for all items except the last one. When eight items were recalled, noise improved recall of the last two items but impaired the recall of others. At least one possible explanation of the storage load difference is that the strategy for dealing with the task changes. However, noise had no effect on which strategy was preferred, which does suggest that task difficulty determines strategy and noise has no further effect. Smith (1983b) favours a mechanical view for these results. He introduces the term "hidden defect theory" to describe an effect which occurs due to change in components required by the task and suggests that: "the present data appear to support a hidden defect theory rather that a strategy choice theory (p. 444)." Broadbent (1983) comments that noise may strengthen an existing tendency so that the part of memory that is least favoured is that given low priority. This might imply that the presence of stress augments the features of strategies.

Manipulation of instructions to produce priority bias has been informative. Smith (1983a) examined combined task performance in noise where variables such as task difficulty and task priority are varied. The evidence suggested that the effect of noise on a cognitive vigilance task paired with a proportion estimation task, was to impair performance on the vigilance task but not on the estimation task. Changes in task parameters did not affect this. However, performance on the vigilance task was influenced by instructions indicating priority. When it was a high-priority task there was a large improvement in performance, whereas when instructions indicated that it was low priority, performance was impaired.

When the same vigilance task was paired with a running memory task a different pattern of results occurred, in that when the vigilance task was given high priority, the improvement which resulted was to the detriment of the running memory task. The reverse effect was obtained when the running memory task was given high priority. The results give support to the strategic model of attentional allocation, but indicate the importance of particular dual-task combinations.

Smith (1983b) devised an experiment in which biased probabilities were introduced into the second of three blocks of trials of a choice reaction task. In the first block, the three trials occurred with equal probability. In the second block one source produced more signals than the other two. In the third block of trials the signals were equiprobable across sources. In the first block of trials (with no signal bias) there was no effect of noise but in the second block reaction time in noise was faster to the source with high probability, and slower to the low-probability source. There was comparable inequality in reaction time in the third block of trials where the signals were equiprobable across sources. The last effect was interpreted by Smith (1983a) to imply that increased sampling of (originally) biased sources leads to increased subjective probability that those sources contain higher signal rates – the cognitive model of signal occurrence across source is to some extent self-confirming. This is true when the subject is confronted with a new task, and has to acquire acceptable strategies for responding, but there are some cases where previously learned strategies may be utilised (appropriately or inappropriately).

The possible influence of previously learned strategies as determinants of current response is indicated by the results of studies by Smith and Broadbent (1982). A list of class words each followed by a single letter was presented and subjects were required to generate a relevant example of the class beginning with the letter. By manipulations of the letters it was possible to present problems in which there was only a very rare member of the class beginning with the specified letter. One group of subjects was found to perform better in noise on the easy (dominant instance) conditions (where a letter easily located an example). A second group of subjects, treated exactly the same way and selected from the same population, performed better on the non-dominant items and worse on the dominant ones. In reporting this Broadbent (1983) pointed out that the only identifiable difference was that the first group had previously been involved in an experiment where the main task was to recall lists of instances of categories. Broadbent argued that "they had become practised in the strategy of moving through a category from the dominant to less dominant examples (p. 723)."

Poulton (1982) develops the notion that for within-subject designs, asymmetric transfer effects occur because of the influence of a strategy learned in one condition and used inappropriately subsequently. Asymmetric transfer generally occurs because learning in the condition paired with stress is different from learning when the stress is not present. According to Poulton's *strategy transfer hypothesis*, asymmetric transfer is likely to have greatest influence when two or more conditions require different strategies, when they are unobtrusive, and when conditions are interleaved randomly within a block of trials. Poulton presents many careful and detailed arguments from experimental data. It would be impossible to cover the arguments here; the reader is referred to Poulton's own account. An illustration of the effect of what Poulton terms "influential companions" in producing asymmetric transfer in within-subject designs, is illustrated by reference to an experiment by Nillson et al. (1975) on free recall of words in a list, presented either separately or sequentially. For separate presentation of 10 two-syllable nouns, words in serial positions 7–10 are better recalled than those which are in positions 2–6. In simultaneous presentation, all words are better recalled but there is a superior priming effect for the first two words in the list. When the simultaneous condition is performed after experience of two separate conditions, the words in positions 7–10 are again better recalled, and there is also a priming effect. Poulton argues that although not complete, there is some transfer from previous experience of the separate conditions. The level of efficiency of the simultaneous, after separate, condition for the last four words is somewhere between the values for the "separate" and the values for "simultaneous" alone. One explanation suggested is that subjects concentrate on the last four words in the list as in the separate condition—but the previously acquired strategy is no longer appropriate for the simultaneous condition. However, there is also the possibility of direct interference (retroactive or proactive) due to the complexity of two tasks, which are similar in some respects and different in others.

4. COGNITIVE ELEMENTS IN STRATEGIC RESPONSE

In this chapter an attempt has been made to provide a review of some of the main findings from the experimental research literature which suggest that attention and memory, the fundamental ingredients of plans, are likely to change in stressful conditions. The changes are not always negative; there are stressful conditions which *favour* aspects of attention and memory. There is no justification for the conclusion that people always behave incompetently in stress or that the outcome of a stressful scenario will necessarily be negative.

A second aspect of this chapter has been to pursue the issue of whether behavioural characteristics in stress occur because of mechanical or "direct hit" effects, or whether there are strategic elements. Evidence has largely been from examination of performance in noise; conclusions might prove to be circumscribed. Nevertheless, there are hints at the use of strategies arising from experiments where priority bias is changed by instructions, or from the detail of dual-task interaction where demand is high. Equally, evidence from experiments on memory and attentional sampling suggests that subjects may operate strategically to find out what is going on and to produce responses consistent with the demands for "success."

Strategic behaviour must involve a number of elements. First, in the absence of instructions, the evidence provided by the "task" must be collected and summarised to form an impression of priorities. The total context of the task, including instructions as to priorities, the criterion for success and the long term implications, combines to determine perceived *demand characteristics*. Demand is not envisaged as a passive quality—it is deduced and depends on individual motivations.

As a result of both sets of evidence personal goals can be specified. The discrepancy between goal and reality is then defined and this provides the input for the selection of appropriate action. There may be a further stage of qualifications due to perceived cost of particular actions. A person may revise a decision to take a particular course of actions because of the demands made.

An important aspect of strategic behaviour is that a person may be operating within a number of different domains of control. Either in real life, or in laboratory conditions, a person's total behaviour reflects the grouping of decisions concerned with control domain and manner of achieving control. These decisions are determined by the specification of personal goals.

9

Speed and Effort Strategies

The three previous chapters have been concerned with ways in which stress is likely to influence competence in daily life. Chapter 8 was concerned with the effects of stress on attention and memory — the essential ingredients of cognitive activity on which competent behaviour depends. Experimental evidence provides some support for the notion that behaviour in stress is strategic and that perceived demand may be an important factor.

A person faced with a potentially threatening encounter may not only behave strategically in mapping out goals and subgoals but may raise the level of energy associated with behaviour. There are a number of identifiable aspects of raised effort – increased speed of response, increased attentional span, increased sampling, increased attempts to note, detect and store information. We argue in this chapter for a view of an individual which is active and information seeking. One way to ensure adequate performance in stress is to raise the effort levels associated with all aspects of the situation. By "effort" is meant utilisation of all aspects of information and energy resources. Stresses provide the need for strategies; effort is an aspect of strategic response.

1. THE CONCEPT OF EFFORT

A. Zipf's Least-effort Principle

The concept of effort was developed in the 1930s when Waters (1937) developed what became known as the "least effort" principle, by examining strategies used by rats to achieve a goal. If a rat was confronted by two

155

paths and one required more activity initially but was more successful, it was more likely to choose that path. Therefore, effort expenditure could result in less effort eventually because the animal could achieve the goal in fewer trials. This notion of strategic behaviour contrasted with Hull's least-work principle. Hull (1943) argued that an animal would seek situations that involved less effort: Whenever two behaviour sequences are possible, the one requiring least effort will be selected.

Zipf (1949) formulated the notion of the least-effort principle, which partly reconciles the two previous positions. A strategy is selected which ensures that overall the minimum effort will be involved in reaching a desired result. On the assumption that any behavioural response involves a number of component operations, Zipf argued that use of cognitive economies could ensure a reduction in mental effort. He illustrated the point by means of an analogy with a workman and his tools. The minimum arrangement of the tools is:

$$W_r = (f \times m \times d)$$

where W_r = the tool's range
  d = distance of tool to artisan's lap
  f = relative frequency with which a given tool (r) is used
  m = mass of tool

Each tool is assumed to represent a cognitive operation specified by a value that indexes the amount of effort required. When the $(f \times m \times d)$ operation is at its smallest value, effort is a minimum. Zipf then specified a number of rules that would help to keep the value of the equation to a minimum. For example, the workman could "close pack" his tools, thus reducing the distance (d) involved. This would make movements more economical. By increasing the versatility of each tool, the number of tools needed could be reduced. These and other principles provided the foundation for the "least effort" law. The most efficient performance is that which achieves a given result with the fewest mediating operations. Zipf proceeded to illustrate the law of least effort with respect to the shortening of the length of frequently used words in everyday speech. Words shortened by the loss of syllables or by amalgamations, such as in brother-in-law, are examples of the way in which the same message is conveyed with reduced effort.

The question of interest is the extent to which reductions and shortenings are strategic or to what extent they are part of a broader strategy – that of speed. Because most communication between individuals is fast, lengthy words will slow speech and so syllables are more likely to disappear as a consequence of the desire to maintain speed.

A second question of interest is the motivating factor in the least-effort principle. One possible principle is 'least expenditure of any resource.' A second possible principle is 'expenditure of resource as needed to achieve a desired result' and therefore to reduce effort needed in the long term.

B. Kahneman's Model of the Allocation of Effort

The model proposed by Kahneman (1973) is notable for its introduction of the notion of effortful aspects of attention and behaviour. The Kahneman model assumes that effort is deployed actively by the individual in response to the changing demands of the environment. Each task confronting an individual is assumed to require a standard allocation of effort. It is the investment of less than the ideal level of effort that leads to deterioration in performance.

The notion of personally deployed effort as a reason for raised arousal, changes the view of the individual as a passive recipient of environmental stimulation (or lack of stimulation) and introduces the notion that a person might have raised arousal as a response to perceived environmental demand. Kahneman proposed that level of arousal is controlled by two factors: (1) the intensity of stimulation and the physiological effects of drugs; (2) the demands of activities an individual is engaged in. Raised effort is assumed to result in reduced capacity and is limited in the effects it can have on performance because there is a ceiling beyond which effort can no longer be effective.

Kahneman further argues that two measures of sympathetic activity provide some measure of effort: Dilation of the pupils of the eye provides the best index, whereas increased skin conductance provides a related but less satisfactory measure. Measures of pupil dilation are argued by Kahneman to provide a sensitive indication of variations between tasks and within tasks. For example, Hess and Polt (1964) and Hess (1965) provided evidence to suggest that there is a positive association between the difficulty of mental arithmetic problems and the magnitude of pupillary dilation when they are being solved. Kahneman and Beatty (1966) provided further evidence to suggest that the presentation of each successive digit in a short-term memory task is accompanied by pupillary dilation. Further, the increase in pupil diameter corresponds to the increasing rate of rehearsal imposed by each additional digit. The speed of pupillary dilation is such that the pupil dilates about 10% of base diameter during the first second following presentation of a familiar name when a response in the form of a telephone number is required from the subject.

One of the interesting issues concerns the effects of stressful circumstances on effort. Kahneman argues that tasks that are dictated by time deadlines may invoke high effort. Short-term memory tasks require high effort because time deadlines are important. Thus, stressful conditions with high demands on memory or with time urgency may necessitate the involvement of effort.

These issues are now important aspects of the understanding of the demand imposed by high workload. Karasbek (1979, 1980) has introduced the idea that job strain is defined with respect to two dimensions, *demand* and *jurisdiction discretion, or control*. When demand is high, a job is more likely to be perceived positively if there is high control, but is perceived as a source of strain if control is low. It may be the case that lack of jurisdiction evident in hierarchical, authoritarian work structures may act to reduce effort as a response to demand. The individual remains paced by events and finds it difficult to raise the necessary effort to cope. Seen in this way, effort is a personal decision in response to demand.

C. Wilkinson's Model of Stress and Effort

One of the paradoxical aspects of separate concepts of "effort" and "arousal" is that both are assumed to energise behaviour, yet effort is argued to create arousal increase in the absence of arousal. Wilkinson (1965) reviewed a number of biochemical, physiological, and psychological studies of the effects of loss of sleep. One of the important observations was that given a task of sufficient interest and incentive, competent performance can be maintained after a sleep-loss vigil. However, performance is maintained at the expense of biochemical energy transfer mechanisms. Wilkinson argued that individuals increase *effort* to *sustain arousal* against the increasing demands of tiredness. The question of interest is how "effort" is generated and whether it can be independent of arousal.

Studies by Murray et al. (1959) on the general behaviour of sleep-deprived subjects showed that if allowed to do so, relative to non-sleep-deprived subjects, sleep-deprived subjects were more likely to change tasks. The effect increased for the early days of the vigil and then decreased. The results are consistent with the idea that the sleep-deprived subjects are capitalising on the stimulation provided by successively changing to new tasks, in order to keep themselves awake. Thus, the response could be argued to be strategic; a manifestation of increased effort to sustain arousal: Sleep-deprived subjects *direct* their efforts, and seek stimulation in order to stay awake.

D. Michael Eysenck's Model of Effort and Anxiety

An approach developed by M. Eysenck (1979, 1981, 1983) is concerned with effort as a factor in performance. Eysenck distinguishes *effectiveness* from *efficiency* as aspects of performance. "Efficiency" is a measure of the quality of performance or behaviour, whereas "effectiveness" involves efficiency as a function of the degree of effort involved. "Effort" is seen by Eysenck in terms of an intensity component that is more than just wakefulness and is in keeping with the Kahneman formulation. The formula:

(processing effectiveness) = (performance efficiency)/(effort)

summaries Eysenck's basic assumptions. He uses the analogy of two cars being controlled by pressure on their respective accelerators. One car drags a trailer. Under these circumstances more work on the accelerator (effort) is required to maintain the same level of effectiveness as the car without the trailer.

Eysenck argues that in the case of anxious individuals, effective demand is greater, largely due to the intrusions produced by task-irrelevant considerations (such as "I will fail"; "everyone will laugh at me"; etc.). Thus, more effort is required to maintain the same level of performance effectiveness. The anxious person is thus seen as analogous to the car with the trailer; she/he is argued to be compensating for his state of less than efficient processing, by raised effort.

Eysenck quotes in support of the effort hypothesis, a study by Dornic (1977). Neurotics and normals were found to perform a task equally well. However, the neurotic subjects rated the tasks as more difficult than normals, as task difficulty levels rose. Eysenck regards this as indirect evidence that neurotic subjects expended more effort. An alternative explanation might be that neurotic subjects protect themselves in advance from the consequence of failure by rating the tasks as more difficult. A further comparison by Dornic involved stable extraverts and neurotic introverts. The complexity of the task was manipulated by the introduction of a number of sources of information and by environmental distraction. The stable extraverts and neurotic introverts did not differ in level of performance but they did differ in perceived effort levels. There was a three-way interaction between task difficulty, distraction, and personality; the neurotic introverts reported higher perceived effort than the stable extraverts.

Eysenck (1979) also investigated the deployment of effort by the less direct means of investigating changes in dual-task performance for anxious as compared with non-anxious subjects. As might be expected, there was no difference in terms of main task performance but there was a detrimental effect of anxiety on the secondary task. This might be taken as some evidence to suggest that the anxious subjects had less capacity available because of the extra effort required by the task.

The assumption that spare capacity is inversely related to effort deployed does raise a conceptual problem. High investment of effort in a complex task should absorb capacity normally required for the task. Therefore, there may be tasks in which increased deployment of effort will not pay off for the subject. It may be these circumstances, where a person is maximally loaded by task and effort, in which deteriorations (usually attributed to overarousal) occur. However, if the effort is sufficient to *expand* capacity, the reduction of already available capacity absorbed by effort is compensated for.

It is assumed by Eysenck that the processing capacity of anxious subjects will be further reduced by worry and task-irrelevant considerations. Therefore, the primary response of non-anxious subjects is *raised effort* whereas the primary response of anxious subjects is *worry*. Raised effort enhances capacity; therefore information about failure should improve the performance of non-anxious subjects. Conversely, for anxious subjects, information indicating failure should lead to increased worry and preoccupation resulting in depressed performance. This prediction does not fit with a number of studies suggesting that feedback indicating failure interacts with personality, producing raised level of performance for non-anxious subjects but lowered levels for anxious subjects (e.g. see Sarason, 1957). Also, as indicated previously, Eysenck also presents evidence to suggest that performance sustained by anxious subjects is characterised by raised effort. Therefore, raised effort *and* preoccupation with task-irrelevant thoughts may be co-determinants of the behaviour of anxious subjects.

E. The Cognitive Basis of Strategic Effort in Stress

One possibility is that raised efforts occurs because a person attempts to sustain performance and to prevent failure. Raised effort is thus a considered decision based on advance expectations suggesting that performance will be impaired by stress. The instruction for raised effort may be available as a code in long-term memory. A person may have codes available which dictate the manner of achieving goals. For example, a person whose mother is dying may respond to a crisis in her breathing by the decision to fetch a doctor, *quickly*. The qualification "quickly" dictates *how* the goal or subgoals will be achieved; for example, running not walking, driving fast, giving rapid instructions. The *manner* of the sequencing of behaviour is assumed to be part of strategic decision.

An experiment by Fisher (1985a) required subjects to provide an estimate of the performance of a hypothetical person about to work in a stressful environment, when given a value alleged to represent performance in "normal" conditions. Irrespective of whether estimates of response speed or response accuracy were provided, subjects tended to provide pessimistic predictions. This was true for a range of stresses—noise; sleep loss; fatigue; social stress. Although the design of the experiment was such that subjects were only making hypothetical predictions, the predictions made were highly consistent and pessimistic. It seems that people *expect* impoverished performance in stress. This may provide the basis for raised effort strategies.

If expected consequences can provide the instruction for raised effort, codes in memory which dictate the manner in which plans are operated may be associated with codes about consequence. A person should speed up if slowing is predicted or become more cautious if errors are predicted. This also implies internal control over effort deployment.

2. THE CONTROL OF SPEED AND ACCURACY

Any assumption that speed or accuracy levels can be varied by a person as a response to changing task demand or instructions, involves the presupposition that subjects can voluntarily change these parameters and that there is internal control over the change so that it can be sustained over time.

A. The Speed/Accuracy Trade-off

General speed and accuracy characteristics of performance are normally described by trade-off or negative relationship in which faster speed is associated with lower accuracy levels (see Pachella, 1972, 1974; Pachella, Smith & Stanovich, 1978). There are some exceptions to this general rule; on recognition tasks, responses that are faster are likely to be more accurate and associated with better confidence ratings (Norman & Wickelgren, 1969). However, on the majority of tasks studied, the negative relationship obtains.

One of the less quoted demonstrations of the speed/accuracy relationship was provided by Hick (1952), who varied the speed of responding in a choice reaction-time task and calculated information transmission rates. When errors increased and therefore less information was transmitted, response speeds were faster. Thus a central foundation was provided for a speed/accuracy characteristic.

Figure 9.1 (from Pachella, 1974) provides an idealised representation of the speed/accuracy trade-off. The form of the function is such that at high response rates a further increase has greater consequence for error rates. Figure 9.2 (from Hale, 1968) illustrates that subjects are likely to have control over the speed/accuracy trade-off but also that setting for speed will produce different empirical relationships. This argues against a single central mechanism on which the balance depends. A sequential decision model such as that of Wald (1947) assumes that there is a speed-error factor in the decision mechanism for responses, and suggests that errors occur

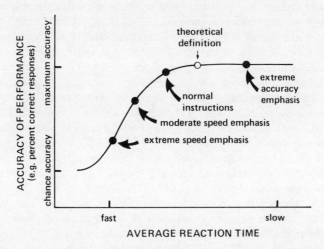

FIG. 9.1 Idealised representation of speed/accuracy trade-off. (Redrawn from Pachella, 1974, with the permission of the author and Lawrence Erlbaum Associates.)

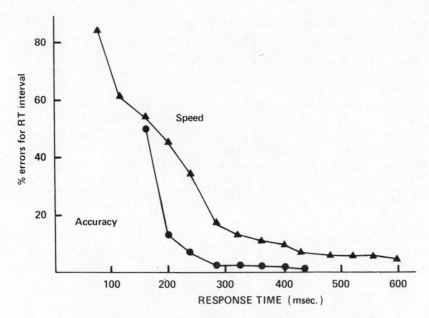

FIG. 9.2   Plots of speed and accuracy as determinants of the proportion of errors to the total number of responses for each 40 msec class interval. (Redrawn from Hale, 1968, with the permission of the author and the American Psychological Association.)

because of "noise in the system"; latency distributions of correct and error RTs should be similar. This is confirmed by an analysis by Fitts (1966), who reported no difference between error and correct RTs, but the weight of the empirical evidence is against this (see Egeth & Smith, 1967; Hale, 1968; Laming, 1968; Rabbitt, 1966; Schouten & Bekker, 1967). Data by Hale (1969) suggests that the effect of "speed set" is to cause an equivalent speeding of correct and error RTs. Error rates increased and subjects produced error rates of over 50% on some trials. Under "speed instructions," not only did correct and error responses both become faster, but subjects made more errors.

The weight of the evidence supports the idea that subjects have a great deal of control over the speed/accuracy trade-off but that control is not necessarily exercised by change of a parameter in a single central mechanism. However, the consistent reporting of fast error rates and the association with speeded correct responses under "speed instructions" might suggest the operation of a criterion change in decision.

Studies by Conrad (1951, 1954) based on observations of the effects of speeded event rates in bobbin winding, provided a convincing demonstration of the limitation in human ability to hold down error rates against increasing speed. As input rates rise, the incidence of omissions increased after about 130 to 140 signals per minute. One explanation is that a person advances the timing of his decision in order to cope with fast event rates and thus response rate increases. However, if event rates exceed the ability to do this, some signals are omitted. The fact that omissions occur suggests that not all input speeds can be accommodated by adjustments in timing; these data represent a very real limitation in processing ability of the sort described by Welford in his refractoriness experiments (see Welford, 1952).

Studies such as these raise the question of how much control a person has over his own performance. It is apparent that he cannot avoid some errors; subjects typically produce 2–6% errors on a simple task such as naming a letter (Theios, 1973). However, it is also apparent that subjects can work slowly, making very few errors, or rapidly with numerous errors, or somewhere between these extremes.

The demands of many experiments may affect not just speed or error, independently, but may change the speed/error characteristic. This means that the latency may not be a measure of delays in internal processes but may represent *strategy*. Posner et al. (1973) reported that the decrease in reaction time to shorter foreperiods may not necessarily be the result of alertness but of a change in speed/accuracy trade-off. Jennings, Wood, and Lawrence (1976) suggested that inconsistency in results concerning the effect of alcohol could be explained in terms of changes in speed/accuracy trade-off. Pachella (1972) argued that the equality of slopes for memory-scanning functions on yes/no responses might be lost if adjustment for error rate was made.

Evidence on the effects of incentives on performance suggests that in general, speed is increased and accuracy deteriorates as a consequence. An early study by Maller and Zubin (1932) investigating the effect of competitive incentives on an intelligience test showed that the number of problems attempted increased, resulting in increased errors. However, against this, Eysenck and Gillan (1964) showed that on a mirror-drawing task incentive could work the other way; mirror drawing actually slowed and became more accurate.

These two experiments together suggest that because the trade-off function is influenced by factors such as incentives, the adjustment is more likely to be strategically than mechanically determined. However, there is some suggestion that it is easier to influence speed than accuracy, perhaps because accuracy is subject to chance factors and involves an "irreducible minimum" beyond which further improvement is impossible. For example, Adam (1972) investigated the collation of information from record cards and found that if quantity was rewarded there was no change in performance. When quality was rewarded there was a change. Increase in quantity was a more controllable response to incentives.

B. Strategic Timing of Decision

Much more detailed information relevant to understanding the speed/accuracy relationship is provided by examination of the profile of response latencies before and after the occurrence of error.

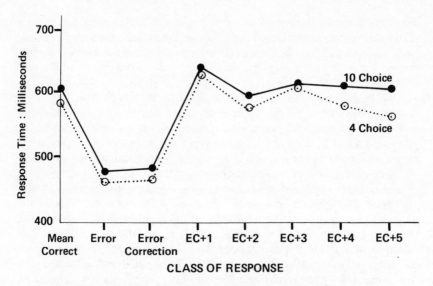

FIG. 9.3 Profile of error and error correction latencies. (Redrawn from Rabbitt, 1966, with the permission of the author and the American Psychological Association.)

As shown in Fig. 9.3, early studies by Rabbitt gave support to the idea that errors occur because a response is made before sufficient evidence on which to base a response has been collected. Rabbitt (1966) showed that for both four- and ten-choice serial response tasks, average error rates were 100–150 msec faster than correct responses. In the same study, the proportion of errors made was 1.4% for a four-choice condition of a serial task and 3.7% for a ten-choice condition.

A model that makes sense of these findings is one that assumes that decisions have to be made with respect to incoming evidence and that it takes time for evidence to accumulate. Decision timing and evidence characteristics are both variables that determine the form of performance features.

Figure 9.4 (from Fisher, 1984a) provides an illustration of a number of ways in which stresses may influence the speed/accuracy trade-off. There are two independent variables: the level of evidence required for a correct decision, and the rate at which this evidence accumulates. Both these variables determine the optimum timing of decision. Responses made in advance of this are based on inadequate evidence and depending on choice available, will be errors on a specifiable proportion of occasions. Figure 9.4 illustrates how the "time zones" for errors effectively shift as a function of evidence characteristics because of changes in the position of optimum decision time. For level of evidence A and accumulation rate X, only very fast responses will fall into the error zone 1, and response rates will be fast anyway. Conversely, for a higher evidence requirement B and slow-rate accumulation Y, there is a slower optimum decision timing and a greater zone for the occurrence of errors (3).

The distinction between mechanical ("direct hit") changes associated with stress, and changes which are strategic in origin can now be illustrated. Mechanical changes will be assumed to be brought about in the following ways:

1. Evidence can degraded by stress and results in a slower rate of accumulation of evidence. For a fixed temporal position of decision, the evidence will be less likely to be complete and errors will result from fast guess decisions.
2. If the task is externally paced, a deadline may be imposed, such that if a subject does not respond within a fixed time, the signal disappears. Thus failure to respond within an externally determined time automatically results in error.
3. If there is no advance knowledge (unprimed), greater level of evidence must be accumulated before an adequate decision can be made. Thus a fixed decision position could be inadequate for the uncertainty confronting the subject and an error will occur.

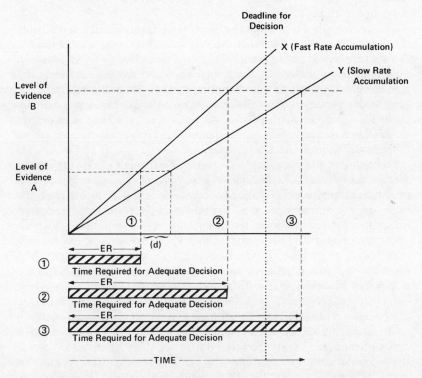

FIG. 9.4   Schematic diagram of the microstructure of speed/accuracy in terms of decision timing and evidence characteristics. (First produced in Fisher, 1984a.)

Thus by 1, degrading the evidence; 2, introducing external pacing; 3, increasing conditions of uncertainty, the occurrence of error increases. A passive mechanical model will explain the change. If however, the person reacts strategically in shifting his decision position to match the circumstances he is confronted with, he may overcome these effects. Thus, effort may be deployed to change decision timing in keeping with perceived requirements. If the evidence is masked and difficult to discriminate, a person should slow his response rates. If the situation is novel and recognition of critical factors requires maximum cognitive activity, a person should slow his response rates. Equally, instructions concerning speed/accuracy priority result in strategic adjustment. If accuracy has priority, decision timing should be equal to or greater than optimum. If speed has priority, the timing of decision should be advanced.

Yellott (1971) proposed that for a given set of conditions two "strategies" are possible; the first is to maintain rapid response times by fast guessing, and the second is to delay responding and wait for adequate evidence. The first strategy will result in a proportion of errors that will vary as a function of the degree of choice; the second in delays in responding, the size of which may vary as a function of the degree of interruption, distortion, or delay of evidence.

The question then is whether the timing of decision is fixed and inflexible throughout the task, or whether the subject makes constant adjustments. A view proposed by Swensson (1972) is that a deadline is self-determined in self-paced conditions and that if the evidence is inadequate, a response is made anyway. An explanation by Broadbent (1971) of the occurrence of errors in high noise on a five-choice serial reaction task has similar assumptions: The subject has a disposition to respond in some conditions even if the evidence is incomplete. If noise causes interruption in the perception of evidence, response occurs prematurely.

From all that has been said above, decision timing can provide a basis for the strategic employment of effort. In some cases merely leaving decision timing fixed may allow the stressful condition to create errors mechanically—an adjustment is essential. In other cases decisions about speed and accuracy may be a strategic response to perceived priority. To give an example, a man flying his aircraft with a fire in one engine may fly fast, making quick corrective decisions not because the danger is making him tense but because he has made the strategic decision to try to put the fire out by flying in a way that will starve the fire of oxygen.

It also remains conceivable that strategic adjustments to speed or accuracy can be made during the task. Experiments on the effects of bursts of noise on the same five-choice serial response task (Fisher, 1972) suggested that cycles of fluctuating effort occurred during a task as a function of events that occurred within it. Just after the occurrence of a 2-second burst of noise, performance was enhanced, but it slowed gradually again until the next burst occurred. Error occurrence was enhanced during the speeding up of responses. One explanation is that there is a change in decision timing while the task is in progress. A comparable effect was noted for the main task of a dual-task design by Fisher (1984b). The intervals between moments of dual-task concurrence were speeded in noise.

C. Speed as a Lead Factor in Performance

These considerations are important because the functional characteristics of performance are dictated by speed/accuracy parameters. A style of performance may result. A person who is late, packs his papers quickly, runs out of the house barely stopping to shut the front door, opens the car door, and starts the engine before he has even shut the door or put his seat belt on. The component activities acquire a different "flavour" and may be combined differently.

The speed of performance may be an important factor that determines a number of phenomena in stress. Fisher (1983b) investigated the effect of loud noise on a standard card game, where target pairs were collected from a face-down array of playing cards. In noise, relative to quiet, the inspection and collection of cards was speeded so that the task was completed more quickly and inspection time per card was reduced. However, more cards were inspected overall in noise. Thus, the overall profile of performance was different; in noise, subjects inspected more cards but they completed the task more quickly. The first question is whether the apparent drop in memory efficiency, which meant that more cards had to be inspected repeatedly, was because subjects had not given themselves sufficient time to inspect, remember, and replace each card. Perhaps they were more impulsive than when they performed the task in quiet, but the rate at which they sampled cards paid off in the end. The second question is whether the speeded response pattern came about as a "mechanical" result of being in noise (noise → raised arousal → greater sampling speed), or was a strategic response to the belief that, for example, memory was likely to be impaired by noise (noise → decision → greater sampling speed).

On the same task the pattern of card selection was different. Inspection in noise favoured cards situated in a central position of the spatial array of cards. Analysis was confined to the first 30 cards because later sampling is increasingly constrained by the detection and removal of pairs which create gaps in the array, and by working memory of initial cards sampled. The percentage of cards inspected in the central segment was 78% in noise and 52% in quiet.

A possible explanation is that, as predicted by the Easterbrook hypothesis (Easterbrook, 1959), heightened arousal in noise mechanically creates attentional restriction. However, an alternative explanation is that since subjects are working faster, there is less time for widely spaced card selections. As Zipf (1949) argued, minimum work to achieve a desired end is an ideal strategy. By working fast and confining sampling to central parts of the array, movement time is reduced and cues can be built up in which each card is linked conceptually to its neighbour. The question of interest is whether such a pattern of behaviour is enforced by speed and is thus mechanical, or whether the total pattern of behaviour, raised speed, reduced inspection, confined centralised sampling, is part of a strategic response.

Speed could logically act as a lead factor in performance or could be part of a series of strategic adjustments to performing a task in stress. The alternatives are indicated as follows:

1. Noise → arousal ⌐→ speed increase
                   L→ central sampling   ⎫
                                                                        ⎬ non-strategic
2. Noise → arousal → speed increase → central sampling   ⎭

3. Noise → (decision) ⌐→ speed increase
                      L→ central sampling   ⎫
                                                                        ⎬ strategic
4. Noise → (decision) → speed increase → central sampling   ⎭

Unfortunately, the above design does not provide a means for differentiating mechanical from strategic models. Designs with changed instruction conditions are more likely to be informative.

3.   EFFORT, DISTRESS, AND HEALTH

A.   The Effort–Distress Model

Selye (1974) made a distinction between "eustress" involved in tasks which require creative effort imposing demand as a consequence, and stress which arises because of unpleasant circumstances. Raised demand may be assumed to be increased in both pleasant and unpleasant circumstances.

More recently, Frankenhaeuser and Johansson (1982) provided evidence to link the catecholamine response (adrenaline and noradrenaline) to raised effort levels, and the corticoid response to conditions of effort where distress is involved. A stressful situation may be challenging, effortful, and with positive outcome, or unpleasant, distressing, and with negative outcome. Hormone levels and thus eventually health and efficiency could reflect these features.

Frankenhaeuser and Johansson argue that control is the fundamental factor. High-control tasks induce effort but not distress, whereas low-control tasks involve effort and distress. The main principles of their effort–distress model is illustrated with respect to laboratory studies (Frankenhaeuser et al., 1980; Lundberg & Foresman, 1979; Lundberg & Frankenhaeuser, 1980). The first paradigm involved a low-control situation; the subject performed a one-hour vigilance task in which the signal was an intensity change in a weak light. The high-control condition was unfortunately not the same task with a different control level but a different task. It involved a design such that a subject performed a choice reaction task with a high degree of personal control allowing modification of the rate at which the stimulus occurred by a decision made every 5 minutes.

Analysis of the results of the study in terms of self-report data and hormone excretion levels showed that in the low-control task, self-reported distress and effort is raised (although it is not clear why distress is a factor in a vigilance task where there are no adverse consequences). In the reaction-time task, distress is actually lower than base level whereas effort levels are raised by 400%. The hormone characteristics show a compatible pattern. The vigilance task is associated with raised cortisol and adrenaline whereas the choice reaction task is associated with lowered cortisol levels relative to base, but raised adrenaline levels. It is unfortunate that these findings relate to two different tasks since the role of control as a factor cannot be directly identified.

In a field study, Johansson and Sanden (1982) investigated a group of operators involved in planning, production, and control. The working conditions created high stimulation levels and increased time deadlines. There was a high degree of control associated with the work. By contrast, process controllers in the same industry worked under monotonous conditions, remained passive, but were required to detect critical signals associated with disturbances in the process. Frankenhaeuser and Johansson argued that this was directly parallel with the low-control vigilance task described earlier (except that it might have been the case that in a real situation there was greater cost attached to a missed signal). The study showed that the active planning task was associated with primarily positive feelings and with raised catecholamine levels. There were also more feelings of rush and irritation during work. By contrast, passive, understimulating process monitoring was associated with feelings of monotony and uneasiness. There was a small increase in adrenaline and cortisol.

B. Strategic Determinants of Mental and Physical State

The argument that has been developed earlier is that perceived control is an important aspect of a person's reaction to stressful events and that for a given situation there are a number of ways in which control may be exercised – personal, interpersonal, and socio-political. In some cases the situation could be assumed to be unsolvable, which means that there is no means for mastery and change in any domain. A person faced with terminal illness, or facing a disaster, could be in these circumstances and is effectively helpless. In other situations, some degree of personal, interpersonal, or socio-political control is possible.

The Frankenhaeuser model provides an initial conceptual framework for understanding how decision making in stressful environments might influence the short or long term health of the individual. If we add to this the ideas concerning the perception and operation of control, there is a possible basis for relating strategy to mental and physical well being in specific situations.

The model assumes that situations characterised by a response of raised effort carry the penalty of raised catecholamine levels. As will be described in Chapter 12, this could increase the functional strain on cardiovascular systems. Constant abuse due to raised levels of effort might create changes of a structural kind.

Effort and distress together might be expected to carry the penalty of raised adrenaline levels together with raised ACTH and cortisol levels. The latter have been shown to suppress the immunological response (Amkraut & Solomon, 1975), which in turn could increase the probability of infectious illness and even the occurrence of cancerous disease. (See Chapter 12.)

Thus, the alternative features of *effort*, or *effort and distress* might have different implications for both mental and physical health. Figure 9.5 illustrates the two major routes to mental and physical health types as described in this section.

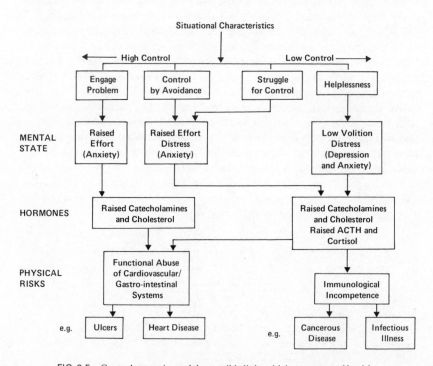

FIG. 9.5   Control strategies and the possible links with hormones and health.

Four possible attitudes to control are envisaged as being the result of cursory or detailed exploration of control facilities and skills in the three domains, personal, interpersonal, socio-political. The four attitudes are:

1. *Helplessness*, associated with passivity and depression and high probability of emotional distress because of punishing aspects if situations cannot be controlled.
2. *Struggle for control*, associated with a belief that control might be possible but difficult. The individual produces raised effort levels and processes feedback about the prospects for control. Distress may be characteristic if failure is evident. Sense of challenge and achievement are alternative features, if success is apparent.
3. *Control by avoidance* is envisaged as a special aspect of trying to achieve control. A person simply opts out, avoids the encounter, ducks the responsibility for action. If the threatening event is not self-limiting a person in this situation may remain in anxiety and fear, because as argued in the early chapters of this book, successful avoidance does not provide information to indicate to a person that control is possible. Therefore, a person may incur distress and high anxiety. Phobic patients may be in such states.
4. *Engage the problem*. This is assumed to have positive connotations. The individual may raise effort levels, and find the situation pleasant and challenging even when demand is high. The potential stress may end up being an enjoyable, rewarding experience with a positive outcome, which may in the end lower the risk for the belief in loss of control in a future encounter.

These four attitudes are portrayed in Fig. 9.5 as if linked to objective control levels, but of course this may not be the case. The individual may "get it wrong" and struggle for control when control is objectively impossible or abandon attempts when there are solutions within his or her capability.

In summary, the gain of raised effort strategies might be effective use of resources and the prevention of adverse effects of stress. The cost may be the raised arousal penalty in the long term because of the potential raised risk of functional damage to bodily systems.

If raised effort strategies are not successful and failure occurs, there is the additional possibility of the perception of loss of control resulting in distress. Effort with increasing distress may provide conditions resulting in cortisol secretion with raised risk of immunological changes due to the secretion of ACTH and cortisol. These issues are developed in Chapter 12.

10 Helplessness-Resistant Strategies

In the previous chapter the main interest was effort as an aspect of the strategic response to stress. In this chapter we develop the idea that effort as a response to stress may take many forms and may actually be an important aspect of a wider helplessness-resistant approach to life events. The main evidence is from laboratory-based research in which the thinking and decision making of depressed and non-depressed normal populations has been examined. A number of different ways in which helplessness may be resisted are described. It is then argued that what is needed is understanding of why some individuals may develop these approaches whereas others do not. A number of forms of illogical reasoning are identified, some of which act to promote pessimism and some of which help to maintain optimism.

1. THE CONCEPT OF LEARNED HELPLESSNESS

A. Learned Helplessness in Dogs and People

The learned helplessness hypothesis was first established from work with animals by Seligman and Maier (Maier and Seligman, 1976; Seligman et al., 1971; Seligman, 1975). The research initially took place against a background of learning theory and led to the conclusion that if exposure to aversive events occurs under conditions where the animal has no means of terminating the event, the organism learns that reinforcement is independent of its behaviour. The interpretation given to the research findings was that animals and people are sensitive to response–outcome probabilities; presentation of randomly associated probabilities or equal probabilities leads to a perception of helplessness. The motivational component involves passivity and inertia assumed to arise from reduced capacity for initiating voluntary responses. The cognitive element is a deficit which is manifest in difficulty in learning contingent relationships in the future.

The main experiment on which the learned helplessness hypothesis rests involved dogs divided into two groups. One group was submitted to a prior treatment of inescapable shocks while restrained. The other was given no such pretreatment. Both groups were then subjected to an avoidance learning task in which when the floor of the cage was electrified, escape was possible if a barrier was jumped. The untreated dogs learned the escape procedure normally but the dogs pretreated with uncontrollable shock failed to learn, showed passivity, and were slow to learn even if the experimenters pulled them across the barrier to safety.

Using a triadic design with three groups of dogs, a further check on the helplessness hypothesis was made. This time the pretreatment of uncontrollable shock was given to two groups, one of which could escape shock by a voluntary response and one of which could not but were yoked to the first group in that the same shock was received. A third group received no prior treatment. The learned helplessness model would predict that the group exposed to the pretreatment with no opportunity for control would be unable to learn the subsequent avoidance task. This was confirmed by the results; six out of the eight dogs failed to learn avoidance responses at all. Seligman concluded that it was not pretreatment with shock per se but pretreatment with uncontrollable shock that was the determinant of subsequent impairement.

Experiments on learned helplessness were also carried out by Hiroto (1974) using human beings, with noise as the aversive stimulus. Using a design involving a finger shuttle box where a given avoidance response could terminate exposure to noise, Hiroto found that even although the instructions indicated to subjects that the noise was controllable, those subjects who had been pretreated with uncontrollable noise were slow to learn escape procedures relative to those who had not. The uncontrollable pretreatment had impaired learning. Hiroto and Seligman (1975) showed that trauma is not the essential factor; a condition of pretreatment with an unsolvable discrimination learning task was also effective as a means of impairing subsequent learning.

These experiments support the notion of the transmission of helplessness; normal subjects may be quite inappropriately tuned by uncontrollable experiences to react as helpless when learning and control are objectively possible: "Uncontrollability distorts the perception of control (Seligman, 1975, p. 37)." However, the explanation remains unclear. It is conceivable that the contingency data suggest to a person that control is not possible in situation A and this generalises to situation B. This may mean that the two situations are not discriminated: The dogs may not have been sensitive to the differences between the pretreatment condition and the facilities in the escape condition.

Alternatively, there may be a tendency to rule out the use of normally effective strategies early on as a result of a pretreatment. These strategies are then suppressed because they are shown to be non-successful. Seen in this way, uncontrollable experiences damp down the use of potentially effective strategies. A cognitive model would assume that any situation brings a number of potentially applicable strategies into focus. Uncontrollable experiences create low probability weightings for these useful strategies. The effective result is that they are temporarily damped and are less likely to be brought into use in new situations. Helplessness is transmitted as a low level of dominance in the memory for appropriate strategies. Therefore, the organism appears slowed, perhaps confused, and learning is damped.

These considerations are important because the fundamental claim made by Seligman (1975) was that the laboratory phenomenon of learned helplessness provides a model of depression in man; no distinction between types of depression was made. The idea that perceived lack of contingency creates depression raises a problem: Occasions of uncontrollability are a feature of life. The question of why we are not all helpless and therefore, by definition, depressed, is a critical argument against the learned helplessness model, and is acknowledged by Seligman.

Chance events are uncontrollable and there is no correspondence between action and outcome. Therefore, it could be argued that if depressed subjects have acquired an expectation of being helpless, they should behave in tasks requiring skill in the same way as they do for chance tasks. They should not use the evidence suggesting success has occurred, in making future predictions for success. Miller and Seligman (1973) found that whereas non-depressed subjects distinguished chance and skill tasks when providing verbalised expectancies for future success on the basis of previous success trials, depressed subjects did not. This implies that depressed subjects either do not note the main features of the situation confronting them or they fail to use the evidence adequately in making the inference as to whether "chance" or "skill" is involved. This may be an important factor determining the origins of depression and could be a primary cognitive factor.

B. The Illusion of Control

At least one result of Seligman's development of the notion of learned helplessness was increasing interest in the factors that determine the perception of contingency between action and outcome. The interpretation of learned helplessness is that there is a reduction in the ability to detect contingent relationships. Since Seligman argued that helplessness provides a laboratory model of depression, it would follow that depressed people should also show a reduction in the detection of contingent relationships.

A series of experiments by Alloy and Abramson (1979) was designed to investigate the hypothesis that depressed students underestimate contingency in a contingency-learning task. The experiments consisted of a series of problems in which depressed and non-depressed students had to judge the objective level of contingency between pressing or not pressing a switch and the onset of a green light. In the first experiment there were three levels of control. If subjects err in their judgements it could be because they have not noted the structure of events (inadequate data) or because they have made incorrect inferences.

Judged control was accurate for both depressed and non-depressed students although there was a tendency for both groups to underestimate control at the 25% contingency level. This result was obtained regardless of whether the response associated with higher frequency of outcome was pressing or not pressing a button. However, a second experiment showed that non-depressed students overestimated the contingency between response and outcome when non-contingent outcomes were frequent or desired, but underestimated the degree of contingency when contingent outcomes were not desired. Therefore, subjects do not always judge contingency accurately in all conditions. Affective state and frequency of reinforcement interact to produce systematic errors in the judgement of non-contingency.

The most important and interesting finding was that it was *non-depressed* subjects who showed a tendency to make judgemental errors in that they over estimated control when positive outcomes occurred. Depressed subjects, by contrast, were unaffected by what the authors describe as "density of reinforcement" and accurately detected *lack* of relation between responses and outcomes. The use of invalid heuristics by non-depressed subjects in arriving at their judgements of control was corroborated by answers to open-ended questions designed to probe the reasons for the judgements. Some non-depressed students appeared to abandon rational strategies in favour of intuitive strategies in making their judgements. The authors argue that it is the *organisation* of the data rather than an inadequate data base, which was responsible for the effect. The important point is that the non-depressed were over optimistic about control when positive events were forthcoming whereas depressed subjects continue to be accurate and unaffected.

An interesting further point of difference emerged, which the authors felt gave some support to the learned helplessness model of depression. Although there was zero control in all problems, non-depressed subjects changed their judgements as a function of conditions. In the 25–25 problem condition, 50% of both depressed and non-depressed students actually said they had zero control. In the 75–75 problem, 50% of depressed students made the same decision but only 6% of non-depressed students did.

A sex difference was evident in that non-depressed females provided greater evidence of the illusion of control. This is perhaps all the more suprising in that the evidence suggests that females tend to be more prone to depressive disorder than males, yet it appears that they are abandoning rational strategies in positive outcome conditions. The authors interpret the result as being consistent with a finding reported by Langer (1975) that males, unlike females, did not demonstrate an "illusion of control" when the demand for rationality was very high.

A third experiment involved a design where there was no contingency between response and outcome but the onset of a green light was associated with either gain or, in another condition, loss of money. Again, non-depre-

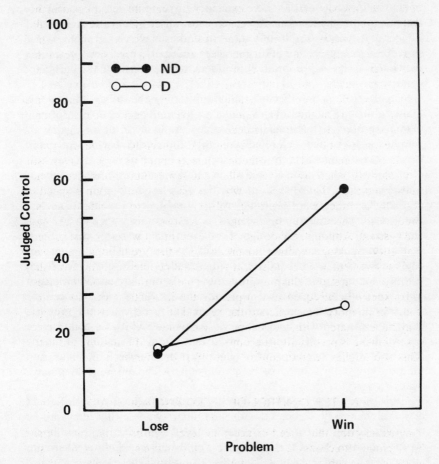

FIG. 10.1   Data showing judged control for depressed (D) and non-depressed (ND) students as a function of success characteristics. (Redrawn from Alloy & Abramson, 1979, with the permission of the authors and the American Psychological Association.)

ssed subjects overestimated control in "gain" situations. As shown in Fig. 10.1, depressed subjects were found to be more certain of their judgements of control in the "lose" rather than the "gain" condition. The questionnaire at the end showed that non-depressed subjects believed that factors other than their own responding were more important in the lose than in the gain condition. There was no such difference for depressed subjects.

The experiments demonstrate the importance of the role of valence rather than frequency of events attached to outcome. The authors generally interpret their results to support the notion of the "illusion of control" formally developed by Langer (1975). Langer developed this notion from studies of the behaviour of normal people in chance situations. "Illusion of control" was defined as "an expectancy of personal success probability inappropriately higher than objective probability would warrant (p. 311)." Langer reported the results of a series of studies in which factors from skill situations such as competition, choice, familiarity, involvement, caused individuals to be inappropriately confident and demonstrate the illusion of control.

Langer quotes a number of studies supporting the notion that people frequently treat chance events as controllable. For example, Goffman (1967) reported that casinos in Las Vegas were likely to dismiss gamblers who had a run of bad luck. Henslin (1967) studied dice players and noted players behaving as if there was control over outcome; a soft throw was often made for small numbers and a hard throw was made for large numbers.

Langer argued that when characteristics of skill situations are introduced into chance situations, people behave as if skill were involved. The first study involved competition. Subjects were presented with a chance task and made to compete with either a confident, or a nervous, confederate. A main prediction was that subjects would bet more against the nervous confederate than against the confident confederate. Results showed that this was the case; the mean bet for subjects against the confident player was 11.04 cents but against the nervous, anxious player was 16.25 cents.

A second study explored the hypothesis that if subjects were given the choice of which lottery ticket to buy, they would sell it at a higher price than if they were not. Results showed that the mean amount of money required for a lottery ticket which had been chosen was 8.67 dollars and for a ticket given without choice was 1.96 dollars. The difference was statistically significant.

A third study involved lottery tickets which had familiar symbols (letters of the alphabet) as compared with unfamiliar symbols (line drawings or novel symbols). Langer argued that familiarity with the symbols should favour increased belief that the ticket would be successful and therefore greater willingness to keep it. This was born out by the results.

One of the problems with Langer's studies is that there are a large number of alternative explanations for reported findings. Langer's own interpretation favours the idea that people will attribute skill to chance situations.

This is the basis of the illusion of control. This same reasoning lies behind Alloy and Abramson's notion that overestimation of contingency evidenced in their studies when positive or rewarded outcomes occur, is part of an illusion of control. The important point is that depressed subjects do appear to be objective about the data. The authors use the term "sadder but wiser" to describe the mental state of the depressed and see the results as being largely against a learned helplessness model of depression.

Langer considers the possibility that the illusion of control is the reverse of learned helplessness because it is an erroneous impression of dependence between action and outcomes. In the case of learned helplessness there has been carry-over from a low control to a potentially high control situation. In the case of the illusion of control there may be generalisation from high control experiences to low control conditions. In both cases the cognitive factors of past experience have remained influential.

A different way of viewing the illusion of control is that it is what is sometimes described as a self-serving motivational bias which provides a basis for resisting helplessness and depression. Individuals who are likely to resist depression exploit positive features of a situation as much as possible. They resist the effects of uncontrollable situations by creating evidence of control whenever there are positive features. Non-depressed people will thus find the best and resist the worst in any situation.

An experiment was designed by Fisher and Ledwith (1985) to investigate the effect of loud noise on the perception of contingency. It was argued that if it was the *stimulating (arousing) properties of incentives* that were responsible for the illusion of control it should be possible to replicate the effect with loud noise. Alternatively, if the effect is based on the *informative aspects of incentive* (perhaps suggesting to subjects that they are performing well), the effect should not be apparent in loud noise. The initial experiment involved a design whereby subjects selected a red key on the left of an Apple microcomputer or green key on the right. An event then occurred on the left or right of the monitor in the appropriate colour. There were three levels of contingency, 25, 50 and 75%.

The first quite unexpected result is that the group working in noise had attempted to predict the temporal sequence of events across the 40 trials. Since the experimenters had preprogrammed the outcomes for trials scheduled as non-contingent (to avoid response bias), some predictability was introduced inadvertently into the sequence and subjects took advantage of this and correctly pressed the key which was followed by the compatible event on the display more times than should have been possible. In fact, prediction accuracy or *success* should have been defined by $OC + (1 - OC)/2$, where OC is objective contingency (because half the programmed non-contingent trials should seem contingent to the subject). Subjects in quiet conditions made no such gains and so it seemed that noise had the effect of encouraging subjects to put more effort into the situation and find out more about the structure of the task.

This finding made it difficult to find out whether the illusion of control was apparent in noise: Although when estimates of contingency were subtracted from "success" data, results showed that subjects in noise overestimated their own success level in the 25% condition.

The experiment was repeated using a random-event generator to provide the outcome for non-contingent trials. Results showed that no gains could be made by predicting the sequence; in noise as in quiet, success levels were predicted by $OC + (1 - OC)/2$. Results consistent with the illusion of control hypothesis were found for noise in that there were overestimations of success data for the 25% and 50% conditions.

The issue of why this should occur in noise is an interesting one. Perhaps noise does not simply act as an arousing stimulus but is after all a "special kind of incentive" (see Broadbent, 1971). A second series of experiments was run by Fisher (to be published) and reported that depressed students (greater than 8, on the Beck depression inventory) did not raise effort levels in noise on the preprogrammed version of the task. Nor did they overestimate contingency data (illusion of control). Collectively, the evidence suggests that the response of non-depressed subjects on a contingency estimation task in noise was different: There was: (1) raised effort to predict the sequence; and (2) overestimation of contingency data. Both could be argued to be part of a strategic response to taking part in an experiment in stress.

A finding which might help to make sense of the illusion of control effect in loud noise is that people may expect to perform less efficiently in stress. In an experiment by Fisher (1985a) subjects were asked to predict the performance of a hypothetical person for a second set of trials, given an overall estimate alleged to represent performance for a first set of trials. The second set of trials was alleged to have been conducted in one of a number of stress conditions, noise, fatigue, sleep loss, incentive, social stress. Results suggested that irrespective of whether performance was assessed in terms of "error" or "latency" variables, subjects predict performance impairment in a range of stressful conditions. This may provide the basis for understanding the illusion of control. If even non-depressed people are sometimes pessimistic, maybe various strategic responses are brought into action to prevent a negative outcome. One such strategic response is raised effort; the other involves optimistic distortion of performance-related data.

This view is to some extent supported by a subsequent finding (in the same article) that when non-depressed and depressed subjects assess their own likely performance in one of a number of specified stressful conditions, under circumstances when they believe they will have to carry out the task subsequently, the non-depressed are less pessimistic than the depressed. Maybe the non-depressed are ready to rise to the challenge and bring optimistic strategies into play. A prediction of challenge and raised effort brings about a sense of optimism. This is not evident in the mildly depressed.

In general, the self-serving motivational bias hypothesis proposed originally by Schwartz (1981), might help to explain raised effort and optimistic
data distortion strategies found to occur in loud noise. Maybe the operation
of such a strategy will help to ward off the development of pessimistic
expectancies about personal performance in stressful conditions and is in
that sense "depression-resistant." We must emphasise at this point that
there are only a few pieces in the jig-saw; the data may be circumscribed
and the generality of these and related phenomena needs careful testing
in other contexts.

C. The Revised Helplessness Model

Since Seligman's book on learned helplessness was published, a number of
difficulties with the concept and its application to the human condition
have been identified. This has led to a reformulated model in which the
attribution made concerning outcome is a critical factor. This has brought
into focus the notion of *personal rather than universal helplessness* and has
helped to provide a basis for understanding some of the major symptoms
of neurotic depression. The interested student should follow up some of
the research that has reported difficulties with anomalies with the learned
helplessness model in Abramson et al. (1978); Miller and Norman (1979);
Roth (1980); Peterson (1982).

The results from Seligman's work with dogs suggested impairment of
learning, passivity, and lack of volition to accompany the pretreatment of
uncontrollable shock. The *criterion for the definition of passivity* is not clear,
because dogs receiving shock should show other signs of pain and distress.
Cats made anxious by uncontrolled shock (Masserman, 1943) clawed and
leaped at the cage when shocked. This was part of the behaviour that caused
them to be described as anxious and later, when this behaviour was inappropriate, as "neurotic." Moreover, *the motivational deficit in human beings* is
not characteristic. Human subjects frequently continue to initiate responses.
Learning is slower but not entirely absent (see Hiroto, 1974; Peterson,
1978, 1982) and a belief in the lack of correspondence between response
and outcome is not a necessary condition of helplessness (Peterson, 1982).
This, combined with the notion that the concept of generalised helplessness
may be circumscribed, has led to the development of alternative explanations of the cognitive origins of depression.

One explanation is that pretreatment of no control leads to specific
suppression of strategic responses. The suppression is specific to the conditions in which the treatment took place or to the circumstances surrounding
the experiment. In the early chapters of this book it was argued that human
subjects in conditioning experiments may be noting and making use of cues
to gain a notion of what is happening and what the demand characteristics
are. If this is true in conditioning experiments, how much more likely is it

when people are being subjected to uncontrollable pretreatments? They probably develop new strategies (suppressing others) only to find that the new ones are no longer appropriate in the second phase of the experiment. This should lead to confusion, some passivity, and slower learning.

D. Uncontrollability and Self-blame in Depression

According to a reformulation proposed by Abramson et al. (1978), experience with non-contingency is not in itself a sufficient condition for helplessness. A prerequisite for depression is *personal helplessness*, brought about because a person sees his or herself as *responsible* for the bad outcome. Abramson et al. (1978) refer to attributions which are internal (self-blaming), stable across time, and global. As argued by Garber and Hollen (1980) this would lead a depressed person to expect to be helpless (personal helplessness) in situations where other people are not helpless (universal helplessness). This may help with a particular logical difficulty observed in the thinking of depressed individuals found to have low self-esteem in situations which there is objectively low control over unpleasant circumstances. For example, in a study of working-class women in London, who were experiencing poverty and deprivation (Brown & Harris, 1978), the investigators noted that low self-esteem was a central feature of the depressed women although the circumstances surrounding them were objectively uncontrollable.

Beck's cognitive model of depression, developed in the later 1960s and early 1970s, derived largely from observations of thoughts, beliefs, and behaviour of clinical patients, is based on pessimism and self-blame as core features of depression. One of the early studies by Beck (1967) involved comparison of the symptoms of 50 depressed and 30 non-depressed patients. A list of distinguishing symptoms was compiled and given to 100 patients. As a result of their endorsements the revised inventory was given to 966 psychiatric patients. Key features distinguishing the depressed were tendencies for self-blame, low opinions of the self, negative expectancies of the future, indecisiveness, and loss of volition. The self-esteem factor was a particular feature: 38% of non-psychiatric patients and 81% of severely depressed patients had low self-image.

Beck developed a model of depression in which a number of negative beliefs were identified and seen as primary. The depressed person denigrates the past and present, has low self-esteem, and is pessimistic about the future. These beliefs form the basis of the "negative cognitive triad" proposed by Beck as the foundation for depressed mood, motivation, and behaviour (see Beck, 1970) and reflect in thought and dream content of patients. The emphasis on low self-esteem fits with the reformulated helplessness model in which global, stable, internal attributions are of primary causal significance.

One of the problems with exploring the relationship between self-esteem and depression is that questionnaires for measuring depression usually involve items relating to low self-esteem. In other words, low self-esteem is inextricably linked to depression. So attempts to compare low self-esteem with depression by obtaining correlations are likely to involve item contamination and circular reasoning. MacLachlan (1985), used inter-judge agreement to identify self-esteem items on the Beck depression inventory; when seven self-contaminating items were removed, the correlation between the remainder of the items and the self-esteem inventory was −0.05 and was not significant. This is an important finding because it suggests a lack of association between depression and self-esteem items when contamination is prevented.

A point made by Abramson and Sackheim (1977) is that the apparent paradox of perceived uncontrollability and self-blame can be resolved by distinguishing universal uncontrollability and personal uncontrollability; the depressed person perceives helplessness because of lack of personal skills. This seems difficult to reconcile with the lack of correlation between depression and self-esteem in MacLachlan's results and underlines the need to explore personal assessments of performance in the depressed in more detail.

Garber and Hollen (1980) investigated changes in expectancies during skill- and chance-determined tasks for depressed and non-depressed subjects. In a skilled task, depressed subjects showed little expectancy change in estimating the probability of their own success. In contrast, when estimating the probability of another person's success on the same skilled task, the estimates of depressed and normal subjects did not differ. Thus, the authors conclude that depressives' cognitive distortions are specific to their beliefs about their own skilled activity rather than a general belief about response–outcome independence: "personal" but not "universal" helplessness. A comparable conclusion could be drawn from the study (described previously) by Fisher (1985a).

An experiment by Fisher (unpublished) investigated the focus of pessimism in greater detail using a very simple experimental design requiring a subject to type a word and then without seeing the result visually, to decide whether or not an error had been made. Fisher argued that if depressed subjects had a sense of personal helplessness, they would over-report correct words as errors, but would not report more errors as correct. A task was chosen which involved the repeated typing of a preselected word. The same word was typed and judged 100 times. At the end of the trials subjects were each asked to provide an estimate of how many errors they thought they had made. The task thus afforded three measures of the performance of depressed and non-depressed subjects: (1) errors produced; (2) detection efficiency (corrects reported as errors; errors reported as corrects); (3) overall estimates of errors.

It was deemed important that neither the depressed nor the non-depressed subjects realised that the main reason for the experiment was to investigate the effects of depression on the perception of task performance. If subjects were preselected for depressed features this would provide them with some advanced notion that the effects of depression were to be investigated. Instead, a technique was used which involved asking for students to take part in an experiment involving error detection. The Beck depression questionnaire was administered either before or after the experiment. As a result, partitioning of subjects into depressed or non-depressed based on whether or not they scored greater than 8 on the questionnaire was made at the stage of the analysis of the results.

Word-typing errors averaged out about 7% for both the depressed ($N = 26$) and the non-depressed ($N = 42$) groups. Detection efficiency (correct detection of errors) was over 96% accuracy for both groups. There was no evidence that the depressed group over-reported errors on a trial-by-trial basis. The depressed did not report more correct words as errors. However, they did provide a greater pessimistic estimate at the end of the task than the non-depressed. The experiment indicates that the depressed are not unduly pessimistic about their own performance when assessing it on a trial-by-trial basis. Only at the end of the trials when a global estimate was provided, was the global estimate more likely to be disparate with trial-by-trial reports. The focus of pessimism would seem to be the global assessment of performance.

One possible explanation is that when asked to make a public statement about performance, the depressed provide a pessimistic account as part of a protective strategy: If a person comes out of an examination room saying "I did not do a good paper," he is protected from part of the consequence of failure by the public statement; he showed he knew what "good" was but could not achieve it this time. When success is forthcoming, this strategy should have further positive gains ("I did well and yet I did not think so because I know what 'good' standards are.") However, the strategy could work to disadvantage in case of failure. Other people note the failure, which confirms the person's pessimistic assessment as objective, and they may begin to react to the person as a potential examination failure. Thus an originally protective strategy becomes a source of the development of low self-evaluation.

2. HELPLESSNESS-RESISTANT TECHNIQUES

We can now begin to identify strategies which might help a person resist adverse effects associated with threatening encounters. These are itemised in the next sections.

A. Avoidance of Negative Encounters in Life

There are a number of identifiable ways in which, faced with a low-control situation, a person might *resist* helplessness and depression. The first involves *avoiding a scenario where success is deemed as unlikely.* Kanouse and Hanson (1971) have investigated the properties of a distribution of life event outcomes. The result of their analysis suggests that most outcomes are good but that extremely bad outcomes are more frequent than extremely good ones. Kanouse and Hanson argue that in general, people will work their way into "good" environments and out of "bad" ones. They will not seek *very* good outcomes; this would shift the psychologically neutral point for judgements (Parducci, 1963, 1965) and will mean that more intermediate forms of experience are seen as bad.

An assumption of importance imbedded in the Kanouse and Hanson analysis is that people may *seek* or *reject* encounters with life events. Avoidance of situations with negative outcomes is potentially a depression-resistant process. For example, a person who fears that he will fail at making a speech, may avoid jobs or roles where public speaking will be incumbent on him. He thus creates a stream of potential life encounters in which he avoids negative outcomes. This view stresses the possibility that human beings are *active creators of life scenarios.* Therefore, one aspect of helplessness resistance that could be trained is avoidance of "negative outcome" encounters. Use of avoidant strategies implies some control over decision making in life. There may be cases where the necessary control is denied. Thus, some people may be forced into encounters perceived as likely to be negative, which they do not like. Stewart and Salt (1981) considered the possibility that women in traditional roles are more likely to have low control over the structure of life. Their investigations produced results suggesting that women who are single and work are more likely to incur stress-related disorders typical of men who work; whereas women in traditional roles have problems characterised by low control and react with depression. Family-centred problems are like this because there is often low control over the activities of children.

Studies by Fisher et al. (1985a, b, c) have identified a number of factors related to homesickness in university students and children attending boarding school for the first time. High control over the decision to move reduces homesickness in students. Geographical distance of the move to university is positively associated with homesickness, yet the number of home visits does not distinguish those who are homesick from the rest. It may be that the *perceived potential for visits home* is a factor of importance, because this preserves control over life ahead and prevents a person from feeling distressed because he or she is trapped in the situation. Ability to approach, engage, or avoid changes in life may be an aspect of strategy with implications for short- and long-term reaction.

In general, very little is known about decision making in opportunities that present themselves in life, but it is in avoidable (controllable) situations that situations likely to produce helplessness may be resisted. More needs to be known about the way in which people might explore problems in advance and avoid conditions likely to trap them and create helplessness. The avoidance of helplessness in advance requires control but also necessitates planning.

Fisher (1984a) introduced the term "control by avoidance" to cover situations in which there is avoidance of encounters with threat. Such a strategy may be very costly in terms of effort and even if avoidance is successful, the individual receives no relevant feedback to suggest that control is being established. Avoidance of negative encounters in life may have properties in common with subjective perception of loss of control because of the loss of feedback. Experiments by Brady and colleagues on ulcers in executive monkeys (Brady, 1958; Brady et al., 1958) showed that the animals made responsible for pressing a lever to avoid shock were more likely to develop ulcers than their yoked controls who experience identical shock. Studies by Mason et al. (1968a, b) revealed that after six 72-hour avoidance learning sessions, urinary epinephrine and norepinephrine levels were raised during avoidance experiences. These levels showed relatively little diminution across time, thus indicating relative absence of habituation.

Phobic responses could be argued to be clinical manifestations of "control by avoidance." A person could be expected to be behaving normally if he operates an elaborate strategy to avoid encounters that are associated with negative outcomes. For example, if water is contaminated with bacteria or where rats carrying hepatitis are prevalent, a normal person might be expected to go to elaborate lengths to avoid contact with bacteria. The fact that efforts for avoidance are increased would be expected in view of the seriousness of a slip. A phobic individual is distinguished in that: (1) the source of threat is not recognised by a "normal" population; (2) the behavioural strategy is seen as over-elaborate and utterly inappropriate by normal observers. Yet if the belief the phobic person has in the dangers of the encounter are accepted, the operation of elaborate strategies for avoidance is understandable.

Because of the close association between avoiding bad outcomes in life and developing phobic attitudes, some further comments on phobic responses are useful. Phobic behaviour has been investigated more intensively in recent years and a number of models have been developed. The "preparedness theory" developed by Seligman (1971) has emphasised the features of objects likely to be associated with threat and phobic avoidance. The concept of preparedness as introduced by Seligman (1971) is operationally defined in terms of ease of learning and relative resistance to unlearning. Evolutionary pressures are assumed to favour avoidance of stimuli known to be potentially threatening to pretechnological man. Thus stimuli such as small animals and reptiles are likely sources of phobic events. However, the earlier question "why are we not all helpless?" can be translated into "why are we not all phobic?" Clearly threat-avoidance strategies are only operated by some.

Traditional learning theory emphasises that there is a primary drive to avoid pain, which becomes rapidly associated with signals present at the time (see Dollard & Miller, 1950). However, successful learning and avoidance should have drive-reduction properties; the model does not explain the escalation of anxiety or the *elaboration of strategies* which increasingly dominate phobic behaviour. Additional concepts such as that of incubation (Eysenck, 1979) are required. The incubation model explains the rise in anxiety and increasing elaboration of behaviour in terms of reinforcement. Eysenck refers to incubation as a "growth of fear over a time interval which follows some aversive stimulus (p. 159)." The increase in fear is assumed to be spontaneous.

A two-stage model is needed to account for the development of a phobic condition. First there is sensitivity (preparedness) towards a particular object or event, which results in fear that is unrealistic concerning likelihood of control. Avoidance strategies are brought into operation but if successful they will not necessarily lower the level of fear. For this reason the practising of avoidance of negative aspects of life may have counterproductive and negative implications in the long term. Avoidance of too many avoidant strategies could be a good stress resistant approach.

B. Raising the Effort Levels

Figure 10.2 illustrates the potential decisions which an individual might employ as part of a raised effort strategy: "Raised effort" may be a *master strategy* from which subordinate strategies such as "raise response rates," "concentrate harder," "notice the structure of the task," "read the instructions carefully," might stem. An individual will need to appraise the cost of raised effort and, as the lower expanded representation shows, may needs to decide *how* raised effort should be employed.

Raised effort assumes that the task is to be engaged and that the person is engaged in "the struggle for control." Effort may be rewarding and the result positive for a person when success is the outcome, but may be an input which can add to distress when the outcome is negative ("I tried to save her life but I just did not do the right things; it would be better for me if I had never tried.") Thus, although in general raised effort levels are "depression resistant," there are penalties for struggle and failure.

C. Optimising the Evidence about Control

It is possible that when a person tackles a situation, strategies for optimising the gains of "good" outcomes will be implemented. These strategies may not necessarily produce the desired main goal or "aim," but may act to minimise distress, to maintain esteem and sense of achievement, and to increase the potential for positive "side effects." To use an illustration of a person whose mother is terminally ill; it may not be possible to achieve a cure, but it might be possible to maximise the "good" aspects ("At least

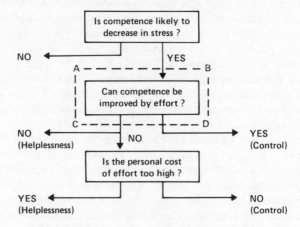

FLOW DIAGRAM OF DECISIONS WHICH CHANGE PERCEIVED CONTROL OR PERCEIVED HELPLESSNESS

Is competence likely to decrease in stress ?

NO YES

A — — — — — — — B

Can competence be improved by effort ?

C — — — — — — — D

NO (Helplessness) NO YES (Control)

Is the personal cost of effort too high ?

YES (Helplessness) NO (Control)

FLOW DIAGRAM OF COMPONENT QUESTIONS LEADING TO DECISIONS ABOUT EFFICACY OF RAISED EFFORT

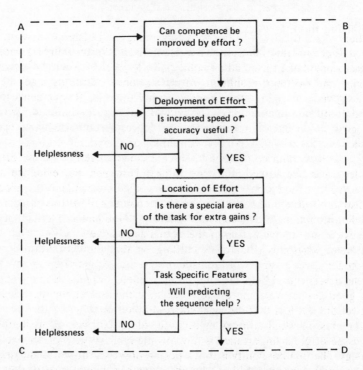

A B

Can competence be improved by effort ?

Deployment of Effort

Is increased speed or accuracy useful ?

Helplessness NO YES

Location of Effort

Is there a special area of the task for extra gains ?

Helplessness NO YES

Task Specific Features

Will predicting the sequence help ?

Helplessness NO YES

C D

FIG. 10.2 Decisions likely to be involved in raised effort strategies.

she enjoyed the last months of her life; I was around to make her comfortable; I found the treatment that caused the symptoms to abate.") These assessments arise from inputs provided by actions and outcomes as events progress within a particular life event scenario.

D. Avoiding Self-blaming Attributions

From what was said previously (section C), it should be evident that avoidance of self-blame might: (1) increase the potential for optimism in future encounters; (2) help to ward off distress associated with feeling responsible for a bad outcome.

Kanouse and Hanson (1971) observed across a series of studies that negative information about a person or object carried greater weight than positive information in making an appraisal. The same is true for risk taking; costs appear to be given greater weight than gains. It might follow that a strategy designed to resist depression should incorporate either a *bias against negative features* or should involve *active distortion of negative information*. It might be argued, for example, that self-blaming attributions and the negative thoughts about the self that result should be avoided because representations attract undue weight in all impressions of the self in the future.

There is a difficulty with the view that being "self-blaming resistant" is always beneficial, in that, as shown by Bulman and Wortman (1977), accepting personal blame for a bad outcome helps to *preserve* a sense of control. Bulman and Wortman examined the attributions of causality made by 29 accident victims, against their judged ability to cope. Respondents were asked to attribute blame and causality. Social workers and nurses provided ratings of coping and behaviour. Results suggested that self-blame was a predictor of good coping. An obvious explanation is that by feeling responsible, the individual could feel a sense of control over the cause of the accident and thus avoid it in the future. However, the evidence also suggested that good copers did *not* feel they could have avoided the accident. In response to the question "Why me?", responses fell into six categories: "predetermination," "probability," "chance," "God had a reason," "deservedness," and "re-evaluation of the events as positive."

In some ways this research is baffling, in that the attribution is self-directed and yet a variety of fatalistic or external explanations are evoked for the actual causal links leading to the accident. A paradox reappears in that good copers were more likely to blame themselves for the accident and yet did not feel that the accident could have been avoided.

If a stress-resistant strategy involves avoiding self-blaming attributions, one issue of great importance is how people might evolve or acquire the strategy. The first possibility is that a person observes the world and gradually acquires concepts of blame by observing selective aspects of the outcome of events encountered in life. Those life events which are particularly memorable because of their impact or consequence might be expected to have greater implication for the model formed. For example, a person might be less likely to remember that he was to blame for a trival error, say dropping an object such as a pen, than for an error which has great consequence in that it causes an accident.

Weiner et al. (1971) investigated the reaction to failure by individuals in terms of the attribution of blame. Four causal elements of ascription were identified as providing the basis of interpretation and prediction of outcome: ability; task difficulty; effort; and luck. The first two elements are assumed to be stable and the last two elements are assumed to be unstable. A basic assumption is that attribution to chance and luck will create instability as far as future predictions are made. To illustrate the implication of Weiner's descriptive classification, a person may well believe that by increasing his effort levels he can affect performance in the desired direction. This should give him reason for optimism in future predictions because it provides a basis for assuming there is personal control. Equally, however, failure in the face of raised effort should lead to logical acceptance of personal responsibility for failure.

Experiments conducted by Weiner and Frieze (as reported by Weiner et al., 1971, 1972) involved providing subjects with information about a hypothetical person who achieved a percentage of success at a task and a percentage of success for previous tasks. Additionally, information was provided about the percentage of other individuals allegedly successful at the task. No information about the task was given. Manifest discrepancies between previous and present success increased the frequency of attributions to luck or effort (leaving it open as to whether the hypothetical person was responsible). When past and current success were less disparate, "ability" or "task difficulty" provided the basis of ascriptions made. (Again this would leave it open as to whether the hypothetical person was responsible or not). Further information was then found to be important. The perception of prior success and the success of others on the task would increase the probability of an ascription to ability.

Thus, it might be possible to itemise conditions in which a person would feel personally responsible for a success or a failure. If he fails where others succeed (a classroom experience for some children), he has evidence for personal helplessness and personal blame. If he fails where others fail, he has evidence for universal helplessness and no blame. The same would be true if he fails under conditions where no one could be expected to succeed: A person might be willing to undertake a task where he cannot succeed if he is protected by the knowledge that neither could anyone else, because he gains credit for the effort but does not incur the *costs* of failure. The evidence reviewed in early chapters suggested that "fear of failure" individuals may protect themselves in this way. Perhaps there are disingenuous ways of conducting personal performance, designed with consequence in mind. "Disingenuous strategy" might provide a means to avoid responsibility for failure but gain credit for effort.

An additional disingenuous strategy might be to underestimate performance publicly. By setting the expectations of others for underperformance, a person may be more protected against an attack for failure. As described previously in this chapter, Fisher (unpublished) found that the only difference between the assessments of depressed and non-depressed subjects for the detection of errors in a task involving a repeatedly typed word in the absence of visual feedback, was in the estimate provided at the end, not in trial-by-trial reporting. It is possible that public statements of failure may begin as protective, "disingenuous strategies," but may bounce back on a person because of the effect it has on other people. The choice of such a strategy could be a disaster in the long term (see section C).

The disingenuous (initially protective) strategy could go wrong and increase the risk of undervaluation of self and of successes that do occur. An additional protective element which would fortify such a strategy against possible adverse effects would be to provide a reason for failure. The student who comes out of the examination room with the message "I know I failed, I swotted the wrong questions," or "I know I failed, I was awake all night last night with toothache," is providing both a protection from the shock of failure and a reason for its occurrence. Because of the qualifying statement it is less likely that this strategy could work adversely for the individual.

For deeper understanding of the inferential reasoning paths that could protect against depression, there needs to be further identification of the relationship between behavioural and characterological blame and of the way in which information about mitigating circumstances is used. Bulman (1979) argued that the form of attribution that correlates with depressive symptoms is blame directed at the self rather than at the situation or at behaviour. She proposed that characterological blame is associated with helplessness and depression, but behavioural blame is not. Since character is blamed, the transmission of helplessnes should be guaranteed. If behaviour is blamed, future situations remain potentially controllable; a person could improve his behaviour. Bulman reported that depressed college students were more likely than non-depressed students to make a characterological attribution for bad events, but the two groups were not distinguished by behavioural blame.

This hypothesis was confirmed by Peterson, Schwartz, and Seligman (1981), who conducted a longitudinal study and found that for 87 female undergraduates there was a correlation between depressive symptoms and blame directed at their own characters; blame directed at behaviour correlated with *lack* of depressive symptoms. Further, negative events that were attributed to behaviour were seen as more controllable, with less stable and less global causes. Interestingly, characterological blame increased with the greater frequency of negative events in the year.

One important area to examine might be the *way* in which behavioural blame progresses to the point of characterological blame. In other words, at what point does the tendency to behavioural blame become so pronounced that it is a profound self-denigrating tendency? We have itemised ways in which behavioural blame might be beneficial in that:

1. It could help a person to retain control for the future ("It was my fault for not putting the brakes of the car on, I'll never drive like that again").
2. It could be part of a "disingenuous strategy"—"I cannot have passed the test, I did so badly," implies knowledge of what success is; and protects against the shock of failure while increasing the value of possible success.

It has been assumed that acceptance of behavioural blame is either logical or strategic. A possibility not so far considered is that it arises from a fault in reasoning. This explanation is totally different and would suggest that there is a primary cognitive failure which increases the probability that behavioural blame will occur. There is some indirect evidence from Fisher (1985a) to suggest that depressed people might not utilise information adequately in making allowance for performance which is less than competent. Students acting as subjects were asked to assess the competence of a typist allegedly producing typescript in either normal conditions or in conditions of high street noise. Four prepared typescripts containing four levels of error (2%, 5%, 10%, and 15%) were used. Each subject judged the typist by being shown one typescript. Errors were always letter transposition errors and were ringed in red in text and then expressed as a percentage at the end. Each subject then made a judgement about the competence level of the typist on a five-point rating scale from "very competent" through to "very incompetent." It had been established by two previous studies referred to in the same article that *both normal and depressed subjects* anticipated *deterioration in performance* when a hypothetical person was asked to work in conditions of environmental stress. Noise was one of the stress conditions and was found to be associated with predictions of increased error. Therefore, the issue of interest was whether subjects would make use of this information in the assessment of competence of a typist believed to have produced the typescript while working in high street noise.

As illustrated in Fig. 10.3, depressed subjects ($N = 55$, mean score on Beck depression inventory 14.2) were "tougher" overall in their judgements of the typist than non-depressed subjects ($N = 60$, mean BDI 6.1). In addition, there was less attempt on the part of the depressed to make allowances for the conditions under which the typist was working. By contrast, the non-depressed were more generous and showed signs of utilising the information that stresses such as noise might increase error rates.

If depressed subjects behave in the same way when judging their *own* performance, they might be more expected to gain poor impressions of

MEAN COMPETENCE RATINGS FOR (HYPOTHETICAL) TYPIST
PRODUCING SCRIPTS IN QUIET AND NOISE CONDITIONS

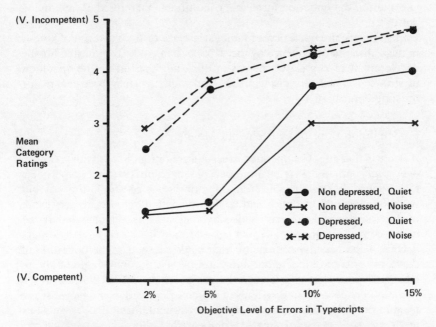

FIG. 10.3   Mean competence ratings for (hypothetical) typist alleged to
have produced typescripts in either quiet, or loud street noise. (From Fisher,
1985a.)

their own capabilities. By contrast a non-depressed person makes allowance
for any extenuating circumstances surrounding performance (such as the
presence of stress) and therefore does not form an adverse impression easily.

It must be emphasised that the study does *not* demonstrate that the
depressed subjects did not make allowances when judging their own performance, only that they did not make allowances when judging the performance of a (hypothetical) other person. The problem with the same design
involving self-assessment of personal performance in the presence of stressful conditions, is that judgement is likely to be based on different base
data (depending on the effects of stress on performance). This presents a
difficulty for the generality of the conclusions.

Even if failure of the depressed to make use of cognitive facts about
performance in stress was found to be applicable to personal performance,
the development of characterological blame from behavioural blame must
still be explained. An obvious explanation is in terms of the inductive
process. The generalisation "all swans are white" arises from combinations
of single experiences of white swans (X is a swan and X is white; Y is a
swan and Y is white; etc.). In the same way a data stream of outcomes

which are bad and for which a person accepts personal blame could lead to a general construct (I under-performed in condition X; I under-performed in condition Y; I under-performed in condition Z; therefore I always under-perform).

In summary the operation of faulty strategies or the existence of a fault in the utilisation of evidence by the depressed might be responsible for the development of depressive themes in thinking. Conversely the operation of strategies which are disingenuous and fault free may be a means for resisting depression.

E. Obtaining Control by Irrelevant Means

A strategy that might be operated in certain conditions is to establish control over *some*, perhaps less relevant, aspect of life. There is no direct experimental evidence that people gain from operating some control in this way but there is anecdotal evidence and it is evident that "control by irrelevant means" may provide an explanation of some aspects of human behaviour in low-control situations.

One of the best illustrations of what could be seen as the operation of this form of control, is the autobiographical account by Dolgun (1965) of his experiences during interrogation in Soviet prisons in the late 1940s, when Stalin had instigated systems of extreme deprivation and punishment. Dolgun relates how he survived the constant unpredictable beating, sleep reduction, solitary confinement in a black-walled cell in near-freezing temperatures. Dolgun was an American, working in the American Embassy in Moscow when he was picked up by the MGB (KGB equivalent). There appeared to be no reason for his capture and the Embassy appeared to have made little attempt to help him, which must have added to the helplessness and hopelessness of the situation. Dolgun appeared to endure the unendurable by a mixture of techniques, some of which could be argued to act to ameliorate the deprivations he had to endure but some of which could not and may have exacerbated it. He used the term "survival strategies" to describe the techniques.

Significant factors throughout might have been his stated anger at the Embassy for failing to help with his rescue and his stated determination to struggle and survive. He reports that he gave himself "pep talks" (Dolgun, 1965): "Easy Alex. Take it easy. You can do it. You went with no sleep for a week and you can do anything you want. You're all right. You've got guts. You're young and you're strong. These Russian bastards are trying to break you but you're on to them aren't you. So as long as you are on to them they can't get you (p. 53)." He evolved techniques for increasing the periods of cat-nap sleep. He was required to spend the day in his cell either standing and walking or sitting on the bed facing the door. He evolved a technique of sitting motionless for increasingly long periods but noting the guard's activities and moving just when the guard thought he was asleep. This way he was able to increase the period in which he could be motionless without the guard believing that he *was* asleep. He was then able to snatch periods of sleep. He refers to this as "conditioning the guards." This could be argued to be a direct attempt to increase the probability of survival by increasing the periods of sleep. Dolgun claimed he could steal up to two or three hours of sleep in a day with one of the guards, and that it probably saved his life.

However, Dolgun also reported a need to achieve a sense of "being on top"; the need was actualised with the more sympathetic of the guards. There were also attempts to challenge or laugh at the interrogator. These challenges could hardly have been conducive to obtaining better treatment, but clearly formed an essential aspect of the "struggle mentality" which helped Dolgun survive. Although not a direct form of control over the deprivations, these strategies might instead provide evidence which helps to sustain hope and to reduce loss of courage. In a sense, this is achieving control by "irrelevant means." Dolgun also reports in some detail how he planned and calculated the mileage for imagined walks around France and how these imaginary walks and the accompanying physical activity were of importance in his struggle to survive the deprivation.

These observations suggest that it might be the case that *control over some less pertinent aspect of life* during a stressful encounter may be beneficial. Perhaps control in one domain can offset its loss in another.

The importance of interest in leisure activities in ameliorating the effect of stress at work was emphasised by Broadbent (1982). In studies of electricity workers a three-way interaction was found between satisfaction with work, satisfaction with leisure, and depression. Stress will principally result in depression among those unhappy with leisure. One possible explanation is that a successful leisure activity (sport, hobbies) might create a domain of raised control, which offsets loss of control in other domains. Moreover, Stewart and Salt (1981) investigated the difference in stress effects for married women who work, single women who work, and married women in traditional roles. The women who were married and who worked were found to be more protected against stress effects in both work and home environments. This could be partially explained in terms of the counterbalance created by control in other domains.

Perceived social support also seems to have an ameliorating effect on stressful events. Brown and Harris (1978) reported in their door-to-door survey of working-class women in Camberwell, London, that those who were depressed were not only likely to be poor, jobless, and with a number of children at home, but were also less likely to report a close confiding relationship with another person (husband or friend). Social support could provide the basis of increased control in another domain and this could be a form of control by irrelevant means.

3. AN ACCOUNT OF DEPRESSION-RESISTANT
DECISION MAKING

The use of the strategies outlined in this chapter could result in positive outcomes for potentially negative encounters. Experiences in an encounter may be challenging and demanding if control is present. Depression-resistant strategies should have the effect of ensuring that some form of control is perceived: Either the *evidence is distorted* in the direction of optimism, or *effort levels are raised* to produce "positive," encouraging data, or *control by irrelevant means* may offset negative feedback. In the cognitive model of health and illness to be developed in the final chapter, these techniques are envisaged as methods of avoiding pessimism and distress as an outcome to a stressful scenario.

The arguments grouped together in this chapter are largely extracted from laboratory studies. The generality of the results must be tested in

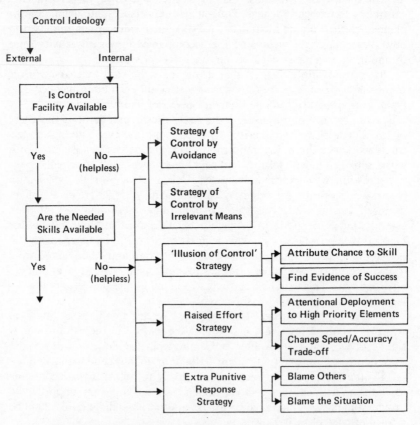

FIG. 10.4   The link with hierarchical decisions about control and the operation of depression-resistant strategies.

real-life contexts in spite of the obvious associated difficulties. One way of envisaging these findings is as "straw men" for arguments from analysis of evidence in life encounters. The synthesis provided here and in the final chapters would be useful if it provoked research and discussion along these lines.

Figure 10.4 illustrates how helplessness-resistant strategies may be linked to decision making about control in a particular situation. For example, if the situation leads to the decision that control is not available, two resistant strategies may be likely. One is control by avoidance; this may incur an anxiety and distress penalty. The other is control by irrelevant means. People suffering adverse experiences at work may be unable to avoid the encounters because of financial needs, etc., but may develop a leisure pursuit in which they have expertise, thus helping to maintain a feeling of high personal prestige.

If facility for control is seen to be available but a person perceives a lack of the skills and resources required, the same two strategies could be invoked. However, if the person engages the problem and struggles for control, techniques of data distortion ("illusion of control"), raised effort, and blame avoidance (extra punitive or external blaming strategies) may be used.

11 Strategy, Style, and Disorder

The view that the individual seeks to obtain control over aspects of a potentially threatening environment might at first seem to portray a self-interested, power-conscious view of the individual as one who exploits his environment. However, the approach taken in this book is that control is a form of stability and predictability which makes it possible for a person to develop and acquire skills and resources. The definition proposed in an earlier book (Fisher 1984a) that "control involves knowing that there is a response available which can change a situation" indicates that the main importance of control is as part of the homeostatic balance with the environment. Stresses and threats represent disequilibrium; the knowledge that corrective responses are available provides a basis for the deduction that equilibrium can be restored.

We have attempted to link "control" with strategic response. Strategies are regarded as means–ends specifications. The underlying behaviour is goal directed and there are sequences of specifiable goals and subgoals. Ideally, these should be determined by the description of the situation but both circumstantial and personal factors may change the mental structures on which the conception and utilisation of strategies depend.

1. PLANS AS THE ELEMENTS OF CONTROL

Before beginning to think of the way strategies might be changed or constrained by personal styles and circumstances, it is useful to return to the concept of the plan as a basic element of a strategy and to consider the basic ingredients on which planned behaviour depends.

The notion that behaviour is purposeful, organised, and designed with consequences in mind was formally developed by Miller et al. (1960). As, described in Chapter 5 (see Fig. 5.1), they envisaged the TOTE unit as central to all aspects of skilled activity. The individual was argued to TEST the discrepancy between intentions and reality, OPERATE to reduce the discrepancy, TEST the discrepancy between intentions and reality after the operation phase and then EXIST. The plan based on TOTE units was argued to have impetus; thwarting could result in raised anxiety due to the release of tension (see Mandler, 1975).

More recently theorists of planning have begun to identify the essential steps in the planning process. "Plan construction" refers to the process whereby plans are conceived. "Plan execution" refers to the process by which plans are carried out. Three steps which best define the planning operation are:

1. Noticing the problem—the mismatch between reality and the desired state of affairs is noted. In stressful environments, the mismatch may be readily defined in terms of homeostatic imbalance.
2. Constructing a plan—a series of procedures are conceived which will reduce the discrepancy between *reality* and the *desired state of affairs* (discrepancy reduction). If a number of procedures are available, the selection of one procedure defines the current strategy. The associated activity might *appear* remote from the final goal. For example, if a person confronted with a wild bear, tipped sugar on the ground around him, this might be seen as useless, irrelevant behaviour, but as strategic if it was known by an observer that bears like sugar. The overall strategy could be to persuade the bear to eat the sugar rather than attack. The strategy "feed bear" relates to the goal "prevent attack."
3. Executing a plan—this involves the production and refinement of sequences of strategic responses linked by "if–then" mental facts: If the bear eats the sugar then he will be preoccupied and then it should be possible to escape by running quickly to the car. Executing the plan implies that qualitative considerations are taken into account (e.g., quickly, slowly, aggressively).

A. Types of Goal and Planning Strategies

The nature of the threat or discomfort perceived as stressful should determine the goal and hence the range of planning possibilities. However, the overall goal or "aim" might itself vary as a function of circumstance. For example, in the case of a person whose mother is terminally ill, peripheral circumstances might change the *aim*: If the mother were over 90 years old, the aim might be to make sure she is kept free from pain and comfortable. If the mother were only 40 years old, the aim might be to seek treatment likely to keep her alive. Equally, there may be personally held ideologies that operate to determine the aim. To use the example of the confrontation with a wild bear, a person who strongly believes that killing animals is wrong, may form the aim "prevent bear from attacking," which may lead to avoidance or distraction strategies. A person who does not believe killing is wrong may formulate the aim "kill bear." Thus, the basic goal on which the blueprint for a strategy is based may differ between individuals in the same situation.

The aim then provides a fact in cognition which is the ingredient for selection of a strategy. If no effective strategy is possible a person may conclude he or she is helpless. In the example of the attacking bear, the person whose goal is to kill the bear but who then realises that there is no weapon may experience helplessness; the person whose goal is to distract the bear may obtain control of the situation more easily. In practice it may be more expedient to use cognitive facts about action to formulate the aim in the first place (no gun; cannot kill bear; sugar is in pocket, therefore use sugar to distract bear).

In this chapter the possibility is considered that both personal styles and situational constraints may *determine all levels of the planning of strategies* from the conception of the goals through to the implementation of the component actions and the qualities that describe action (fast/slow; confident/unsure; strong/weak; etc.). In the next section the evidence for differences in personality is considered in the context of prevailing features of planned activity. Because of the limitations of space, only a brief synopsis is presented of the basis of each personality feature considered; the interested student should consult the key references for further information. One important point about the evidence presented next is that it should not be assumed that the categories of personality are exclusive: there are frequently high inter-correlations reported. Consideration of the evidence would require more space than is available.

2. COGNITIVE STYLES AND PLANNING CONSTRAINTS

A. Content Limitations

i. Need Achievers and Fear of Failure

People may vary in the goals formulated even with respect to such basic distinctions as to whether or not competence is itself desired.

Work on achievement motivation was developed by McClelland et al. (1953) and Atkinson (1957), and was incorporated into a formally stated risk-taking model by Atkinson (see Atkinson & Feather, 1966; Atkinson & Raynor, 1974). Accounts of the research literature on achievement motivation, and particularly the expectancy-value approach, are provided by Feather (1982).

The Atkinson risk-taking model formed the basis of a model of achievement motivation (Atkinson & Raynor, 1974; Atkinson & Birch, 1978). The essential principle of the risk model is that motivational tendency (T_r) is a function of the product of the expectancy of success (P_s) and the incentive for success (I_s). This is weighted by the difference between two motivational factors—striving for success (M_s) and avoidance of failure (M_f):

$$T_r = (M_s - M_f) \times P_s \times I_s$$

Since I_s is assumed to be a inverse function of P_s, a U-shaped preference curve results with a peak at intermediately difficult tasks $(P_s = .5)$ for subjects characterised by the success motive $(M_s > M_f)$, but a negative U-shaped curve implying *avoidance* of intermediately difficult tasks results for those characterised by the motive for avoidance of failure $(M_f > M_s)$.

The basic premise of the theory of achievement motivation is that some individuals seek achievement for its own sake. They will thus undertake tasks which provide them with a reasonable chance of success but avoid those so simple that success is inevitable. By comparison, other individuals seek success because of a strong desire to avoid failure. "Fear of failure" individuals avoid challenging tasks, but undertake tasks where success is inevitable or which are so complex that no one could be expected to succeed. In the latter situation, for the very reason that no one could be expected to succeed, they are protected from the consequence of incompetence. This basic distinction has been found to have empirical reality in situations where choice of degree of difficulty of a task to be undertaken is concerned, where persistence with difficult tasks is measured and in terms of the attributions made concerning the involvement of skill and effort on a task.

High-achievement individuals are indexed by performance on the thematic apperception test. Fear of failure is indexed by means of a questionnaire designed to measure test anxiety (see Atkinson & Feather, 1966). Achievement motivation is argued to be a dimensional, stable, enduring aspect of personality.

Studies of achievement motivation and persistence were initiated by Feather (1961, 1967). He presented subjects with an unsolvable mental problem and measured the period of persistence. The success motive was found to have a complex relationship with persistence in that individuals characterised by high achievement (N_{ach}) showed reduced persistence in conditions of failure. Feather argued that persistence was best defined in terms of competing response tendencies which define the strength of the tendency to complete the task and the strength of the tendency not to complete it (or to complete a different task). Persistence was to be examined in terms of other *alternative* activities. It was assumed that the tendency to keep working at a particular task (task A) would continue as long as the tendency to perform it (T_A) was greater than the tendency to perform an alternative (T_B). Thus, when $(T_A > T_B)$ persistence will occur, but when $(T_B > T_A)$ there will be termination of task A activity. An additional assumption was that the expectation of success would be a factor that weighted the tendency to complete the task. In the main study, half of the subjects began the task with an induced high expectation of success, whereas half began with a high expectation of failure. Subjects high in achievement motive ($M_S > M_F$) persisted longer when the task was presented as relatively easy. Subjects high in fear of failure persisted longer when the task was presented as difficult.

An example of the importance of the achievement motive in the choice about level of difficulty is illustrated by the ring toss game studied by Mouton (1965). Subjects selected a task from one of three difficulty levels after having failed or succeeded on a first task. High-achievement individuals selected a difficult level of the task if they had succeeded on a first task but selected an easier version if they had not. Those characterised by fear of failure selected an easy version after success and a difficult version after failure.

The implicit assumption in work on achievement motivation is that goals on which performance and ultimately assessment of control depend are different. In the case of the high achievement-oriented person, success and competence are part of the plan; the individual does not select to work at, or persist with, a task where success is perceived as unlikely. By contrast, the fear of failure individual could be envisaged as accepting low control in cases where it is seen by others as inevitable: *Failing when it is safe* may be part of the plan; therefore *incompetence* may be planned for in certain circumstances.

ii. Augmenters and Reducers

The possibility that there are individual differences in the perception of stimulation has been developed as a theory of personality and has application for the understanding of pain tolerance, sensation-seeking behaviour, and psychopathology. Petrie (1960) pioneered research on the assumption that socio-cultural influences were largely responsible for the differences in this respect. However, the research led to the postulation of two contrasting styles in terms of response on kinaesthetic figural after-effects. One group of individuals, christened *augmenters*, judged the magnitude of a standard stimulus as larger after stimulation, whereas others, christened *reducers*, judged the standard as smaller. Contrasting responses were also found in the case of the response to pain: Augmenters were found to have increased sensitivity, whereas lowered sensitivity and tolerance were more typical for reducers (Petrie et al., 1958; Petrie, 1960). Finally, the contrasting response styles were evident in sensory deprivation; Petrie reported that augmenters could tolerate longer hours in a tank respirator.

These results fit with the notion that one personality style involves damping or diminishing sensory input, whereas a contrasting style involves augmentation. In spite of some difficulties inherent in the task used by Petrie (see Barnes, 1976), the notion of "strength of the nervous system" as a feature of personality research has received attention in terms of biological correlates (e.g. Buchsbaum, 1978; Zuckerman, 1979; Zuckerman et al., 1980).

Evoked potentials recorded in response to stimulation by means of electroencephalographical techniques, were shown by Buchsbaum et al. (1980) to indicate augmentation in 33.4% of a sample of 209 individuals matched for age and sex. Buchsbaum et al. also reported that evoked potential amplitude correlated with pain responsiveness and with the effects of pharmacological agents in a manner consistent with their known effects.

One of the most reliable associations with augmenting is that of bipolar depressive psychosis. Augmenting patterns have been found among the relatives of bipolar depressives (see Gershon & Buchsbaum, 1977). Lithium, which reduces manic aspects of mood and behaviour, also changes the augmenting pattern to one of reduction (Buchsbaum et al., 1980).

The implication for understanding planning and strategic response is at the level of the perception of the evidence. If an augmenter over-reacts to stimulation, the evidence on which he bases the majority of his daily plans could sensationalise or over-represent reality, resulting in plans not well-tailored to circumstance; goals and sub-goals are likely to contain different elements. The individual may well be attracted to action, heightened social activity, and stimulation seeking as a way of coping with events in life history.

Zuckerman (1983) lists four dimensions of sensation seeking identified as factors in the development of sensation-seeking scales. The first is the desire for thrill and adventure as obtained from activities such as parachuting and diving. These and related activities offer physical sensations produced by defiance of gravity or speeded activity. They may also operate to challenge a person to achieve control by the exercise of competence. This exercise in itself may provide stimulation and subsequent satisfaction. The second is described as "experience seeking" and involves the desire to have new experiences by means of music, art, or travel as well as by drugs or nonconformity. This may be close to the third, termed "disinhibition," which describes pursuit of sensation by social and sexual means and includes drinking alcohol. Finally, there is "boredom susceptibility," which involves a restless response to lack of variety and change and a dislike of dull, routine situations.

Sensation seeking as defined by scores on the Zuckerman scale appears to predict those who will volunteer for unusual activities such as encounter groups, experiments, hypnosis, meditation training. Therefore, it might be expected that plans run by sensation seekers will include adventurous rather than passive elements. Manifest features of strategic response may reflect this overall disposition; action rather than inaction should be the most likely response to a problem.

iii. Extraversion and Introversion

The traits of extraversion, neuroticism, and psychoticism have been identified by H.J. Eysenck (1967, 1973, 1977). Extraversion is the dimension
described by sociability and impulsivity; those who are high on extraversion
as measured by the scales devised and modified by Eysenck and his colleagues, are more likely to seek stimulation and social support, less likely
to plan activities but rather to act on impulse, to persist less, and to be
less likely to withstand a drop in stimulation. By comparison, those who
score high on introversion have a greater tendency to seek solitude and
"quiet" environments, to plan for action, and to show persistence. Eysenck
has provided evidence to suggest that these personality characteristics are
biologically based; for example introverts have been found to condition
more easily than extraverts, which has led Eysenck to postulate that for
the introvert, cortical arousal is high, whereas for the extravert, inhibition
predominates.

According to Eysenck's later model, the hypothetical physiological basis
of extraversion is in terms of arousal level in the brain stem reticular
formation and the cortex. The extravert has a lower resting arousal level
than an introvert, in that both reticular and cortical activation are lower.
This recent development of Eysenck's model (see Eysenck, 1983) is broadly
in line with the two-factor model of tonic and modulating arousal proposed
by Claridge (1967), with the important difference that Claridge developed
evidence based on differences in the sedation threshold and the spiral
after-effect, to suggest that introverts are high in tonic arousal but highly
damped cortically, whereas extraverts are low in tonic arousal but not
damped cortically.

Introversion–extraversion differences should affect ease of learning,
socialisation and stimulation seeking. These factors should influence the
way reality is represented, the goals which are formed and the qualitative
features of plan running: The extravert should be stimulation seeking and
impulsive, with lowered persistence.

B. Speed Constraints

i. Neuroticism and Arousal

It was argued by Fisher (1984a) that the speed and error characteristic
of plans will be influenced by stressful conditions because of decisions made
(e.g. finish a task quickly to limit exposure to stress) or because stress
creates raised arousal and a person has a high disposition to act rather than
remain passive; timing of decision might be advanced or retarded mechanically (see Chapter 9).

The neuroticism factor, which was argued by Eysenck to be orthogonal
to extraversion and defined in terms of autonomic lability, has recently

been explained in terms of the visceral brain or limbic system and its relationship with autonomic activity (see Eysenck, 1983). Eysenck points out that there is a difficulty with assuming that the limbic system has major responsibility for autonomic arousal because of the fractionations that occur between cortical, autonomic, and behavioural systems.

Speculating, we might imagine the individual high in neuroticism to be more likely to produce speeded, error-prone, responses in stress because existing states of tension and arousal increase the tendency to action rather than passivity. An overall strategic characteristic might be: (1) a tendency to choose goals that involve action; (2) a tendency to act with raised speed and decreased caution.

ii. Type A and Type B Personalities

Work on the role of psychological factors in heart disease has given some emphasis to the view that there are two fundamentally different personality styles, which dictate the amount of pressure and strain experienced during life. Type A behaviour is described by Rosenman (1982) as not a personality typology but a "behavioural syndrome" correlated with enhanced neurohormonal responses. It includes ambitiousness; aggressiveness; competitiveness; impatience; raised muscle tension; alertness; rapid speech characteristics; rapid pacing of activities; emotional states of irritation and hostility. The increased pace of activity in the behaviour of Type A individuals is so characteristic that Rosenman et al. (1964) described the behaviour pattern of Type As as driving, competitive, and time-urgent. The Type A behaviour pattern was associated with a two-fold risk for the development of coronary heart disease (CHD) over an 8.5 year period (Rosenman et al., 1975).

The Framingham Type A scale was developed by Haynes et al. (1978) and appeared to provide a reasonable prediction of the incidence and prevalence of CHD after 8 years of follow-up. It included 10 questions on time-urgency and competitiveness. The key features of the scale included being pressed for time, being dominating, eating too quickly, and having a strong need to excel in most things. Type A's were in the upper 50% of the scores, Type B's were in the lower 50%.

Rosenman describes Type A behaviour as a response style that leads to chronic performance at near maximum capacity. Type A's show hyper-responsiveness to challenging situations and are characterised by raised levels of noradrenaline. Type A's also report more stressful life events. Rosenman argues that active coping with stressors leads to raised noradrenaline in Type A's. (See Rosenman, 1982.)

In terms of the characteristics of strategies, it would be reasonable to expect that Type A's would conceive of goals oriented to action and success, especially in competitive situations. As far as qualitative aspects of planning profile are concerned, they would prefer action to passivity, should have a high disposition to respond and to produce fast rather than slow responses.

Again, this would produce the action-oriented, impatient, speeded response profile.

The neurotic extravert and the Type A personality might be expected to have common features in the response to stress. Speed might be an expected characteristic in both cases; but extraverts might be distinguished by impulsivity and sensation seeking.

iii. Inert and Overactive Response Patterns

Early work in the late 1940s by Davis (1948) was concerned with pilot error on a simulated cockpit task. Pilots returned regularly to the cockpit and worked for set periods. As part of the programme of experiments, pilot behaviour was investigated under conditions of fatigue and conditions of overload. Two distinct patterns of behaviour were observed. A test involving 355 pilots was designed to investigate individual differences in feelings and reaction patterns. About 75% who showed no changes in their behaviour were classified as "normal." Of the remainder, a distinction was made between two different reactions based on the ratio of the total duration of errors (the sum of side-slip and air speed in the simulator) to the scores of control movements (the sum of aileron and elevator errors). The 59 subjects whose scores were high relative to the total duration of errors were classed as *overactive*. The 28 subjects whose scores of total duration of errors were high relative to the movement scores were classed as *inert*.

The overactivity reaction was characterised by large scores on all control movements. The errors in instrument reading were small and of short duration. As the task progressed, movements on controls became large and irregular. Responses to instrument deviations were described as excessive, the extent and gradient of the movements increased, and over-correcting was frequent. Movements were described as "restless." The increase in activity was especially evident when demands were made on subjects. Subjects in this category reported feeling excited, strained, tense and irritable, and sometimes anxious. They reported feeling impatient and having a sense of urgency about corrections. The task seemed more difficult because of the excessive movements, but this was blamed on the machine. In spite of these feelings the subjects wished to improve and remained keen to do well. Sometimes aggression was manifest, largely in irregular, violent manipulations of controls such as the fuel cock. Swearing and thumping the instrument panel were apparent.

The inertia reation was observed usually after increased activity. Errors in instrument reading were high; activity on controls was low. Deterioration was selective and the investigators felt that those aspects which subjects felt to be important were preserved. There was less evidence of restless or hurried movement. Subjects reported feeling bored. Strain was replaced by feelings of tedium and tiredness. Subjects even admitted to day-dreaming.

The implications for plan running are that the *overactive pattern* is a form of "running fast" and may be seen as a speed/accuracy trade-off adjustment in favour of speed. Movements are quick and restless with over-correction being characteristic. By contrast, the *inert pattern* (which may be a secondary state) is characterised by slow, lethergic, tired movements. The planning process is slowed but this is not necessarily to advantage, in that sampling errors are apparent and changes in instrument readings are not quickly detected.

These two aspects of response to a difficult task are of interest because the role of personality differences in the execution of plans is underlined. Irrespective of the plans chosen for implementation, the functional characteristics of execution are likely to vary.

C. Attributional Constraints

An additional factor that might influence plan construction is the attribution of responsibility for failed plans previously run. One of the pioneer studies which established a difference between individuals' reactions to the occurrence of failure was the Harvard study by Funkenstein et al. (1957). This study, already described briefly in previous sections of this book, involved the participation of intelligent students, anxious to perform well in front of their tutors. Students attended regular sessions in which they were encouraged to do well in tests of intelligence and ability. On the fifteenth session, a situation of failure was contrived; each subject was presented with an unsolvable problem and encouraged to solve it. On subsequent examination, three classes of response to failure were observed. These were *anxiety*; *anger-in* (self-blaming or intrapunitive response); and *anger-out* (other-blaming or extrapunitive response). Cardiovascular changes symptomatic of the secretion of epinephrine (adrenaline) were found to be characteristic of anger-in and anxiety. Cardiovascular changes symptomatic of the secretion of norepinephrine (noradrenaline) were found to be characteristic of anger-out. Actual levels of epinephrine and norepinephrine were not measured. The authors favoured the idea that response to failure was a cognitive style. Their data showed a high degree of predictive accuracy from friends of subjects suggesting the failure response to be a stable response tendency.

In terms of their ability to master a situation that was emotionally disturbing, some subjects took a positive attitude and decided to beat the experimenter in subsequent tests, whereas others became apprehensive and reported feeling upset for some time and unable to take part in future tests. Funkenstein et al. (1957) quoted a typical response: "I was upset for several days after leaving here. I thought of it all during the week and can't see the sense of these experiments. It's too upsetting and I don't want to take part in any more experiments like the last one. It was horrible (p. 122)."

Funkenstein et al. reported that anger-in was more characteristic of those students within the Harvard catchment who were from a higher socioeconomic class. A high norepinephrine/epinephrine ratio is argued to be typical of infants. The authors argue that the "acculturation" of the child results in the production of the more civilised reactions of anger-in and anxiety, which being self-related results in a great deal of psychological suffering.

The data also showed that there were significant associations between family patterns and the nature of acute emergency reactions experienced under the threat of failure. For the anger-out group the father was perceived as the chief source of authority and their relationship with their fathers was poor. For the anger-in group, the father was perceived as the chief source of authority but the relationship was close and affectionate.

One major implication for the understanding of the planning process is that the attributional bias for outcomes might be expected to affect subsequent plan formulation. If a person blames himself for failure, the likely result is pessimism about future potential for effective response. Avoidance of blame might be a determinant of aim and may influence subgoals.

3. COPING STRATEGIES

In the previous section we identified a number of "dispositions" as not mutually exclusive stable characteristics of a person which might determine the features of strategies used in all life situations including stressful encounters. Generalising, both policy and stylistic aspects of strategy may be differentially reflected. The impulsive person, the sensitisor, or the Type A personality might be expected to prefer action to passivity—"doing" is more important than letting events happen. Equally, the individual characterised by any one of these attributes might *execute* conceived plans differently. The tendency to act rather than not act might lead to a response style which is fast and error prone.

The "goals" that determine the characteristic of strategies may reflect more fundamental aspects of personality. A person who fears failure or who wishes to avoid a situation where blame is attached for failure, may avoid taking responsibility for action. A person who refuses to map out reasonable goals to achieve an aim may be someone who has a master aim not to get into difficult or demanding situations. Avoidance or denial strategies may be the result.

Throughout this chapter we have not introduced the internality/externality distinction, primarily because this has been dealt with extensively earlier in the book. Although the dimension is unlikely to be unitary, there is evidence that internals and externals are distinguished in their approach to negative encounters. In particular, internalisers are more likely to be information-seekers and are more likely to engage a problem rather than avoid it. We might expect this to influence the features of goals that are constructed.

A. Psychoanalytic Approaches

There are many different descriptive and explanatory accounts of coping strategies operated by individuals. The psychoanalysts could be argued to have developed a wholly deterministic view in which the individual is not merely constrained by factors from the past reflecting in his personality; he is determined by them. The Freudian psychoanalytic therapist views the patient as being in a state which is the result of internal adjustments within personality to events in the formative years of life. Thus, mechanisms such as projection, denial, repression, sublimation, represent adjustments produced at an earlier time as a result of tensions between the id, the ego, and the superego. These are not strategies as dealt with so far in this book because the individual is "functionally pre-wired" and is assumed by psychoanalytic theory to have no choice and no knowledge of the cause of personal thoughts, emotions, and feelings. Yet it could be argued that the techniques, once evolved to resolve conflict, although not consciously selected, were once strategic. They are no longer functional as personality dispositions later in life and must be "cured." Persistence of adaptive strategies "out of context" may be a key factor in mental health.

B. Cognitive Approaches to Coping

Lazarus (1966) asserts that the term "coping" refers to "strategies for dealing with threat (p. 151)." Lazarus favours a distinction between "mastery," the major aspect of which is achievement, and "coping," which involves efforts to meet threat. Clinical interest in coping strategies is more concerned with threat than with challenge. Lazarus emphasises the importance of appraisal as a basis for coping processes. Thus, in his view, coping involves awareness and cognitive activity. The reader should refer to the detailed accounts provided by Lazarus of the nature of coping.

An important point emphasised by Folkman (1984) is that a definition of coping should not confound strategy with success of outcome. The effectiveness of the coping strategy is less important than the fact that some attempt has been made to manage demands made. Thus, a definition favoured by Folkman and Lazarus (1980) and Lazarus and Launier (1978) is that coping refers to cognitive and behavioural efforts to master the environment. Folkman points out that this definition differs from popular conceptions of "coping," where successful outcomes mean that coping has occurred and unsuccessful outcomes mean that it has not.

Folkman distinguishes coping techniques aimed at regulating emotions and distress, from those aimed at the problem causing the distress. These two aspects of coping are termed "emotion-focused" and "problem-focused" coping, respectively. In the latter case the meaning or value of a situation may be changed ("failing an examination is not the end of the world"), or the implications of a negative outcome reviewed ("it's an experience that I can learn from and I won't make the same mistake again"). Emotion-focused coping might be difficult to distinguish from defensive or denial strategies. The person is helpless to control the problem via any domain but ameliorates the pain of the thoughts about the problem by trying not to think about it, making himself busy, etc. Use of tranquillisers and alcohol may provide an aid to emotion-focused coping; when all else fails, a powerful form of control might be to damp down the feelings.

4. SITUATIONAL DETERMINANTS OF COPING STRATEGIES

An important aspect of behaviour in stress, emphasised throughout this book, is that stresses create special conditions for strategy in that the termination of the stress is the end-goal or aim. At the same time, stresses may mechanically create conditions of high arousal or high mental load, resulting in changes in efficiency. Circumstance as well as personality factors may act to constrain the main features of strategy.

Fisher (1984a) itemised three principal ways in which changes in arousal or mental load might influence the conception and running of plans. One influence is on *plan ingredients* because of changes in memory and attention. In stress, a person may not note or remember the same aspects of his environment as he would normally. Secondly, there may be changes in *plan running—arousal increase* may cause a person to speed up, "running fast"; *arousal decrease* may cause a person to be slow and to process information poorly. Error rate may relate directly to speed change. Finally, there are changes in plan monitoring; a person may become less aware of his own actions and more prone to produce "automatic," unchecked activity.

If we imagine that every situation that presents itself is associated with an "ideal strategy" for solution based on all available facts surrounding a situation, circumstantial factors and personality dispositions that *favour* approximations to that ideal strategy will be successful. Those which mismatch will be unsuccessful or will create further problems. The balance between ideal and personally favoured strategies may be the ultimate determinant of the long-term effect of life events.

5. A TYPOLOGY OF COPING STRATEGIES BASED ON CONTROL

A. Cognitive Facts in Decisions About Control

The cognitive approach assumes that coping strategies are *rational* responses to the appraisals a person makes about an unpleasant or challenging situation. The control model of coping provides a more specific set of ideas about the cognitive processes involves in coping. A realistic assessment should take account of:

1. Valence of the situation—challenge or threat.
2. The domain of control involved—personal, interpersonal, socio-political (and its compatibility with a person's preferred domain of control).
3. Mode of control (control by avoidance; control by direct action, problem solving and struggle; control by irrelevant means; emotion-focused control).

The notion that decisions are rational raises complex issues concerning subjectivity. Any situation can be described by a large number of facts. The individual might utilise some facts and not others in deciding on the goals. It is possible that what seems irrational to an outside observer may have a perfectly good, logical inferential structure which the individual does not make explicit. We should perhaps operate by analogy with the old legal code of "rational until proven irrational."

B. The Marionette Model of the Ingredients of Strategies

The concept of a marionette provides us with a very useful analogy for depicting constraints which should determine the selection of coping strategies in stressful encounters. A marionette is constrained by the strings attached to its limbs. The number and position of the strings together with the tension imposed on the strings by the operator determine the profile of the activity of the marionette. The analogy is useful but not perfect because in the case of a real marionette, control is total; what we wish to propose is constraint in the conception and execution of strategies.

Three sources of constraint can be identified: (1) personality dispositions and cognitive styles; (2) life experiences and knowledge; (3) current stress influences, including self-assessment of likely sources of influence. We also want to distinguish particular *aspects* of influence on total behaviour. This would be like asking where on the stage the marionette model dances, what description characterises the form of the dance (polka, jive, waltz), and what movement characteristics are manifest (fast/slow; careful/risky; discrete/flamboyant; etc.).

Figure 11.1 indicates a number of aspects where constraints will operate. There is a likely effect on the ingredients for plans, and the style in which plans are run ("policy and stylistic components"). Equally, attributional style may determine which plans we run (avoid self-blame/accept personal responsibility, etc.).

Figure 11.2 illustrates the likely influences of both circumstantial/stress factors and personality constraints on the details of the planning processes. It is assumed that these constraints operate as bias in decision making; a person will be more likely to conceive of one type of goal rather than another or will be more likely to favour executing the strategy in one way rather than another. This in effect means that a *critical path* is dictated through the matrix of decisions concerned with control.

i. Formulating goals

It is assumed that the problem a person confronts occurs because of a mismatch between what is desired (intention) and reality (state of the world). Personality factors, knowledge, and beliefs can determine intentions and thus provide a different initial input. We might imagine there are many situations where personality factors such as competitiveness, attitude to achievement and failure might be critical determinants of goals. One role of confiding relationships with other people might be to provide the individual with new perspectives and introduce new facts in cognition.

ii. Stylistic Determinants of Policy Decisions

Stylistic or qualitative aspects of personality are assumed to influence both the way plans are executed and the formulation of goals. A person who prefers fast action and "doing" rather than being passive is not only more likely to execute plans in a way which emphasises activity, but may conceive of goals oriented round "doing" rather than passivity. It would be simplistic to consider that goals depend solely on the utilisation of facts in cognition.

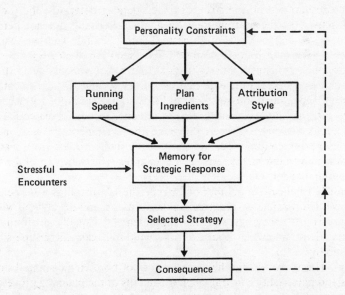

FIG. 11.1   The marionette model of personality constraint on the policy and stylistic components of plans.

iii. Limitations in Domain Selected

The idea that individuals seek control in different domains, fits with research suggesting that internality–externality is not a single dimension, and also aids understanding of cases where control is relinquished without causing stress (riding in public transport, consulting medical or dental help, etc.). The evidence was reviewed in earlier chapters and it was argued that there were three major domains of control (personal, interpersonal, and socio-political). Different conditions and different personality constraints may operate to favour one domain rather than another. It was argued by Fisher (1985b) that lack of wealth and status make seeking control in

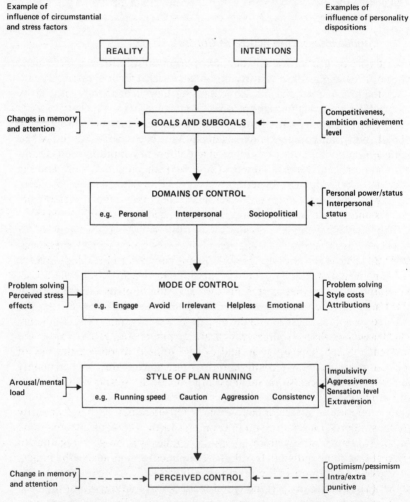

FIG. 11.2   Personality and circumstantial constraint on policy and stylistic elements of strategies.

interpersonal and socio-political domains less likely. A person who lacks money or status may not be able to "buy" help from other people and perhaps has less chance of achieving political change. If an appliance is broken, one person can afford to have it mended; another must try to mend it himself or do without it. Therefore, we might think of circumstantial factors causing "domain limitations." Limitations could be expected to decrease as a function of wealth, status, education, and skill. In accordance with earlier proposals, a person is expected to explore the potential for control in different domains, opting for the one most likely to achieve success. Personal constraints increase the likelihood of certain domains being consulted; circumstantial factors dictate the likelihood of particular domains being appropriate.

iv. Constraints on the Mode of Control

Both circumstantial and personal dispositions may influence the "mode" of control—a person faced with a stressful situation may: (1) struggle with the problem; (2) operate an avoidance strategy; (3) operate control by irrelevant means; (4) become passive.

In recent research on stress and anxiety, response styles such as repression denial and social impression management have been identified and linked with self-reports of both psychological and physical symptoms. Self-deceivers and repressors reported fewer symptoms (Linden et al., 1985) and the style is linked with the hypertensive personality. Thus, use of avoidant strategies based on deception of self and others may involve personality factors and reflect constraint on the mode of control.

The marionette model provides a basis for conceptualising the risk for an adverse response to a stressful encounter. As a result of life experiences and personality, certain settings of the strings are determined and levels of tension on the strings are set. The marionette dances within these constraints. The dance then represents the execution of plans and the form of the dance manifests the parameters of personality and experience. The learned resourcefulness model developed by Rosenbaum (see Rosenbaum, 1983) assumes that resources which are acquired during life history are brought to each new situation and can be utilised to reduce the risk of adverse response. This "counterharm" or resistance feature of personality and experience can also be manifest in terms of the setting on the strings of the marionette.

One important aspect of counterharm resource may be the propensity to resist depression in stressful encounters. In the previous chapter some of the evidence, mostly from laboratory studies was brought together to suggest that some individuals will use techniques for minimising the impact of stressful encounters in life. In stress, subjects with low depression scores show: (1) raised effort; (2) increased tendency to find out about the task; (3) increased tendency to distort the evidence in the direction of optimism (illusion of control); (4) increased tendency to resist blaming attributions;

(5) decreased tendency to be pessimistic about the effects of stress on personal performance as compared with the performance of others ("personal" rather than "universal" optimism).

We assume that these tendencies are represented as bias in decision making and are of personal value for the individual: Life is a bad deal and only the potentially non-depressed resist accepting evidence that will confirm this. In terms of the marionette model, it is assumed that adjustments are made on the tension of certain strings. These adjustments produce the features of the dance of the marionette; perhaps only certain dance steps are used or only some parts of the floor used.

Social psychologists will no doubt argue that the evidence for stress-resistant approaches to life is highly circumscribed and based largely on laboratory conditions. The fact that the evidence is laboratory based does not mean that people are not differentiated in this way in life, but indicates a need for scientific inquiry. Accounts of survivors in disasters, from the Andes air crash disaster to survival of the atrocious conditions of the Nazi death camps, imply that there are important differences in patterns of personal behaviour in survivors and non-survivors. By careful examination of the behaviour of different individuals in life stress encounters, it might be possible to identify some of the resistant techniques described above.

6.   LIFE EXPERIENCES AND DECISION: OPPOSING BELIEFS AND COSTS

The above considerations lead to a concept of stressful experiences in terms of cognitive networks. For every potential stress or threat encountered by an individual there are facts about the problem, about possible courses of action that can be taken, and about the likely consequences of action.

Personal and environmental constraints operate to determine the *particular pathways a person will take in the network of decisions*. These decisions concern the goals and subgoals, the domains of control, the mode of control, and the style of action. An important, so-far neglected variable is that of the *cost* of participation in a scenario, or the "penalty" attached to use of a particular strategy. Decisions about costs provide an additional way in which personality and circumstantial factors unite to determine the form of manifest strategies.

For each set of major decisions, goals, domain of control, mode of control, and execution style, there will be "stop rules," which will cause a person to terminate consideration of a particular possibility. A particular decision considered could be effective but abandoned because of the "cost" factors. A person might consider it perfectly acceptable to attempt to cure his mother's illness by obtaining medical help but decide against it because "Doctors are no good," or because "conventional medicine favours chemotherapy which will make my mother ill." Alternatively, a person might decide against seeking help in favour of personal control (self-help) but then perceive high cost attached to responsibility: "if I tried to make mother better and failed, I would live with the guilt for ever."

Linehan et al. (1983) approached the problem of prediction of those individuals most likely to commit suicide by examining the factors *likely to prevent* a person going through with the decision. A precondition for suicide is argued to be a sense of profound pessimism and hopelessness but not all those who experience these feelings attempt suicide. Linehan et al. concentrated on examining the adaptive, life-maintaining characteristics of non-suicidal people and proposed that those who attempt suicide have a belief system which gives low values on "reasons for living." A "reason for living inventory" designed by the authors involved the following items: (1) survival and coping; (2) responsibility to family; (3) child-related concerns; (4) fear of suicide; (5) fear of social disapproval; (6) moral objections. Those subjects with "para-suicide" histories had lower scores on survival, coping, responsibility to family, child-related, and moral objections. The "fear of suicide" items distinguish those who have thought about suicide from time to time from para-suicides; the former have higher fear scores. Positive beliefs about survival and coping distinguish those with a history of serious suicidal behaviour from those with minimal tendencies.

Taken collectively, the evidence suggests that a system of positive beliefs about the value of living, together with fear of dying, will favour decisions against suicide. The authors did not demonstrate whether a sense of profound hopelessness and depression might influence these previously held beliefs, but clearly demonstrated that survival beliefs, if strong enough, will weigh against the decision to die.

It might be useful to examine *reasons against a particular strategy* in the context of coping with life experiences. The marionette model needs to include the idea of strings which are sited and constrained to prevent movement of specified types. A person may have reasons against phobic avoidance of conditions he dislikes: "it's cowardly to run away; you have got to learn to face it"; or reasons against the struggle for control: "take life as it comes," "you have got to learn to take it." These belief systems dictate the balance of outcomes in particular situations.

Cost may be an important aspect of strategies. If there is high cost attached to failure, alternative domains or methods of control may have to be substituted. Equally, if there is high cost to a particular style of performance (e.g. speed is exhausting), then that aspect may be changed (e.g. take it easy and save effort). Increase in effort may be part of a depression-resistant approach but when this is the case there may be some high-cost penalty involved. It is possible that the non-depressed give a high enough weighting to overall success and that the increased penalty for raised effort is acceptable.

In summary, we might imagine that strategic behaviour involves a number of critical decisions, not necessarily hierarchically ordered. Personality traits and transient states produced by stress, combine to exercise constraints. The constraints create settings on parameters which determine the manifestation of selected strategies. These parameter settings could be argued to provide a representation of the *risk* of negative outcomes, of loss of control, of personal crisis, and ultimately long-term health.

12

A Cognitive Model of Stress and Disease: An Attempted Synthesis

In this book there has been an attempt to understand the effects of stress in terms of the implications for strategies for achieving control. It could be argued that people use strategies to achieve desired goals in all aspects of problems in daily life. Stressful circumstances merely create additional and vital problems for the individual. Whether these problems are seen as challenging and positive or distressing and negative depends on circumstance. A particular feature of circumstance is the perception of control: If control is possible, the stress will be seen as demanding and challenging; if control is not possible but the stress is threatening, high distress is a likely outcome. Yet the perception of control is a demanding and complex cognitive process which either depends on noting contingent relationships between action and outcome or on noting progress made.

Personality and situational constraints are assumed to influence the strategic response to stress: The individual is not free to select strategies. The relationship between a selected strategy and the ideal strategy will determine efficiency and in turn influence perceived control.

In this chapter we consider the implications of some of these ideas for a model of stress and disease and attempt to produce a synthesis. Because this book is intended for advanced students as well as researchers, there is some attempt to provide details of existing models as well as some indication of methodological difficulties in this complex research area. Because of the confines of space, it has been necessary to be selective; where appropriate, references for further reading are indicated.

1. METHODOLOGICAL DIFFICULTIES IN INTERPRETATION OF STRESS AND ILLNESS ASSOCIATIONS

Countless literary and folk-law sources have hinted at relationships between unhappiness and ill health. Many primitive societies incorporate the belief that *disharmony in social relationships* is likely to bring about adverse health effects. Only within the last 30 years or so have scientists begun to take a formal interest in these possibilities. The interest is stimulated by statistical records showing that, for example, the widowed, divorced, single individuals, the coloured minorities, and the poor tend to be more likely to be at risk for a variety of illnesses.

Figure 12.1 shows data redrawn from statistical evidence provided by Berkson (1962) showing the relative increased vulnerability of divorced and single individuals, relative to married US citizens, in terms of a large number of chronic and infectious diseases as well as for aspects of behaviour such as suicide and homicide. The data as shown in the figure indicate sex differences in this respect. Data such as these point to the need to ask the question—what is it about being alone that renders a person vulnerable? More importantly, there is a need to ask what bodily communication processes provide mediating links. The fact that there are sex differences in vulnerability to illnesses suggests a need to understand the role of factors other than those due to being alone or to having experienced disruption in social relationships. Equally, the vulnerability of the single person as well as those who have experienced separation or divorce suggests that change, trauma, and even loneliness itself might be factors.

National Health records in the UK (Connolly, 1975), have provided evidence to suggest not just the vulnerable state of the widower (those over 55 years of age have mortality rates 40% above the expected rate for age-matched married men), but there is a vulnerable period 6 months after bereavement; for the ensuing 8½ years, mortality rates revert to expected levels. A further study cited (but not attributed) by Connolly suggests that in a semi-rural population, the risk of the death of a close relative of the deceased was increased two-fold if the death was in hospital, and five-fold if it had occurred on a road or in a field. Again, social disruption alone is not the only factor implicated.

The statistical records provide perhaps the best clue that there must be an association between life events and vulnerability to ill health. More specific explanations usually raise problems of interpretation. Firstly, the date of the beginning of a life event and the date of commencement of the illness are not always clear; it is possible that the commencement of the illness pre-dates or even causes the illness. If the life event is the death of another person, it is even conceivable that the death is a reaction to (and not a cause of) the behaviour of a respondent with a developing illness. Secondly, in most cases, data suggesting an association between stress and

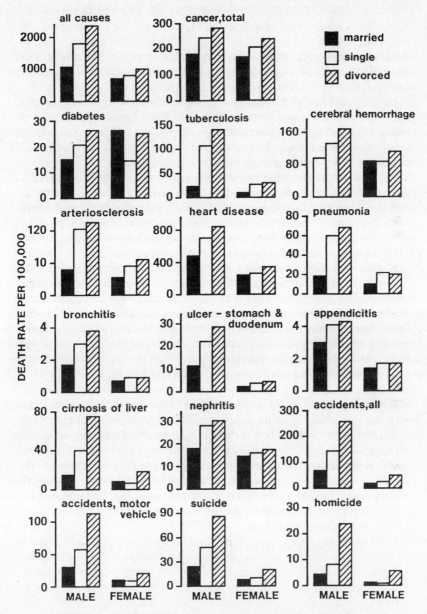

FIG. 12.1 Standardised death rates for different causes of death in the United States. (Data redrawn from Berkson, 1962 (deceased) with the permission of the American Medical Association.)

subsequent illness depend on the recall of the ill or recently recovered patient. It is known that mood state affects the recall of life events (see Lloyd & Lishman, 1975). Further, the effect of having to cope with the symptoms of illness may influence recall of experiences in life; a person may attempt to compensate for, or overreact to, previous life experiences. The "effort after meaning" as a response characteristic of ill people is perhaps enhanced by time spent in bed with little to do.

The view that social change and disruption are somehow linked to high risk of disease is not new. Wolff (1953) provided a very careful review of evidence suggesting that cultural change, developing societies, class mobility, social conflict, and isolation contribute to the risk of ill health. The occurrence of epidemics during periods requiring major readjustment to change and dislocation were originally interpreted in terms of response to adverse conditions such as cold, rain, lack of food, or excessive effort. Increasingly there was acceptance that factors other than adverse environments might be responsible. Sigerist (1932) emphasised that in historical perspective, certain diseases fit into the whole structure of a particular time as if it were part of what was ordered by those in power.

Of particular importance is the development of the notion that even infectious diseases might be affected by cultural and social change. High mortality from tuberculosis has long been associated with migration from rural to urban conditions, or by geographical transitions between countries: High mortality rates were reported in the Bantu natives relocated into the outskirts of the city of Johannesburg; a rise in mortality was reported among the American Indians moved to Indian reservations; and a high rate of tuberculosis was reported among the 1841 Irish immigrants to the USA (see Adams, 1932; McDougall, 1949; Moorman, 1950).

Dubos (unpublished) even noted the relationship between tuberculosis mortality and phases of industrialisation. His investigations led to a somewhat startling observation that the peak incidence of tuberculosis mortality occurs in a society 10–20 years after industrialisation has taken place (see Wolff, 1940). This underlines the need to continue to entertain the hypothesis that poor living conditions as a result of social change are possible determinants of risk. Thus, a model is needed to account for all aspects of mobility in relation to susceptibility to ill health.

2. COMMON DENOMINATORS OF LIFE EVENTS AND ILLNESS

A. Changes in Life History

One noted common denominator of social and cultural mobility is *change*. Social and cultural mobility together with sudden traumatic life events, represent forms of change during the life history of the individual. Change has a number of simultaneous effects: The individual is prevented from continuing with on-going activities, may for a time have no substitute activity, and then may be exposed to new environments which make new demands and over which there is low control. If we reduce all life-event characteristics to the common denominator of change, the question arises of what it is about change that increases the risk of illness.

Research developed by Holmes and Rahe (1967) attempted to quantify the stress levels incurred by experience of different life events. The social readjustment rating scale was designed as a set of 42 life events. Endorsement of one or more of these events gave a crude index of the cumulative experience of change. A refinement of the scale involved estimates of the amount of readjustment entailed by each event. "Marriage" was given an arbitrary score of 500 and subjects assigned scores to the remainder of the events using it as a reference point. This provided the basis for a weighting of events in "life change units" (LCU) represented by the average score for each item divided by 10.

LCU scores have been related to illness occurrence both prospectively and restrospectively (Birley & Connolly, 1976; Rahe, 1972). A fairly common pattern emerges. There is an increase in LCUs for a period of up to one to two years before the occurrence of an illness. In the case of ischaemic heart disease, for example, LCUs increased from 20 to 40 in 3 months prior to the event (see Theorell, 1970).

In general however, the power of LCU scales to predict illness is low. The scale has greatest predictive power in the case of major illness. In any case, the scale, although of practical value, provides little by way of insights as to what it is about change that increases the risk of ill health.

Laboratory work (Mandler & Watson, 1966; Mandler, 1975) has suggested that interruption of on-going activities is a precondition for tension release. Although Mandler's results might be circumscribed, it is possible that social change produces periods of tension and arousal because routines are interrupted. The "mind-grabbing" qualities of previous lifestyle and environment are evident in the phenomenon of homesickness (Fisher et al., 1984, 1985a, c), which is a cognitive-emotional "grief" experience involving frequent mental preoccupation with the "home" or previous environment. Even children at boarding school who do not report homesickness, do report greater periods of worry attached to "home" as compared with "school"-oriented problems when they attend boarding school for the first time: The "old" environment continues to have psychological influence.

B. Social Disruption Models

Greater attention has generally been paid to social disruption and isolation as the common denominators of adverse life events including social and cultural evolution. Slightly different "common denominators" have been identified by researchers. The descriptive labels vary slightly but there are common themes associated with disequilibrium, disruption, loss of social integration and consistency. The emphasis in these models is on the ingredients that create threat rather than on analysis of the responses the individual might make to such a threat. Thus we argue that the models fall short of providing the basis for a complete explanation of social change, life events, and the association with illness.

i. Wolff's Social Anxiety Model

Wolff (1953) formulated four main postulates, which he argued could represent the basis of a "social change" model of illness propensity:

1. The changes for man affect the folklore and taboos of his culture.
2. Many of the dangers are overexaggerated, creating anxiety.
3. Formalised methods for dealing with it are prescribed by the culture.
4. In changing or deteriorating cultures, the method of resolution of tension ceases to be operative therefore the anxiety factors persist.

Wolff (1953) thus argued that conditions that violate laws and taboos create anxiety leading to illness: "when a culture either changes rapidly or deteriorates, the anxiety-resolving systems break down before the culturally engendered anxieties became attenuated (p. 12)."

An example given by Wolff to illustrate this point is of a taboo in Hopi Indian culture concerning avoidance of treading on a snake's track. In the event of an accident of this sort, pain would occur in the ankles and feet and would be dealt with by the medicine man. When cultural development led to the loss of the medicine man, the taboo still continued and no therapeutic procedure for coping with pain in the ankles and feet existed.

One important way in which Wolff's approach is different from more recent approaches is that there is some emphasis on the importance of coping responses. Wolff argues that a "conspicuous portion of man's illness is a function of his goals, his methods of attaining them and the conflicts they engender (p. 12)." These ideas fit with the control-based model to be developed in this chapter, in that Wolff does not assume that social change is a sufficient condition for illness; it is that social change prevents or alters the social facility for coping with disruption, thus leading to the persistence of anxiety.

ii. Dodge and Martin's Social Integration Model

The model developed by Dodge and Martin (1970) was largely stimulated by observations of the rise in chronic disease levels in modern, industrial civilisation in the USA. Regional (inter-state) differences as well as sex and marital status differences in chronic disease are apparent in the statistical records. The approach is detailed and it is impossible to present an adequate representation within the confines of this chapter. The interested student is advised to read the original book.

Dodge and Martin report the persistence of variations in chronic disease (cardiovascular disease, cancerous disease, diabetic disease, gastrointestinal ulcers) across US states as a function of sex, race, age, and marital status. The differential statistics they see as posing two problems:

1. The need to account for variations in time, of the incidence and prevalence of chronic disease morbidity and mortality.
2. The need to account for differences in disease morbidity and mortality in subpopulations as a function of age, sex, race, and marital status.

In their account they emphasise the possible influences of differences in lifestyle, nutrition, and climate, the likely influence of availability of medical resources, and the necessary wealth and geographical location which enable these resources to be fully utilised. They present a social integration model of the origins of disease: The empirical evidence rests on observed patterns of correlations concerning suicide rates, infant mortality rates, and chronic disease levels between states. Infant mortality rates are used as an index of general health; high rates of infant mortality represent a poor health milieu. Suicide rates are argued to provide a benchmark of social stress. The two death rates, when brought together with the death rate from chronic disease, provide the basis for explanation in terms of either "health milieu" or "social stress." According to Dodge and Martin (1970): "The more a chronic disease is distributed differently than the infant mortality rate and similarly to the suicide rate, the greater is the expectation that the cause of death is stress linked (p. 183)."

An example of the way arguments proceed from evidence is given by heart disease: arteriosclerotic heart disease rates show a distribution across the 31 states which is different from infant mortality rates but is similar to the suicide rates. This suggests ateriosclerotic heart disease to be linked with stress rather than with the health milieu of the community.

The findings of importance concern the role of variables such as age and marital integration. Thus, malignant neoplastic disease (cancer) is distributed differently across the states than infant mortality and is correlated positively with suicide incidence, although only for the older age group. With regard to marital status, age-standardised death rates from heart disease and neoplastic disease are inversely related among marital status to a measure of marital integration with age. Whatever immunity (or lack of immunity) is provided by marital status, varies with age.

Dodge and Martin favour a social-disruption hypothesis to account for the better correlational patterns between suicide rates and chronic disease than between infant mortality rates and chronic disease. They argue that life experiences, perceptions, and adaptive capacity play an important part as determinants of the risk of disease but that social integration is the major risk variable. "Almost all of man's goals, interests and objectives are

achieved through social participating with his fellows (p. 59)." Social participation is hypothesised as highly valued and banishment is punishing.

The first postulate of the social integration model is that *the incidence of chronic disease varies with level of socially induced stress*. Therefore, loss of social support by banishment, death, or divorce would provide a precon-dition for increased risk of ill health. A second related postulate is that *the extent of socially induced stress varies inversely with the stability and dura-bility of social relationships in that population*.

The authors then argue that in order to maintain stable and durable relationships with others, individuals must conform to rules and expecta-tions. This leads to the third postulate: *the stability and durability of social relationships within a population vary with the extent to which individuals conform to the socially sanctioned demands made by others*. The authors point out that people have to fulfil multiple roles. Every individual occupies a number of statuses simultaneously and this increases the likelihood that demands made in one role interfere with demands made by another. This leads to a fourth postulate: *the extent to which members of a population conform to demands made by others, varies inversely with the extent to which members of the population are subjected to role conflicts*. This in turn is linked to a fifth postulate which proposes that *the extent of role conflict is linked with the extent to which an individual occupies incompatible statuses*.

These postulates are linked to two final postulates concerning status integration. A person does not normally occupy incompatible statuses simul-taneously and there are assumed to be social checks against this. However, in some cases, particularly in urban societies, there may be less coherent status integration. Incompatible roles and poor status integration are argued by the authors to be linked with increased incidence of chronic disease.

The authors are largely concerned with chronic disease, by which is meant long-duration disease processes—heart disease, cancerous disease, diabetes. They envisage an aetiological complex of three elements: (1) the disease-producing agent; (2) the nature of the environment in which host and agent are brought together; (3) the resistance and susceptibility of the host. A scale is proposed in which at one end are acute diseases caused by antigens and at the other end are chronic diseases that can be caused by stress alone. The authors argue that there is an empirically demonstrated relationship between measures of status integration (not clearly defined) and stress-related chronic disease; correlations are negative and high for arteriosclerotic heart disease and malignant neoplasms (cancer), but low for leukaemia and aleukaemia. The authors do not provide detailed analysis for biological links with the disease process.

iii. Totman's Social Consistency Model

The position taken by Totman (1979) has much in common with the approach of Dodge and Martin in its emphasis on breakdown of social rules as a determinant of disease. Totman reviews the evidence from a number of areas of research concerned with illness patterns following significant life events. He notes that social factors exert a protective influence on health and that the individual at risk is one who has incurred social mobility, status incongruity, or a high degree of social change, and is unable to relate to his changed situation in a meaningful way.

Totman proposes a structural theory based on the assumption that the understanding of other people's actions depends on relating what is perceived to social rules and conventions. People have a propensity to form concepts. Judgements may be described by a hierarchical model; at the top are very general judgements; further down the hierarchy are very fine discriminations. For a person to make sense of another person's actions, he must have a set of "prescriptive rules," which could be represented as values on the structure of norms. Consistency is an important feature of Totman's model. For rules to exist, they must be resistant to change; although some clarification of rules can occur as a result of habitual action. Major changes in rules will be brought about by a change at a high level of structure. Two situations are envisaged: One is where a person acts consistently with internally represented rules and there are no mismatches. The other is where radical modification of rules is required. According to Totman (1979) it is the latter situation which is likely to produce "inconsistent, fitful and uncertain social behaviour (p. 176)."

With regard to the origins of disease, Totman argues that the critical factor is the absence of registered consistency. Tenure of inflexible or rigid rules which are restrictive or which supersede the capacity of the individual will render him vulnerable. Equally, changes in the social environment (exits, losses, separations), severance from a reference group, or experience of attack on the rules themselves put a person at risk. Mental states such as depression and helplessness are merely additional symptoms of the physical malfunction. The model could be argued to be concerned rather more with description of preconditions of stress than with the precise mechanisms by which these experiences might create illness.

The control model as proposed here provides a description of the common denominators of change and an explanation of changes in the risk of illness. It assumes that inconsistency between what is expected and what happens creates an experience of loss of control. Loss of control itself can be threatening, (as when brakes fail to work when a car is being driven), but may also be perceived as challenging. A model is needed which includes the notion that a person faced with threats will attempt to change the situation. Coping (or failure to cope) is regarded as an important determinant of illness. However changes in circumstances must be linked to the biological states which are preconditions for disease. Biological models linking perceived threat to illness provide a further link for the control model. These are therefore considered first.

C. Biological Pathology Models

A biological account of how it is that stress increases the risk of a heart attack, or helps a virus establish itself, must ultimately be concerned with routes from threat experience to the development of malfunction.

i. Sterling and Eyer's Arousal Pathology Model

Sterling and Eyer (1981) have attempted to provide a unified account of the social origins of disease and the underlying arousal pathology this results in. Sterling and Eyer extend the idea developed by Cannon (1932, 1936) that physiological changes in stress are part of a highly functional emergency response. They argue against the traditional physicians' view that "internal constancy" of the body, determined by the operation of self-regulatory feedback loops, is occasionally disrupted and should be corrected by drugs or surgery. Instead they argue that the symptoms of disruption make sense as part of the coping resources of the individual.

Sterling and Eyer describe a number of autonomous regulatory controls which act to self-limit physiological response. For example, a rise in the concentration of glucose in the blood stimulates the pancreas to secrete insulin. Insulin encourages the uptake of sugar by muscle, fat, and liver cells, thus providing the basis of a negative feedback loop due to drop in concentration of glucose in the blood.

Having described a number of autoregulatory systems, Sterling and Eyer identify the major forms of brain control over these mechanisms and then pose the interesting question of why it is that there needs to be neural control of self-regulatory mechanisms. One answer, they argue, lies in the *efficiency of response*; stimulation of a hormone-releasing agent can *anticipate* a need. Anticipatory changes can reduce the size and length of fluctuations. A second, perhaps more important, answer is that most processes cannot be kept constant but must vary in accordance with environmental demand. For example, blood pressure changes around a base level during the 24-hour period. The authors argue that this reflects shifts in demands made on a person. Autoregulation would prevent adaptive changes in blood pressure. The sustained rises in blood pressure are initiated by neural control of all peripheral autoregulatory mechanisms.

The argument is an important one; the brain's response to perceived demand is to overrule autoregulatory processes and allow the demand to be reflected in physiological response. This in turn means that under constant or frequent demand the self-regulatory processes might be temporarily blocked, allowing high and possibly damaging levels of function to occur.

Recent evidence reviewed by the authors suggests that all of the hormones suppressed during high arousal are those which promote synthetic or *anabolic* processes requiring energy. These processes help to replace cells, store energy as fat, maintain the immune system by cell and antibody production in bone marrow, and maintain low levels of fatty acids and cholesterol. By contrast, increased catabolic activity is associated with hormones which are associated with high arousal; adrenaline, glucagen and cortisol antagonise the effects of insulin. Free fatty acids, blood sugar, and cholesterol levels rise, cellular activity slows, the thymus shrinks, and level of antibodies in the blood falls. Production of erythrocytes (red blood cells) increases and the adrenal glands may swell to maintain catabolic hormone production.

These changes, not unfamiliar to most students interested in the physiological basis of the stress response, provide us with a basis for understanding the risks of biochemical, tissue and system damage in stress. This is not to deny the role of diet and excercise as contributing factors in disease, but it is to argue that constant exposure to internal catabolic processes can instigate long-term damage. Sterling and Eyer (1981) argue that for health to be maintained, periods of stress must be balanced by periods of relaxation: "otherwise there would be no repair of accumulated damage and no vigilance against pathogens (p. 13)."

The objective determinants of pathogenic states of arousal are the demands made on the individual and the resources available. The authors report the main findings of Weiss on ulceration in rodents (see Chapters 1 and 2 of this book) and cite his results showing that raised demand and helplessness through lack of instrumental facility are responsible for increased ulceration.

The emphasis on these variables means that the approach of Sterling and Eyer is much closer to the one favoured in Fisher (1984a), namely that it is the "doing," as much as the perceiving, which is the likely determinant of health and illness. Studies of the effects of geographical transitions show that a move itself is *not* a sufficient condition for adverse reaction; it is the context of the move and the individual's attempt to cope with it effectively that are important (see Stokols et al., 1983; Fisher et al., 1985a, c).

Sterling and Eyer emphasise both "perceiving" and "doing" aspects of a threatening situation. People are able to empathise in relation to the context of film material when no "doing" is required; exposure to content of symbolic material is a sufficient condition for an arousal pattern. Equally, the operation of coping strategies may be a highly influential determinant of arousal response. The authors cite a study on the parents of children with leukaemia (Wolfe et al., 1964) in which those who made an attempt to deny the realities of the situation show high levels of cortisol; those who used one of a number of identified denial strategies had lower cortisol levels. There were high correlations between level of cortisol predicted on behavioural observation and actual levels measured.

The way in which disease is engendered by heightened states of arousal has often been described in terms of "somatisation"; overactivity results in functional change, leading eventually to anatomical change. Sterling and Eyer do not use this term but do provide accounts of various ways in which anatomical changes leading to disease may occur.

ii. A Dichotomous Model of Arousal Pathology

In earlier chapters in this book and in Fisher (1984a), the basis for proposing different patterns of arousal was discussed. Two main bodily arousal systems can be identified. There are important differences in the pathology resulting from prolonged or repeated arousal. Moreover, the relationship with the characteristics of planning and decision features is different.

The sympathetico-medullary route concerns the stimulation of the autonomic nervous system resulting in the secretion of the catecholamines (adrenaline and noradrenaline) and associated release of sugars, fatty acids, and cholesterol. This is the hormone route first investigated in detail by Cannon (1932, 1936) and it is this route which might, by prolonged stimulation, bring about somatisation, as described on page 229.

In addition, high levels of sympathetico-medullary arousal could, by the action of associated high catecholamine levels, lower the resistance to infection because of changes produced in the spleen and the reduction of effective lymphocyte (white blood cell) activity (Wang et al., 1978). Thus, continuous or frequent experience of stress may result in: (1) increased risk of pathological changes in organ structure and function later on in life; (2) increased risk of successful antigen challenge in the short term.

In Chapter 10, it was argued from laboratory work that the non-depressed might resist adverse effects expected in stressful conditions by raised effort levels. These effortful behaviours are most likely to be associated with raised catecholamines and the experience of challenge. An outcome of effortful activity may be raised levels of hormone with the long-term risk of "arousal pathology"; the effort pays off, performance is successful, the stress is attenuated; there may be some pleasure and satisfaction in coping in such circumstances.

The second hormone route is the pituitary–ACTH–adrenal cortex route, described by Selye (1956). This is the hormone route associated with increased risk of lowered resistance to infection because of the combined effects of ACTH (adrenocorticotropic hormone) and hormones such as cortisol. Amkraut and Solomon (1975) reported that injections of ACTH in rodents effectively suppressed the immune response. Rassmussen (1957) investigated the stressful effects of shock, constraint, or loud noise in rats trained to learn an avoidance task. The stressful experiences were associated with high levels of corticosteroids. The results of 6-hour stress sessions daily were hypertrophy of the adrenal glands, leukopenia, and hypertrophy of the spleen and thymus. More importantly, there was increased susceptibility to herpes simplex, poliomyelitus, coxsackie B, and polyma virus infections. There were no changes in resistance to influenza and related respiratory viruses.

As described in previous chapters, avoidance (control by avoidance) and absence of control may be conditions likely to be associated with psychological distress reactions. Absence of control may not itself be a sufficient condition; a critical qualifying factor is the cost or outcome of not coping. Thus, absence of control which results in pain, life threat, or loss of prestige may be more likely to be associated with distress and cortisol release than conditions where there are no particular implications.

Increased *intensity, duration*, and *frequency* of states of pathological arousal should favour illness. Firstly, there will be increased chance for "somatisation" to take place so that functional abuse results in structural damage. Secondly, there is a raised probability that a state of suppressed immune response will be in existence at the time of occurrence of an antigen. The waiting-time paradox described by Feller (1966) assumes that if there is a distribution of different-sized time intervals generated and an event occurs randomly, then it will be more likely to occur during a long time interval. If we imagine that a distressed individual has a large part of his life in a biological state characterised by raised catecholamines and cortisol, then the probability is increased that an antigen will survive.

Periods of rumination and worry associated with stressful life events will increase the likelihood that hormonal states conducive to antigen development exist for long periods of time. A study by Pennebaker and O'Heeron (1984) was concerned with health and illness patterns in spouses of accidental death and suicide victims. It was found that the more the subjects discussed the deaths with friends and the less they ruminated about the deaths, the fewer the reported health problems. The authors speculate that the two processes are related; failure to confide increases the propensity to ruminate. In terms of the relationship with health, it can be argued that rumination provides a way to extend the period of psychological distress associated with a stressful experience. Worry in advance or retrospectively may extend the period of a hormonal state conducive to successful antigen establishment. Incompetent, ineffective behaviour in stress also increases the risk of arousal pathology because control over the situation is relinquished. This represents a second way in which action may influence the risk of illness.

Immunological incompetence has implications for cancerous diseases as well: WHO reports indicate that 60–80% of all cancers are caused by environmental determinants such as carcinogens, radiation and viruses. The immune response may be involved in the routine detection and check of malignant cells. In patients given immuno-suppression treatment to lower the chance of rejecting a transplanted organ, there is 100% increase in cancer rates (see Burnett, 1970; Harris & Sinkovics, 1970).

iii. Personality Factors and Arousal Pathology

Personality factors may be evident in the form of constraints on behavioural style which create associated arousal patterns. Glass (1977) presented evidence from work with Type A and Type B individuals to suggest that Type A individuals exert greater effort to control stressful events. Glass argues that if the situation is objectively uncontrollable, the relentless striv-ing and time-urgency of Type A individuals leads to frustration and "psychic exhaustion," which end with abandonment of effort. Glass argues that in these circumstances Type A individuals respond with frustration and show greater signs of helplessness than Type B individuals. He identifies hyper-responsiveness followed by hyporesponsiveness as typical of Type A person-ality in a non-rewarded, low-control situation. Glass (1977) emphasises the importance of eliciting conditions as well as predispositions: "Type B will in some situations accelerate the pace of their activities in order to master a prescribed task (p. 38)."

Some of the experimental results suggest that Type A personalities use strategies similar to depression-resistant strategies (described in Chapter 10). Perhaps there are constellations of personality characteristics variously termed "Type A"; "depression-resistant"; "internality"; "high achieve-ment"; which are associated with effortful, challenging behaviour. The in-dividual in this grouping struggles for control, raises effort levels, and persists with high activity. Glass cites a study by Krantz (1975) in which subjects were exposed to slides of lists of words or pictures and required to recall out the items after each exposure. Type A's remembered more items than Type B's. One interpretation is that the effect is due to raised effort levels.

The achievement-oriented aspects of Type A behaviour were emphasised by results of choice reaction-time experiments designed to investigate time urgency; Type A's were found to react more slowly when the need for patience was a feature of the task but otherwise demonstrated time urgency and impatience, especially when delayed in the execution of tasks.

Experiments also showed that a pretreatment of non-contingency in prob-lem solving caused Type A's to increase their efforts on a subsequent task. However, additional experiments showed that when cues about control are less salient, Type A's show depressed control efforts. Glass argues that in life, the time-urgent, striving, struggle behaviour may, because of the associ-ation with high catecholamines, increase the likelihood of coronary heart disease due to haemodynamic effects such as raised cardiac rate, blood pressure, elevation of lipids and free fatty acids, damage to the intima (inner layer) of the coronary arteries, and facilitation of aggregation of blood platelets. Adrenaline levels may diminish as a function of the develop-ment of successful control (see Frankenhaeuser, 1971; Fisher, 1984a). When control is lost there may be a physiological state characterised by *cholinergic activity* in which depletion of active striving characterises behaviour, and helplessness is the prevailing psychological state. Glass (1977) emphasises the importance of cycles of alternations of effort and helplessness as critical in determining the risk of coronary heart disease. The increased risk is due to the arousal pathology associated with high catecholamines but also with the effects of shifts between sympathetic and parasympathetic activity. Increased tendency of Type A individuals to blood clotting and raised noradrenaline levels in stressful situations supports the proposed link between personality style and arousal pattern.

3. THE CONTROL MODEL OF STRESS AND ILLNESS

In this section we intend to bring together many of the major findings in this book towards understanding the basis of the probabilistic association between stressful life events (including occupational stress) and mental and physical health.

Although the evidence suggesting that social disruption and change are conditions associated with illness patterns in populations who experience them, models formed exclusively on the particular properties of these conditions are descriptive rather than truly explanatory. We argue that for a complete explanatory model it is necessary to trace the psychological states associated with the perception of these threats through to the physiological preconditions of illness. In the previous section, models of arousal pathology were considered and it is clear that both "somatisation" and immunological incompetence will be more likely to occur if: (1) autoregulation processes are overridden; (2) stress hormone secretions are prolonged; (3) stress hormone levels are high; (4) high stress hormone levels occur frequently in life. These factors should be borne in mind as we try to integrate some of the main findings of successive chapters towards an explanatory model of stressful experience and illness.

A. The "Mental Health Vulnerability" Clue

A prospective study (Fisher et al., 1985b) on the role of circumstantial and personality determinants of adverse reaction (homesickness) to a geographical transition to university in young adults (first-year students) provided an occasion for the examination of vulnerability factors.

One interesting aspect of the study was that by obtaining a set of scores on a scale designed to measure cognitive failure (absentmindedness) 2 months before arrival at university and 6 weeks after arrival, it was possible to contrast two hypotheses. The first, the *stress-inefficiency hypothesis*, assumes that a move is stressful and if stress causes raised inefficiency, cognitive failure levels should rise. The second, contrasting hypothesis, is based on the assumption that cognitive failure is a stable, durable feature of personality and that high levels of cognitive failure predict high risk of symptoms of mild mental disorder in stressful environments. This view, advanced by Broadbent et al. (1982), is based on high retest concordance on the cognitive failures questionnaire (CFQ) and high concordance between respondent and close relatives regarding the cognitive failure level of the respondent. On this "stress-vulnerability" view, those who react adversely to a move should have higher cognitive failure scores prior to the move.

"Homesickness" is a complex cognitive-motivational-emotional state, largely associated with grieving for or missing and ruminating about the previous (still existent) home environment. It is an adverse reaction in that it is described by those who experience it as akin to depression. Symptoms such as crying, vomiting, and loss of appetite are not uncommon in severe cases. It was assessed by scores on a 4-category scale from "not homesick" to "extremely homesick".

The stress-inefficiency model predicts that those who experience homesickness have higher scores than those who do not, on the cognitive failure questionnaire at the second time of testing (CFQ2), i.e. after 6 weeks at university, but are not distinguished from the non-homesick on the first test occasion (CFQ1), prior to arrival at university. By contrast, the stress-vulnerability hypothesis predicts that those who are homesick are distinguished by raised scores in cognitive failure (CFQ1) prior to arrival at university.

Results showed that for both subject groups, CFQ2 scores were significantly greater than CFQ1. The important point is that CFQ1 scores do not differentiate homesick and non-homesick groups.

However, as part of the same study the Middlesex Hospital questionnaire was used (MHQ; Crown & Crisp, 1966) since it provides overall and subscore measures of psychoneurotic symptoms. This scale includes the following subcategories: phobias, obsessions, anxiety, depression, somatic symptoms, hysteria. In terms of a number of subscores, there were indications of the vulnerability of the homesick group two months prior to transition to university. In the case of the students who were homesick (relative to non-homesick) there were raised MHQ1 subscores.

In other words, those who, by reporting homesickness, are indicating negative reactions to the move are predicted by mild symptoms of mental disorder two months prior to the event. All subject groups show rises in cognitive failure and depression, perhaps suggesting that the transition involves adjustments to a new situation perceived as stressful by all. Covariate analysis showed that when the MHQ1 scores for the homesick and non-homesick groups were held constant the *gain*, or degree of increase, in MHQ scores after the transition to university was greater for the homesick group, confirming greater vulnerability to the effects of the move in those with high MHQ1 initially.

A clue about differential modes of reaction to experienced stress is provided by these data. The main findings of interest are that a) all those who undergo the transition to university show a rise in cognitive failure and psychoneurotic symptoms; b) those who report homesickness have greater psychoneurotic symptoms prior to the transition and greater gain in increased psychoneurotic symptoms after the transition. It seems as if all students are affected adversely by the move but that those already vulnerable show greater adverse reaction and report homesickness. A possible explanation is that the homesickness reaction is dominated by past-oriented, nostalgic cognitive activity which represents desire for the previous and the secure and a turning away from challenge. Non-homesick individuals although affected by a transition react positively and perceive a sense of challenge.

B. Predisposing Factors and Extrinsic Risk

There is now considerable evidence to suggest that the risk of adverse reaction to a stressful event in life might be predisposed by early trauma. Exits and losses in early life are factors identified as likely to lead to adverse reaction to life stress. For example, Brown (1961) reported that 41% of 216 depressed patients had lost at least one parent before the age of 15. This compared with 12% in a sample of the general population. Beck (1967) compared cases of mild and severe depression on the Beck Depression Inventory. Results showed that 27% of those with severe depression reported loss of a parent before the age of 16, compared with 12% in the non-depressed group. For both males and females, paternal loss appeared with greater frequency and female sufferers were "more prevalent." The vulnerability produced by early loss does appear to be of a general nature and does not easily predict diagnostic groupings within clinical states (Gregory, 1966).

The relationship of early loss and subsequent vulnerability is not generally understood. Loss of a mother before the age of 11 is likely to have a more profound effect than loss of a close relative (Brown & Harris, 1978). These authors argued that the mother provides a source of comfort and support; a source of control is provided which is perhaps essential to early development processes. There is some support for this: Navran (1954) reported greater dependency in women who had lost their mothers before the age of 10 years. It is possible that general attitudes to means and methods of obtaining control are strongly influenced by both the guidance and protection afforded by a close parental relationship. Bowlby (1973) considers that early traumas move the child from an "optimum development pathway." The child perhaps is transferred to a psychosocial milieu which nurtures faulty strategies. A child unprotected by parents may, for example, always act to avoid confrontation with adults. Thus, he may show loss of confidence; be afraid to say what he really thinks; try to please; etc. Perhaps it is in the context of these early experiences that we should examine the development (or lack of development) of the kind of depression-resistant approach to life indicated by laboratory studies (reviewed in Chapter 10).

Fisher (1984a) attempted to incorporate the findings on vulnerability into a "risk model"; reaction to a current stressful event was envisaged as being the result of cumulated risk factors acquired during early life (extrinsic risk) as well as of the intrinsic properties of the immediate stress (intrinsic risk). Thus, some people might react adversely to a relatively mild event, whereas others might be predisposed to cope effectively with a very severe event and even see it as challenging.

If we imagine that there is vulnerability represented as a psychological risk level, a question of importance is to what extent vulnerability is specific and how it is represented in cognition. Using a lock-and-key analogy, is vulnerability so specific that only a certain key will open the lock (i.e. a person is at risk for adverse reaction to a certain kind of stress), or is it so general that any key will open the lock (i.e. general insecurity, loss of confidence, coping inadequacy)?

It was proposed by Fisher that vulnerability might be represented as bias in the decision about the possibilities for control in threatening situations. Now we extend this view to suggest that vulnerability is represented in the parameters of strategic response—formulation of goals, decisions about domain of control, decisions about kinds of control to be operated, and decisions about the way in which component actions are carried out.

In the previous chapter we developed a marionette model of strategic response in which long-term personality factors and immediate circumstances combine to constrain the parameters of selected strategies. Thus a person who likes action rather than inaction might rush around applying different remedies; a person who is competitive may respond with competitive goals; etc. Irrespective of whether the life event is an accidental encounter or involves long-term experience of social disruption and alienation, faulty strategies strongly represented in cognition may cause the vulnerable person to produce strategies that *the greater proportion of a population would not produce in the particular situation.* We could think of the memory of an individual, including a vulnerable person, as analogous with a record where the grooves are deepened in time so that early inappropriate strategic themes dominate thinking, reflecting in policy and stylistic decisions. The vulnerable person is the one who "gets it wrong."

In reviewing the notion of "arousal pathology" and its possible causal roles in the development of illness, it was argued that we need to define and understand conditions which will increase the *frequency, intensity,* and *duration* of such states. Incompetent, misdirected, or inadequate strategies will achieve just that result. A person who produces inappropriate behaviour in response to a major long- or short-term threat loses the initiative; "control" becomes externally located. If the threat is not self-limiting, the situation worsens, thus propagating the state of arousal.

These considerations suggest that the emphasis on understanding the probabilistic relationship between social change and the propensity to illness should be on action: Attempts to rectify social disruption involve strategies. Dominant mental structures that are inappropriate for situations will perpetuate adverse states. Additionally, anxiety levels associated with stress experiences may increase the tendency to produce dominant themes in memory or at very high levels to produce ragged, disorganised, unplanned activity. Either way, efficiency and competence will suffer.

It follows from previous arguments that factors which directly raise the risks of chronic or acute illness include unsolved, prolonged, immediate stress and early (predisposing) trauma. Perhaps early trauma sensitises the mechanisms of arousal pathology or perhaps there is impairment of the learning of successful strategies which prevent or limit "arousal pathology." The latter explanation does raise the question of the criterion for success. The parents of children with leukaemia who behaved as if their children were not dying and continued to make plans for their future (see discussion in section 2C), could on first consideration, be argued to be using inappropriate strategies. Yet, cortisol levels were lower than for parents with realistic strategies and the risk of arousal pathology creating "somatisation" or "immunological incompetence" should be lower. Studies of surgical patients awaiting impending operations (Janis, 1958) have suggested that those who worry *effectively* prior to surgery, may be more anxious prior to the event than those who practise denial strategies, but the gain is better reaction to post-operative discomfort, less hostility towards the surgeon, and better rates of recovery. In the short term, the denyers have the benefits; in the long term the outcome may favour the "worryers."

Vulnerability may be represented as bias in perceived salience: Most stressful events provide dual or multiple tasks. For example, planned activity, instrumental in solving the problem, is required at the same time as techniques for dealing with the emotional problems created (see Fisher, 1984a, Ch. 8; Mackay, 1980). In some individuals, selected strategies may reflect the need to deal with emotions; for others, the instrumental approach might predominate and directly determine emotions.

C. Effort and Control as Determinants of Arousal Pathology

In section 2C, two kinds of arousal pathology were identified and some of the implications for illness characteristics were discussed. These two kinds of pathology may be linked to states of decision making and to emotional responses to specific situation. The effort and distress model, as proposed in Chapter 9, is based on work from Frankenhaeuser's laboratory which suggests that when control is available, raised demand translates into raised effort and is associated with high catecholamine levels; but when control is not available, raised demand might translate into *raised effort and raised distress* associated with raised catecholamine and cortisol levels. Figure 9.5 explores possible links with decision making about control; the decision to engage the problem results in raised effort and raised catecholamine levels as long as success is forthcoming, but in raised effort and distress if the struggle is producing negative feedback. Control by avoidant strategy is likely to result in raised effort and distress because coping responses do not produce feedback: A person never receives the feedback to show that the avoidant responses are successful (see Chapters 1 and 2). Helplessness or failure to engage the problem may be associated with low effort but raised distress if the penalty of no control is high (uncontrolled pain and discomforts) or if there is cost to social prestige.

If adverse psychological states prevail (as might be expected with the kinds of social stresses discussed in Sections 1 and 2 of this chapter), then there is raised probability of specific arousal pathologies persisting. One possible guarantee of persisting pathological arousal processes is if the stressful conditions are unremitting features of a person's job. Broadbent (1982) argued that stress at work leading to states such as anxiety or depression has implications for clinical psychology. A person who spends up to 40 hours per week of his or her working life in states of effort or distress is also at risk for physical illness.

Analysis by Karasek (1979, 1980) of job descriptions provided by Swedish and American workers indicated two independent dimensions of strain, one of which reflects work demand, the other of which reflects discretion or control. Job strain is more likely to be reported when demand is high and discretion is low. High demand in the presence of high discretion is more likely to be perceived positively. Although in theory we might argue that white-collar workers are more likely to have high discretion than blue-collar workers so that raised demand will not cause distress (see Fisher 1985b), in practice this may be an oversimplification. Demands of white-collar workers and professional jobs may *create* conditions of low discretion. The need to meet deadlines with reports; the need to maintain status within the hierarchy and the need to produce high-quality work that is assessed by others, are forms of restriction and could result in distress as well as effort.

D. Effort, Control, and the Marionette Model

In describing two dimensions of potential strain—demand and effort—one assumption has been that these are *properties of situations*. In fact, as argued earlier, we believe that these are *interactional concepts* as much determined by people as by situations. A person at work who receives event rates at speeds he or she cannot cope with, could be said to have work characterised by high demand. The fact of importance is whether he or she *accepts that demand*. Finding economies (see Chapter 9 on Zipf's law), opting out, operating a strategy of frequent absenteeism, feigning headaches, use of "slap happy" work techniques, might be different ways of reducing demand (personal domain). Confrontations with the management or consultation with unions (interpersonal domain) provide higher-level ways of changing demand. The point is that a person can *choose to accept the demand*. Those who are poor and not in positions to risk job loss may not in effect have much choice, but then the decision to accept demand may be part of a higher-order strategy (retain wealth, keep family, raise status, etc.).

Laboratory studies suggesting that complex tasks can be performed adequately against the effects of sleep loss (Wilkinson, 1964) raised the issue that it was not the complexity of the task per se which was critical; complex boring tasks were not effective in the same way as complex tasks offering interest and incentive. The motivational properties of tasks are important determinants of demand. Potentially, demand can be *accepted, rejected,* or *created* by the individual. The Type A individual (see Chapter 11) whose behaviour is competitive, assertive, "fast running," might be creating constant demand.

Often stress may appear to *impose* raised demand: Moving to a new environment involves packing and arranging the transportation of self and possessions, seeking accommodation in the new environment, finding out about new social and job opportunities, etc. However, it is the *acceptance* of that demand that is the important factor. A person might sit around until the last moment hoping someone else will do the work, and not accept the demands imposed. By contrast, another person might react by frantic activity and overwork.

Cognitive structures may constrain master-control decisions that dictate daily policy: A person accepts by his presence, prevailing control levels ("voting with his feet"). Electing to accept a job on an assembly line in a factory implies *acceptance of lack of jurisdiction* over how time is to be spent at work. Accepting the reasons for lack of choice (poverty, need to keep a family) is simply another element of the master-control decisions.

In the case of both "demand" and "control," personality constraints may operate to determine what a person will accept. In effect, what becomes the key factor is *effort*. A person who is highly motivated might accept demand and override jurisdictions imposed by society. In Chapter 9, we considered the possibility that there is a grouping of decisions concerned with optimistic maximising of success—raised effort, blame-resistance, data optimisation. Individuals who adopt such an approach may define a particular path through the matrix of decisions involved in gaining control.

In the following paragraphs an attempt is made to develop a cognitive model of illness that involves a synthesis of ideas developed in previous chapters concerning decisions about control and the implications for strategic response. Central elements are effort and control judgements which determine "policy" and "stylistic" features of strategies.

E. The Control Model, Arousal Pathology, and the Risk of Illness

The following postulates provide the basis for a synthesis of policy and style components of strategy as determinants of risk of illness:

1. Life stress situations, including social change and disruption involve, as common denominators, change in *level of perceived control*. Additionally, individuals become at risk for subsequent stresses which may

occur because the *means for control* is reduced (no one to confide in; no one to discuss problems with).

2. Individuals react to life threats by attempting to implement strategies. Although this is also true of the response to non-stressful problems, in threatening situations these strategies will have high cost attached to failure.

3. Strategies are characterised by "policy" and "style." As part of strategic policy, a person envisages end-goals and subgoals and seeks control in different domains (social, interpersonal, political). As part of policy, instrumental and emotional goals may be simultaneously planned for.

Policy decision is further characterised by mode of control: Whether a person *engages/fails to engage* the problem, operates *control by irrelevant means*, or *control by avoidance.*

Style of response involves qualitative aspects of the running of plans described by adjectives such as: *irritable, quiet, sad, frantic, fast, cautious*, etc.

4. Personality and circumstantial factors (including stressful conditons) constrain both the features of policy decisions and style (marionette model). In turn these features dictate the *success* of a particular strategy. By determining competence these factors determine persistence and intensity of critical features of arousal pathology and hence influence the risk of illness.

5. The link with physical illness is best understood in terms of *arousal pathology.* Two systems are identified—sympathetico-medullary (catecholamines) and hypothalamic-cortical (cortisol). There is a tendency for catecholamine arousal to be associated with increased risk of system malfunction via the process of "somatisation." There is a tendency for cortisol arousal to be associated with increased risk of infection via the process of immuno-suppression (immunological incompetence).

6. Any process which increases the *persistence, frequency,* or *intensity* of arousal pathology is likely to *increase* the persistence and intensity of hormone states and thus increase the risk of ill health.

Some processes may serve to increase the risk of arousal pathology. Of particular importance in this respect are *excessive rumination or worry, obsessionality, and incompetence.* Incompetence is envisaged as a major element of the link between stress, arousal pathology, and both mental and physical illness because failure to attenuate or terminate the stress can lead to a more protracted, intense, negative experience.

7. Two types of arousal pathology are identified with *demand* and *control.* In high demand, catecholamine level is raised when control is present but cortisol level and catecholamine levels are raised when control is low or absent. These two hormone states are associated with subjective perception of effort and distress respectively.

8. "Demand" and "control" *are not determined by situations* but are interactional and involve *personal response to situations.* Demand and loss

of control may be accepted/rejected or determined by other policy decisions a person makes. Therefore, "marionette" constraints determine the balance of accepted demand (effort) and control as constantly experienced. Thus conditions of demand translate into subjective effort and conditions of objective control may contribute to level of strain or distress.

It is envisaged that strain as compared with distress as a response to perceived low control is further determined by properties of the situation. Thus perceived low control in the presence of high demand accepted by the individual may translate into effort. By contrast low control over a major threat may result in effort *and* distress. These are important considerations because the total psychological characteristics determine the form and persistence of arousal pathology and hence the risk associated with different types of illness.

9. In formulating the marionette model the impression given was that strategic response to perceived threat is highly idiosyncratic; each marionette dances differently as a function of the tension and positioning of the strings. However, from evidence reviewed in Chapter 10 it appears that there may be groupings of strategic response which favour resisting depression and accepting challenge and groupings which favour the reverse. The depression-resistant approach involves raised effort, data distortion, resistance to the development of self-blaming attributions. This strategic approach should dispose the individual against depression or distress at the cost of continued raised effort. In turn this may favour illnesses which arise from functional abuse of bodily systems rather than from sources which depend on the effectiveness of the immune response. This proposition is speculative and is influenced by our findings from the longitudinal study of cognitive failure and psychoneurotic symptoms in homesick and non-homesick students. The results indicated that although all students show some adverse reaction to the stress of the transition to university, those already shown to have raised psychoneurotic symptoms prior to the move show greater gain in symptoms following the move and report homesickness: A possible explanation is that this represents turning away from challenge.

10. Depression resistance and the acceptance of challenge may evolve as a result of personality and the total of life experiences. Individuals may evolve skills and resources which have the propensity to turn an adverse potential experience to advantage. These skills predispose the non-vulnerable individual to rise to the occasion accepting demand and actively finding or creating the means for control. Conversely some individuals are not so predisposed; if life is a bad deal they see it as such and fail to rise to the occasion. The answer to the problem of what conditions predispose individuals one way rather than another may lie as much with the way in which the statistical evidence provided by the features of life events is summarised (see Chapter 4, section 2) as with the actual experiences which occur.

In summary, it is argued that social change and disruption are not sufficient conditions for illness. For any situation that confronts an individual,

SS-I

chosen action is the important factor; "risk" factors are manifest in the chosen path through a matrix of decisions concerned with the policy and style of instrumental activity. The "grooves in the record" may deepen with constant use, thus increasing the probability that the stress-experienced person will have strong manifest patterns both in everyday life and in the response to threats. If these patterns involve: (1) low rumination/worry/obsessionality; and (2) high success, the extrinsic risk for illness will be low. If these patterns involve or create conditions resulting in high rumination and worry or low competence, the risk for illness is high.

4. SUMMARY

Constrained Resources Model

The ideas developed across successive chapters of this book provide the basis for a *constrained resource* model of the reaction to stressful life events that predicts both short-term and long-term outcome. In the earlier chapters the emphasis was on how people assess and represent the evidence provided from daily life concerning control. It was argued that even in simple learning situations there is evidence to suggest that people may act strategically, attempting to control the production of responses in relation to perceived demand. This view which centres on the notion of awareness as a mediating process, brings learning into the context of daily planned activity in which aims and ambitions are influential.

It was also argued that the evidence suggests that people are poor at statistical representation of evidence concerning control. Bias in the perception of evidence is likely. A number of sources of bias were described, some of which were linked to fallacies in analytic reasoning. The use of "rule of thumb" techniques for the assessment of control could be argued to be a cognitive economy in that the individual is less overwhelmed by the data provided. However, a disadvantage in relying on an account of progress (progress model), or on expectancies between action and outcome (ideomotor model), is that bias may be more strongly implemented: A person may decide that there is high control simply because events seem to be turning out as desired or because actions initially produce expected results.

Thus, there may be distortions in the developmental evolution of strategies throughout life history. Moreover, genetic or experiential factors may combine to determine constraints on likely strategies available in memory. Thus a person becomes increasingly likely to respond in predictable ways to environmental contingencies. This model predicts high intra-individual correlations both longitudinally and transversely in the strategic response to life events.

In the central chapters of the book, it was argued that the immediate effect of stressful events is to change the fundamental ingredients on which planning processes depend. Thus the individual in stress is strategically limited. However, the main body of evidence suggests, if anything, that the individual will be more likely to produce dominant strategies or deploy attention in line with existing cognitive structures indicating priorities. Only in states of extreme panic is behaviour likely to be characterised by disorganised, fragmented activity. Therefore we might think of stressful events as tending to produce states of thinking that continue to favour the strategies already available in cognition. In other words, manifestation of developmental bias becomes more apparent. This allows the person with competent strategies to succeed more often than fail whilst the person with inappropriate strategic blueprints in cognition becomes increasingly at risk. In general, outcome for the individual should be determined by the approximation of personally-favoured strategies in relation to the ideal required by an occasion. One implication for intervention and help is that situations of *strategic incompatibility* may be created by helper and the individual being helped. This argument would favour the view that self-help must be involved, because an individual continues to act within his own cognitive framework.

Finally, all these notions are set in the context of different typologies and stylistic aspects of control. The points made above may apply to decisions about domains of control (personal, interpersonal etc.), mode of control (take action, remain passive, operate avoidance, etc.) and style (action/inaction; fast/slow; cautious/risky; etc.). It is proposed that there may be groupings of decision making about control that favour being depression resistant. Thus, evolving bias may favour effective and protective strategies when life events are difficult.

An identified need in interpreting the evidence suggesting that there is a probabilistic relation between stresses in life history and the risk of illness, is to concentrate on the responses of individuals rather more than the common denominators of situations. Demand and control are argued to be *interactional concepts*; the individual may create or avoid demand and may accept or change control levels. Stressful life events may provide situations of different demand/control balance but it is the interactional aspect that is argued to be important; some individuals may struggle to engage the problem whereas others give up and feel helpless. It is argued that it is in this area that research effort would be most advantageous. I have tried to link strategies with the risk of ill health by examining the possibility that situations which cause effort and challenge (but are not distressing) are more likely to operate via the catecholamine hormone route, perhaps raising the risk of *somatisation* whereby functional abuse of biological systems may lead to anatomical changes which increase the risk of chronic disease such as heart disease. Alternatively, effort accompanied by distress may operate by the cortisol hormone route as well as the cafecholamine route, to produce change in immunological incompetence and thus the additional raised risk of infectious illness through failure to cope with antigen challenge. Thus, we have attempted to develop a cognitive model of the relationship between life stresses and ill health.

References

Abramson, L. Y. & Sackheim, H. A. (1977) A paradox in depression: Uncontrollability and self-blame. *Psychological Bulletion, 84*, 835–851.

Abramson, L. Y., Seligman, M. E. P., & Teasdale, J. D. (1978) Learned helplessness in humans: Critique and reformulation. *Journal of Abnormal Psychology, 87*, 49–74.

Adam, E. E (1972) An analysis of changes in performance quality with operant conditioning procedures. *Journal of Applied Psychology, 56*, 480–486.

Adams, W. F. (1932) *Ireland and the Irish immigration to the New World*. New Haven, Conn.: Yale University Press.

Allan, L. G. & Jenkins, H. M. (1980) The judgement of response contingency and the number of the response alternatives. *Canadian Journal of Psychology, 34*, 1–11.

Alloy, L. B. & Abramson, L. Y. (1979) Judgements of contingency in depressed or non-depressed students: Sadder but wiser? *Journal of Experimental Psychology* (General), *108* (4), 441–485.

Amkraut, A. & Solomon, G. F. (1975) From the symbolic stimulus to the parthophysiologic response immune mechanisms. *International Journal of Psychiatry in Medicine, 5*, 541–563.

Atkinson, J. W. (1957) Motivational determinants of risk behaviour. *Psychological Review, 64*, 359–372.

Atkinson, J. W. (1982) Old and new conceptions of how expected consequences influence actions. In N. Feather (Ed.), *Expectations and actions: Expectancy-value models in psychology*. Hillsdale, N. J.: Lawrence Erlbaum Associates Inc.

Atkinson, J. W. & Birch, D. (Eds.) (1978) *An introduction to motivation*, New York: Van Nostrand.

Atkinson, J. W. & Feather, N. T. (Eds.) (1966) *A theory of achievement motivation*. New York: Wiley.

Atkinson, J. W. & Raynor, J. O. (Eds.) (1974) *Motivation and achievement*. Washington, DC: Winston.

Averill, J. R. (1969) Autonomic response patterns during sadness and mirth. *Psychophysiology, 5*, 399–414.

Averill, J. (1973) Personal control of aversive stimulation and its relationship to stress. *Psychological Bulletin, 80* (4), 286–303.

245

Ax, A. F. (1953) The physiological differentiation between fear and anger in humans. *Psychosomatic Medicine, 15*, 433–442.

Bacon, S. J. (1974) Arousal and the range of cue utilisation. *Journal of Experimental Psychology, 102*, 81–87.

Baddeley, A. (1968) How does acoustic similarity influence short term memory? *Quarterly Journal of Experimental Psychology, 20*, 249–264.

Badia, P., McBane, B., Suter, S. & Lewis, P. (1966) Preference behaviour in an immediate versus variably delayed shock situation with or without a warning signal. *Journal of Experimental Psychology, 72*, 847–852.

Ball, T. S. & Vogler, R. E. (1971) Uncertain pain and the pain of uncertainty. *Perceptual Motor Skills, 33*, 1195–1203.

Bard, P. & Mountcastle, V. B. (1947) Some fore brain mechanisms involved in the expression of rage with special reference to suppression of angry behaviour. *Research Publications Associated Nervous and Mental Disease, 27*, 362–404.

Barnes, G. E. (1976) Individual differences in perceptual reactance: A review of the stimulus intensity modulation individual difference dimension. *Canadian Psychological Review, 17*, 29–52.

Beck, A. T. (1967) *Depression: clinical, experimental and theoretical aspects.* New York: Harper & Row.

Beck, A. T. (1970) The core problem in depression. *Science and Psychoanalysis, 17*, 47–55.

Berkson, J. (1962) Mortality and marital status. Reflections on the derivation of etiology from statistics. *American Journal of Public Health, 52*, 1318.

Berlyne, D. E. (1960) *Conflict, arousal and curiosity.* New York: McGraw-Hill.

Berlyne, D. E., Borsa, D. M., Craw, M. A., Gelman, R. S. & Mandell, E. E. (1965) Effects of stimulus complexity and induced arousal on paired-associate learning. *Journal of Verbal Learning and Verbal Behaviour, 4*, 291–299.

Berlyne, D. E., Borsa, D. M., Hamacher, J. H. & Koenig, I. D. (1966) Pair-associate learning and the timing of arousal. *Journal of Experimental Psychology, 72.*

Birley, J. L. T. & Connolly, J. (1976) Life events and physical illness. In O. W. Hill (Ed.), *Modern trends in psychosomatic medicine 3.* London: Butterworth.

Boggs, D. H. & Simon, J. R. (1968) Differential effect of noise on tasks of varying complexity. *Journal of Applied Psychology, 52*, 148–153.

Bonvallet, M. & Allen, M. B. (1963) Prolonged spontaneous and evoked reticular activation following discrete bulbar lesions. *Electroencephalography and Clinical Neurophysiology, 15*, 968–988.

Bonvallet, M., Dell, P. & Hiebel, G. (1954) Tonus sympathetique et activité electrique corticale. *Electroencephalography and Clinical Neurophysiology, 6*, 119–144.

Bower, G. H., Gilligan, S. G. & Monteiro, K. P. (1981) Selectivity of learning caused by affective states. *Journal of Experimental Psychology, General, 110*, 451–473.

Bowlby, J. (1973) *Attachment and loss. Volume 2: Separation anxiety and anger.* London: Hogarth Press.

Brady, J. V. (1958) Ulcers in "executive monkeys". *Scientific American, 199*, 95–100.

Brady, J. V., Porter, R. W., Conrad, D. G. & Mason, J. W. (1958) Avoidance behaviour and the development of gastroduodenal ulcers. *Journal of the Experimental Analysis of Behaviour, 1*, 69–72.

Brewer, W. F. (1974) There is no convincing evidence for operant or classical conditioning in adult humans. In W. Weiner & D. Palermo (Eds.), *Cognition and the symbolic processes.* Hillsdale, N.J.: Lawrence Erlbaum Associates Inc.

Broadbent, D. E. (1951) The twenty dials and twenty lights tests under noise conditions. *Applied Psychological Unit Report,* No. 160.

Broadbent, D. E. (1953) Noise, paced performance and vigilance tasks. *British Journal of Psychology, P44*, 295–303.

Broadbent, D. E. (1954) Some effects of noise on visual performance. *Quarterly Journal of Experimental Psychology, 6*, 1–5.

Broadbent, D. E. (1957) The effects of noise on behaviour. Chapter 10, In J. Harris (Ed.), *The handbook of noise control*. Maidenhead: McGraw-Hill.

Broadbent, D. E. (1958) *Perception and communication*. Oxford: Permagon Press.

Broadbent, D. E. (1963) Differences and interactions between stresses. *Quarterly Journal of Experimental Psychology*, *15*, 205–211.

Broadbent, D. E. (1971) *Decision and stress*. London: Academic Press.

Broadbent, D. E. (1976) Noise and the details of experiments: A reply to Poulton. *Applied Ergonomics*, *7*, 231–235.

Broadbent, D. E. (1977) Precautions in experiments in noise. *British Journal of Experimental Psychology*, *68*, 427–429.

Broadbent, D. E. (1978) The current state of noise research: A reply to Poulton. *Psychological Bulletin*, *85*, 1052–1067.

Broadbent, D. E. (1982) *Some relations between clinical and occupational psychology*. Paper delivered at the 20th International Congress of Applied Psychology. Edinburgh, July 25–31.

Broadbent, D. E. (1983) Recent advances in understanding performance in noise. *Proceedings of the Fourth International Congress on Noise as a Public Health Problem*. Turin, Italy, June 21–25.

Broadbent, D. E. & Gregory, M. (1965) Effects of noise and of signal rate upon vigilance organised by means of decision theory. *Human Factors*, *7*, 155–162.

Broadbent, D. E., Cooper, P. F., Fitzgerald, P. & Parkes, K. R. (1982) The cognitive failures questionnaire (CFQ) and its correlates. *British Journal of Clinical Psychology*, *21*, 1–16.

Broen, W. E. & Storms, L. H. (1961) A reaction potential ceiling and response decrements in complex situations. *Psychological Review*, *68* (6), 405–415.

Brown, F. (1961) Depression and childhood bereavement. *Journal of Mental Science*, *107*, 754–777.

Brown, I. D. (1964) The measurement of perceptual load and reserve capacity. *Transactions of the Association of Industrial Medical Officers*, *14*, 44–49.

Brown, I. D. (1978) Dual task methods of assessing work load. *Ergonomics*, *21* (3), 221–224.

Brown, G. W. & Harris, T. H. (1978) *Social origins of depression. A study of psychiatric disorders in women*. London: Tavistock.

Buchsbaum, M. S. (1978) The average evoked response technique in differentiation of bipolar, unipolar and schizophrenic disorders. In H. Akiskal (Ed.), *Psychiatric diagnosis: exploration of biological criteria*, pp.411–432. New York: Spectrum.

Buchsbaum, M. S., Davis G. C., Goodwin, F. K., Murphy, D. L. & Post, R. M. (1980) Psychophysical judgements and somatosensory evoked potentials in patients with affective illness and normal adults. In C. Perris, L. van Knorring & D. Kemali (Eds.), *Psychophysical pain judgements and somatosensory evoked potentials in patients with affective illness and normal adults*, pp.66–72. Basle, Switzerland: Karger.

Bulman, R. J. (Janoff-Bulman) (1979) Characterological versus behavioural self-blame: Inquiries into depression and rape. *Journal of Personality and Social Psychology*, *37*, 1798–1809.

Bulman, R. J. & Wortman, C. B. (1977) Attributions of blame and coping in the real world. Severe accident victims react to their lot. *Journal of Personality Social Psychology*, *35*, 251–363.

Burnet, M. (1970) *Immunological surveillance*. New York: Pergamon Press.

Bursill, A. (1958) The restriction of peripheral vision during exposure to hot and humid conditions. *Quarterly Journal of Experimental Psychology*, *10*, 113–129.

Callaway, E. & Dembo, D. (1958) Narrowed attention: A psychological phenomenon that accompanies a certain physiological change. *Archives of Neurological Psychology*, *70*, 74–90.

Callaway, E. & Stone, G. (1960) Re-evaluating the focus of attention. In L. Uhr, & J. G. Miller (Eds.), *Drugs and behaviour*. New York: Wiley.

Cannon, W. B. (1932) *The wisdom of the body* (2nd edition). New York: Norton.

Cannon, W. B. (1936) *Bodily changes in pain, hunger, fear and rage.* New York: Appleton-Century-Crofts.

Carnegie, D. (1948) *How to stop worrying and start living.* Surrey, UK: The World's Work Ltd.

Chapman, L. J. (1967) Illusionary correlation in observational report. *Journal of Verbal Learning and Verbal Behaviour, 6,* 151–155.

Claridge, G. (1967) *Personality and arousal.* Oxford: Pergamon Press.

Connolly, J. (1975) Circumstances, events and illness. *Medicine, 2* (10), 454–458.

Conrad, R. (1951) Speed and load stress in sensori-motor skill. *British Journal of Industrial Medicine, 8,* 1–7.

Conrad, R. (1954) Speed stress. In W. F. Floyd & A. T. Welford (Eds.), *Symposium on Human Factors in Equipment Design.* London: H. K. Lewis & Co.

Cooper, C. (Ed.) (1982) *Stress at work.* Chichester and New York: John Wiley & Sons.

Cooper, G. & Smith, P. (1985) *Job stress in blue collar workers.* Chichester: John Wiley & Sons.

Corcoran, D. (1962) Noise and loss of sleep. *Quarterly Journal of Experimental Psychology, 14* (3), 178–182.

Courts, F. A. (1942) Relationships between muscular tension and performance. *Psychological Bulletin, 39,* 347–367.

Cox, T. (1978) *Stress.* London: Macmillan Press.

Crandall, V. C., Katkovsky, W. & Crandall, V. J. (1965) Children's beliefs in their own control of reinforcements in an intellectual–academic achievement situation. *Child Development, 36,* 91–109.

Crown, S. & Crisp, A. H. (1966) A short clinical diagnostic self-rating scale for psychoneurotic patients. *British Journal of Psychiatry, 112,* 917–923.

Dae, S. & Wilding, J. M. (1977) Effects of high intensity white noise on short term memory for position in a list and sequence. *British Journal of Psychology, 68,* 335–349.

Davis, D. R. (1948) Pilot error. *Air Publication 3139a.* London: HMSO.

Davis, D. R. & Jones, D. W. (1975) The effects of noise and incentives upon attention in short term memory. *British Journal of Psychology, 66,* 61–68.

Dawson, M. E. (1970) Cognition and conditioning: Effects of masking the CS–UCS contingency on human classical conditioning. *Journal of Experimental Psychology, 85,* 389–396.

Dawson, M. E. & Reardon, P. (1973) Construct validity of recall and recognition past-conditioning measures of awareness. *Journal of Experimental Psychology, 98,* 308–315.

de Charms, R. (1968) *Personal causation.* New York: Academic Press.

Deffenbacher, J. L. (1978) Worry, emotionality and task generated interference in test anxiety: An empirical test of attentional theory. *Journal of Educational Psychology, 70,* 248–254.

Diamond, S. (1939) A neglected aspect of motivation. *Sociometry, 2,* 77–85.

Dickinson, A. (1980) *Contemporary learning theory.* Cambridge: Cambridge University Press.

Dickinson, A., Shanks, D. & Evendon, J. (1984) Judgement of act–outcome contingency: The role of selective attribution. *Quarterly Journal of Experimental Psychology, 36A,* 29–50.

Dodge, D. L. & Martin, W. T. (1970) *Social stress and chronic illness.* Indiana: Notre Dame Press.

Dolgun, A. (1965) *Alexander Dolgun's story. An American in the Gulag.* New York: Knopf.

Dollard, J. & Miller, N. E. (1950) *Personality and psychotherapy.* New York: McGraw-Hill.

Doris, J. & Sarason, S. B. (1955) Test anxiety and blame assignment in a failure situation. *Journal of Abnormal and Social Psychology, 50,* 335–338.

Dornic, S. (1974) Some studies on the retention of order information. In P. M. A. Rabbitt & S. Dornic (Eds.), *Attention and performance V.* New York: Academic Press.

Dornic, S. (1977) Mental load, effort, and individual differences. *Reports from the Department of Psychology, The University of Stockholm,* No. 509.

Duffy, E. (1962) *Activation and behavior.* New York: Wiley.

Dulany, D. E. (1974) On the support of cognitive theory in opposition to behaviour theory: A methodological problem. In W. Weiner & D. S. Palermo (Eds.), *Conditioning and the symbolic processes*. Hillsdale, N.J.: Lawrence Erlbaum Associates Inc.

Easterbrook, J. A. (1959) The effect of emotion on cue utilisation and the organisation of behaviour. *Psychological Review, 66*, 183–201.

Edwards, W., Lindman, H. & Phillips, L. D. (1965) Emerging technologies for making decisions. In *New directions in psychology II*. New York: Holt, Rinehart & Winston.

Egeth, H. & Smith, E. E. (1967) On the nature of errors in a choice reaction time. *Psychonomic Science, 8*, 345–346.

Ells, J. G. (1973) Analysis of temporal and attentional aspect of movement control. *Journal of Experimental Psychology, 99*, 10–21.

Epstein, S. (1962) The measurement of drive and conflict in humans: Theory and experiment. *Nebraska Symposium on Motivation*. Lincoln, Nebr.: University of Nebraska Press.

Epstein, S. (1967) Toward a unified theory of anxiety. In B. A. Maher (Ed.), *Progress in experimental personality research*, Vol. 4. New York: Academic Press.

Epstein, S. & Clarke, S. (1970) Heart rate and skin conductance during experimentally induced anxiety: The effects of anticipated intensity of noxious stimulation and experience. *Journal of Experimental Psychology, 84*, 105–112.

Eysenck, H. J. (1967) *The biological basis of personality*. Springfield, Ill.: C. C. Thomas.

Eysenck, H. J. (1973) Personality, learning and anxiety. In H. J. Eysenck (Ed.), *Handbook of abnormal psychology*. London: Pitman.

Eysenck, H. J. (1977) *You and neurosis*. London: Maurice Temple Smith.

Eysenck, H. J. (1983) Extraversion, neuroticism and psychoticism. In A. Gale, & J. Edwards (Eds.), *Physiological correlates of human behaviour*, Vol. 3, pp.13–30.

Eysenck, H. J. & Gillan, P. W. (1964) Speed and accurary in mirror drawing as a function of drive. In H. J. Eysenck (Ed.), *Experiments in motivation*. Oxford: Pergamon.

Eysenck, M. W. (1974) Extraversion, arousal and retrieval from semantic memory. *Journal of Personality, 42*, 319–331.

Eysenck, M. W. (1975) Effects of noise, activation level and response dominance on retrieval from semantic memory. *Journal of Experimental Psychology, 104*, 143–148.

Eysenck, M. W. (1979) Anxiety, learning and memory: a reconceptualisation. *Journal of Research in Personality, 13*, 363–385.

Eysenck, M. W. (1981) Learning, memory and personality. In H. J. Eysenck (Ed.), *A model for personality*. New York: Springer.

Eysenck, M. W. (1983) Anxiety and individual differences. In G. R. J. Hockey, *Stress and fatigue in human performance*. Chichester: John Wiley & Sons.

Feather, N. T. (1961) The relationship of persistence at a task to expectation of success and achievement related motive. *Journal of Abnormal and Social Psychology, 63*, 552–561.

Feather, N. T. (1967) An expectancy value model of information seeking behaviour. *Psychological Review, 74*, 342–360.

Feather, N. T. (1982) Human values and the prediction of action: an expectancy value analysis. In N. Feather (Ed.), *Expectations and actions*. Hillsdale, N.J.: Lawrence Erlbaum Associates Inc.

Feller, W. (1966) *An introduction to probability theory and its applications*, Vol. 2. New York: John Wiley & Sons.

Fenz, W. D. (1964) Conflict and stress as related to physiological activation and sensory, perceptual and cognitive functioning. *Psychological Monographs, 78* (8), 1–33.

Fenz, W. D. (1969) Die funktion der erfahrung bei der kontrollierung der inneren erregung. *Psychologische Beitrage, 11*, 588–594.

Fenz, W. D. (1975) Strategies for coping with stress. In I. G. Sarason & C. D. Spielberger (Eds.), *Stress and anxiety*, Vol. 2. Washington: Hemisphere Publishing Corporation.

Fenz, W. D., Kluck, B. L. & Bankart, C.P. (1969) The effect of threat and uncertainty on mastery of stress. *Journal of Experimental Psychology, 79*, 473–479.

Fernichel, O. (1945) *The psychoanalytic theory of neurosis*. New York: Norton.

Finkelman, J. & Glass, D. (1970) Reappraisal of the relationship between noise and human performance by means of a subsidiary task measure. *Journal of Applied Psychology*, *54*, 3.

Fishbein, H. D. (1967) Effects of differential instructions and number of acquisition trials on extinction and reacquisition of the conditioned eye lid response. *Journal of Experimental Psychology*, *75*, 126–127.

Fisher, S. (1972) A distraction effect of noise bursts. *Perception*, *1*, 223–236.

Fisher, S. (1975) The microstructure of dual task interaction. 1: The patterning of main task responses within secondary task intervals. *Perception*, *4*, 267–290.

Fisher, S. (1977) The microstructure of dual task interaction. 3: Incompatibility and attention switching. *Perception*, *6*, 467–477.

Fisher, S. (1980) The microstructure of dual task interaction: 4. Sleep deprivation and the control of attention. *Perception*, *9*, 327–337.

Fisher, S. (1983a) Pessimistic noise effects: the perception of reaction times in noise. *Canadian Journal of Psychology*, *37* (2), 258–271.

Fisher, S. (1983b) Memory and search in loud noise. *Canadian Journal of Psychology*, *37* (3), 439–449.

Fisher, S. (1984a) *Stress and the perception of control*. London: Lawrence Erlbaum Associates Ltd.

Fisher, S. (1984b) The microstructure of attentional deployment on a dual task in loud noise. *Canadian Journal of Psychology*, *38*, 561–578.

Fisher, S. (1985a) The perception of performance in stress: The utilization of cognitive facts by depressed and non depressed students. *Perception*, *14*, (in press).

Fisher, S. (1985b) Control and blue collar work. In C. Cooper & P. Smith (Eds.), *Stress and blue collar workers*. Chichester: John Wiley & Sons.

Fisher, S. & Ledwith, M. (1985) The perception of control in loud noise. *Perception*, *13*, 709–719.

Fisher, S., Frazer, N. & Murray, K. (1984) The transition from home to boarding school: A diary study of spontaneously reported problems and worries in boarding school children. *Journal of Environmental Psychology*, *4*, 211–221.

Fisher, S., Frazer, N. & Murray, K. (1985a) Homesickness and health in boarding school children. *Journal of Environmental Psychology* (in press).

Fisher, S., Frazer, N., Murray, K. & Hood, B. (1985b) A prospective study of vulnerability to homesickness in first year residential students (submitted for publication).

Fisher, S., Murray, K. & Frazer, N. (1985c) Homesickness, health and efficiency in first year students. *Journal of Environmental Psychology*, *5*, 181–195.

Fitts, P. M. (1966) Cognitive aspects of information processing. III: Set for speed versus accuracy. *Journal of Experimental Psychology*, *71*, 849–857.

Folkhard, S. & Greeman, A. L. (1974) Salience, induced muscle tension and the ability to ignore irrelevant information. *Quarterly Journal of Experimental Psychology*, *26*, 360–367.

Folkman, S. (1984) Personal control and stress and coping processes. A theoretical analysis. *Journal of Personality and Social Psychology*, *46* (4), 839–852.

Folkman, S. & Lazarus, R. S. (1980) An analysis of coping in a middle aged community sample. *Journal of Health and Social Behaviour*, *21*, 219–239.

Forster, P. M. & Grierson, A. T. (1978) Noise and attentional selectivity: A reproducible phenomenon? *British Journal of Psychology*, *69*, 489–498.

Fowler, C. T. H. & Wilding, J. M. (1979) Differential effects of noise and incentives on learning. *British Journal of Psychology*, *70*, 149–153.

Frankenhaeuser, M. (1971) *Behavior and circulating catecholamines. Review from Brain Research*. Amsterdam: Elsevier Publishing Company.

Frankenhaeuser, M. & Gardell, B. (1976) Underload and overload in working life: Outline of a multidisciplinary approach. *Journal of Human Stress*, *2*, 35–46.

Frankenhaeuser, M. & Johansson, J. (1982) *Stress at work: psychobiological and psychosocial aspects*. Paper presented at the 20th International Congress of Applied Psychology, Edinburgh, July 25–31.

Frankenhaeuser, M. & Lundberg, U. (1977) The influence of cognitive set on performance and arousal under different task loads. *Motivation and Emotion*, *1*, 139–149.

Frankenhaeuser, M. & Rissler, A. (1970) Effects of punishment on catecholamine release and the efficiency of performance. *Psychopharmacologia* (Bol), *17*, 378–390.

Frankenhaeuser, M., Lundberg, U. & Foresman, L. (1980) Dissociation between sympathetic adrenal and pituitary adrenal response to an achievement situation characterised by high controllability. *Biological Psychology*, *10*, 79–91.

Freeman, G. L. (1948) *The energetics of human behaviour*. Ithaca, N.Y.: Cornell University Press.

Freka, G., Beyts, J., Levy, A. B. & Martin, I. (1983) The role of awareness in human conditioning. *Pavlovian Journal of Biological Science*, April/June, 69–75.

Funkenstein, D. H., King, S. H. & Drolette, M. E. (1957) *Mastery of stress*. Cambridge, Mass.: Harvard University Press.

Garber, J. & Hollen, S. D. (1980) Universal versus personal helplessness in depression: Belief in uncontrollability or incompetence. *Journal of Abnormal Psychology*, *89* (1), 56–66.

Garcia, J. & Koelling, R. A. (1966) Relation to cue to consequence in avoidance learning. *Psychonomic Science*, *4*, 123–124.

Geer, J. H., Davidson, G. C. & Gatchel, R. I. (1970) Reduction of stress in humans though nonveridical perceived control of aversive stimulation. *Journal of Personality and Social Psychology*, *16*, 731–738.

Geer, J. H. & Maisel, E. (1972) Evaluating the effects of the prediction control confound. *Journal of Personality and Social Psychology*, *23*, 314–319.

Gerson, E. S. & Buchsbaum, M. S. (1977) A genetic study of average evoked response: Augmentation reduction in affective disorders. In C. Shagass, S. Gershon & A. Friedhoff (Eds.), *Psychopathology and brain dysfunction*, pp.279–290. New York: Ravon Press.

Glass, D. (1977) *Behaviour patterns, stress and coronary disease*. Hillsdale, N.J.: Lawrence Erlbaum Associates Inc.

Glass, D. C., Rheim, B. & Singer, J. E. (1971) Behavioural consequences of adaptation to controllable and uncontrollable noise. *Journal of Experimental Social Psychology*, *7*, 244–257.

Glass, D. C., Singer, J. E. & Friedman, L. N. (1969) Psychic cost of adaptation to an environmental stressor. *Journal of Personality and Social Psychology*, *12*, 200–210.

Glass, D. C. & Singer, J. E. (1972) *Urban stress: experiments on noise and social stressors*. New York: Academic Press.

Goffman, E. (1967) *Interaction ritual*. New York: Anchor.

Gopher, D. & North, R. A. (1977) Manipulating the conditions of training in time sharing performance. *Human Factors*, *19*, 583–593.

Gore, P. S. & Rotter, J. B. (1963) A personality correlate of social action. *Journal of Personality*, *31*, 58–64.

Grant, D. A. (1973) Cognitive factors in eyelid conditioning. *Psychophysiology*, *10*, 75–87.

Greenwald, A. G. (1970) Sensory feedback mechanisms in performance control: with special reference to the ideomotor mechanism. *Psychological Review*, *77*, 73–99.

Gregory, I. W. (1966) Retrospective data concerning childhood loss of a parent. II: Category of parental loss by decade, birth, diagnosis and MMPJ. *Archives of General Psychiatry*, *15*, 362–367.

Gregory, W. L. (1978) Locus of control for positive and negative outcomes. *Journal of Personality and Social Psychology*, *36*, 840–849.

Gregory, W. L. (1981) Expectancies for controllability, performance attributions and behaviour. In H. M. Lefcourt (Ed.), *Research with the locus of control*, Vol. 1, *Assessment Methods*. New York: Academic Press.

Haggard, E. A (1943) Experimental studies in affective processes: I. Some effects of cognitive structure and active participation on certain autonomic reactions during and following experimentally induced stress. *Journal of Experimental Psychology, 33*, 257–284.

Hale, D. (1968) *Speed/error trade-off in serial choice reaction tasks*. Paper to the Experimental Psychology Society, Nottingham, July 1968.

Hale, D. J. (1969) Speed/error trade-off in a three-choice serial reaction task. *Journal of Experimental Psychology, 81* (3), 428–435.

Hamilton, P. (1967) *Selective attention in multisource monitoring tasks*. Ph. D. Thesis, University of Dundee, Scotland.

Hamilton, P., Hockey, G. R. J. & Quinn, G. (1972) Information selection, arousal and memory. *British Journal of Psychology, 63*, 181–190.

Hamilton, P., Hockey, G. R. J. & Rejman, M. (1977) The place of the concept of activation in human information processing theory: An integrative approach. In S. Dornic (Ed.), *Attention and performance, Vol VI*. New York: Academic Press.

Hamilton, V. (1974) *Socialisation anxiety and information processing: a capacity model of anxiety-induced performance deficits*. Paper presented at a conference on the Dimensions of Anxiety and Stress, Athens, Greece, September.

Hamilton, V. (1983) *The cognitive structures and processes of human motivation and personality*. Chichester: John Wiley & Sons.

Hamilton, V. & Warburton, D. M. (Eds.) (1979) *Human stress and cognition: An information processing approach*. Chichester and New York: John Wiley & Sons.

Harris, J. & Sinkovics, J. (1970) *The immunology of malignant disease*. St Louis, Mo.: Mosby.

Hartley, L. R. (1973) Effect of prior noise or prior performance on serial reaction. *Journal of Experimental Psychology, 101*, 255–261.

Hartley, L. R. (1981) Noise, attentional selectivity, serial reactions and the need for experimental power. *British Journal of Psychology, 72*, 101–107.

Hartley, L. R. & Adams, R. G (1974) Effect of noise on the Stroop test. *Journal of Experimental Psychology, 102* (1), 62–66.

Haveman, J. E. & Farley, F. H. (1969) Arousal and retention in paired associate, serial and free learning. *Wisconsin University Center for Cognitive Learning Technical Reports*, 91.

Haynes, S. G., Feinleib, M., Levine, S., Scotch, N. & Kannel, W. B. (1978) The relation of psychosocial factors to coronary heart disease in the Framingham study. *American Journal of Epidemiology, 107*, 384–402.

Hebb, D. O. (1955) Drives and the C.N.S. (conceptual nervous system). *Psychological Review, 62*, 243–254.

Heckhausen, H. (1977) Achievement motivation and its construct: A cognitive model. *Motivation and Emotion, 1*, 283–329.

Hendrick, L. (1942) Instinct and the ego during infancy. *Psychoanalytic Quarterly, 11*, 33–58.

Hendrick, L. (1943) The discussion of the instict to master. *Psychoanalytic Quarterly, 12*, 561–565.

Henslin, J. M. (1967) Craps and magic. *American Journal of Sociology, 73*, 316–330.

Hess, E. H. (1965) Attitude and pupil size. *Scientific American, 212*, 46–54.

Hess, E. H. & Polt, J. M. (1964) Pupil size in relation to mental activity during simple problem solving. *Science, 143*, 1190–1192.

Hick, W. W. (1952) On the rate of gain of information. *Quarterly Journal of Experimental Psychology, 4*, 11–26.

Hiroto, D. S. (1974) Locus of control and learned helplessness. *Journal of Experimental Psychology, 102*, 187–193.

Hiroto, D. S. & Seligman, M. E. P. (1975) Generality of learned helplessness in man. *Journal of Personality and Social Psychology, 14*, 263–270.

Hockey, G. R. J. (1970a) Effect of loud noise on attentional selectivity. *Quarterly Journal of Experimental Psychology, 22*, 28–36.

Hockey, G. R. J. (1970b) Signal probability and spatial location as possible bases for increased selectivity in noise. *Quarterly Journal of Experimental Psychology, 22*, 37–42.

Hockey, G. R. J. (1973) Changes in information selection patterns in multi-source monitoring as a function of induced arousal shifts. *Journal of Experimental Psychology, 101*, 35–42.

Hockey, G. R. J. (Ed.) (1983) *Stress and fatigue in human performance.* Chichester and New York: John Wiley & Sons.

Hockey, G. R. J. & Hamilton, P. (1970) Arousal and information selection in short term memory. *Nature, 226*, 866–867.

Hockey, G. R. J. & Hamilton, P. (1983) The cognitive patterning of stress states. In G. R. J. Hockey (Ed.), *Stress and fatigue in human performance.*

Hokanson J. E. (1969) *The physiological basis of motivation.* New York: John Wiley & Sons.

Holmes, T. H. & Rahe, R. H. (1967) The social readjustment rating scale. *Journal of Psychosomatic Research, 11*, 213–218.

Houston, B. K. (1972) Control over stress, locus of control and response to stress. *Journal of Personality and Social Psychology, 21*, 249–255.

Howell, W. C. & Burnett, S. A. (1978) Uncertainty measurement: A cognitive taxonomy. *Organisational Behaviour and Human Performance, 22*, 45–68.

Hull, C. (1943) *The principles of behaviour.* New York: Appleton-Century-Crofts.

James, W. H. (1957) *Internal versus external control of reinforcement as a basic variable in learning theory.* Doctoral dissertation. Ohio State University.

Janis, I. L. (1958) *Psychological stress* (2nd edition). New York: John Wiley & Sons.

Jenkins, H. M. & Ward, W. C. (1965) Judgement of contingency between response and outcome. *Psychological Monographs, 79*, 594.

Jennings, J. R., Wood, C. C. & Lawrence, E. E. (1976) Effect of gradual doses of alcohol on speed accuracy trade-off in choice reaction time. *Perception Psychophysics, 19*, 85–91.

Jenson, A. R. & Rohwer, W. D. (1966) The Stroop colour word test: A review. *Acta Psychologica, 25*, 36–93.

Jerison, H. J. (1957) Performance on a simple vigilance task in noise and quiet. *Journal of the Acoustical Society of America, 29*, 1163–1165.

Johansson, G. & Sanden, P. (1982) Mental load and job satisfaction of control room operators. *Rapporter* (Department of Psychology, University of Stockholm), No. 40.

Jung, J. (1978) *Understanding human motivation: a cognitive approach.* New York: Collier Macmillan International.

Kahneman, D. (1973) *Attention and effort.* Englewood Cliffs, N.J.: Prentice-Hall.

Kahneman, D. & Beatty, J. (1966) Pupil diameter and load on memory, *Science, 154*, 1583–1585.

Kanouse, D. E. & Hanson, L. R. (1971) Negativity in evaluation. Chapter 3 in E. Jones, D. Kanouse, H. Kelley, R. Nisbett, S. Valins & B. Weiner (Eds.), *Attribution: perceiving the causes of behavior.* Morristown, N.J.: General Learning Press.

Kantowitz, B. H. & Knight, J. L. (1974) Testing, tapping, time-sharing. *Journal of Experimental Psychology, 103*, 331–336.

Kantowitz, B. H. & Knight J. L. (1976) Test tapping time-sharing, II: Auditory secondary task. *Acta Psychologica, 40*, 343–362.

Karasek, R. A. (1979) Job demands, job description lattitude and mental strain: Implication for job redesign. *Administrative Science Quarterly, 24.*

Karasek, R. A. (1980) Job socialization and job strain, the implications of two related mechanisms for job design. In B. Gordell & G. Johansson (Eds.), *Man and working life.* Chichester: John Wiley & Sons.

Kerr, B. (1973) Processing demands during mental operations. *Memory and Cognition, 1*, 401–412.

Kleinsmith, L. J. & Kaplan, S. (1963) Paired associate learning as a function of arousal and interpolated rest interval. *Journal of Experimental Psychology, 65,* 190–193.

Korchin, S. (1964) Anxiety and cognition. In C. Shreerer (Ed.), *Cognition: theory, research promise.* New York: Harper & Row.

Krantz, D. S. (1975) *The coronary-prone behaviour pattern, obesity and reactions to environmental events.* Unpublished doctoral dissertation. University of Texas at Austin.

Kremer, E. F. (1971) Truly random and traditional control groups procedures in CER conditioning in the rat. *Journal of Comparative and Physiological Psychology, 76,* 441–448.

Kryter, K. D. (1950) The effects of noise on man. *Journal of Speech and Hearing Disorders, Monographic Supplement, 1,* 1–95.

Lacey, J. I. (1967) Somatic response patterning and stress: Some revisions of the activation theory. In M. H. Appley & R. Trumbull (Eds.), *Psychological stress: issues in research.* New York: Appleton.

Lacey, J., Bateman, D. & Van Lehn, R. (1953) Autonomic response specificity. An experimental study. *Psychosomatic Medicine, 15* (1).

Laming, D. R. J. (1968) *Information theory of choice reaction times.* New York: Academic Press.

Lane, D. M. (1977) Attention allocation and the relationship between primary and secondary task difficulty. A reply to Kantowitz and Knight. *Acta Psychologica, 41,* 493–495.

Lane, D. M. (1979) Developmental changes in attention-deployment skills. *Journal of Experimental Child Psychology, 28* 16–29.

Langer, E. J. (1975) The illusion of control. *Journal of Personality and Social Psychology, 32,* 311–328.

Langer, E. J. (1983) *The psychology of control.* California: Sage.

Lazarus, R. (1966) *Psychological stress and the coping process.* New York: McGraw-Hill.

Lazarus, R. (1968) *Patterns of adjustment.* Tokyo: McGraw-Hill-Kogakush.

Lazarus, R. S. & Folkman, S (1984) *Stress, appraisal and coping.* New York: Springer.

Lazarus, R. S. & Launier, R. (1978) Stress related transactions between the person and the environment. In L. A. Pervin & M. Lewis (Eds.), *Perspectives in interactional psychology.* New York: Plenum.

Lefcourt, H. M. (1976) *Locus of control: Current trends in theory and research.* Hillsdale, N.J.: Lawrence Erlbaum Associates Inc.

Lefcourt, H. M. (Ed.) (1981) *Research with the locus of control construct.* Vol. 1, *Assessment methods.* New York: Academic Press.

Levenson, H. (1973) Multidimensional locus of control in psychiatric patients. *Journal of Consulting and Clinical Psychology, 41,* 397–404.

Levitt, E. (1968) *The psychology of anxiety.* London: Staples Press Ltd.

Lewin, K. (1935) *A dynamic theory of personality.* New York: McGraw-Hill.

Liebert, R. M. & Morris, L. W. (1967) Cognitive and emotional components of text anxiety: A distinction and some initial data. *Psychological Reports, 20,* 975–978.

Linden, W., Paulhus, D. L. & Dobson, K. L. (1985) The effects of response styles on the report of psychological and somatic distress. *Journal of Experimental Psychology* (in press).

Linehan, M., Goodstein, J. L., Nielsen, S. L. & Chiles, J. A. (1983) Reasons for staying alive when you are thinking of killing yourself. The reasons for living inventory. *Journal of Consulting and Clinical Psychology, 51*(2), 276–286.

Link, S. W. (1978) The relative judgement theory analysis of response time deadline experiments. Chapter 5 in N. Castellan & F. Restle, *Cognitive theory,* Vol. 3. Hillsdale, N.J.: Lawrence Erlbaum Associates Inc.

Lloyd, G. G. & Lishman, W. A. (1975) Effect of depression on the speed of recall of pleasant and unpleasant experiences. *Psychological Medicine, 5,* 173–180.

Lowe, R. & McGrath, J. E. (1971) Stress, arousal and performance: Some findings calling for a new theory. *Project Report AF 1161–67, AFOSR.*

Lundberg, U. & Foresman, L. (1979) Adrenal-medullory and adrenal-cortical response to under-stimulation and over-stimulation. *Biological Psychology, 9,* 79–89.

Lundberg, U. & Frankenhaeuser, M. (1980) Pituitary-adrenal and sympathetico-adrenal correlates of distress and effort. *Journal of Psychosomatic Research*, *24*, 125–130.

McClelland, D. C., Atkinson, J. W., Clark, R. W. & Lowell, E. L. (1953) *The achievement motive*. New York: Appleton-Century-Crofts.

McCleod, P. (1977) A dual task response modality effect: support for multiprocessor models of attention. *Quarterly Journal of Experimental Psychology*, *29*, 651–667.

McCleod, P. (1978) Does probe RT measure control processing demand? *Quarterly Journal of Experimental Psychology*, *30*, 83–89.

McDougall, J. B. (1949) *Tuberculosis—a global study in social pathology*. Baltimore, Md.: Williams & Wilkins.

McGrath, J. (1974) *Social and psychological factors in stress*. New York: Holt, Reinhardt & Winston.

McGrath, J. E. (1976) Stress and behaviour in organisations. In M. D. Dunnette (Ed.), *Handbook of industrial and organisational psychology*. Chicago, Ill.: Rand-McNally College Publishing Company.

Mackay, C. J. (1980) The measurement of mood and psychophysiological activity using self report techniques. In I. Martin & P. H. Venables (Eds.), *Techniques in psychophysiology*. New York: Wiley.

MacKintosh, N. J. (1975) A theory of attention: variations in the associability of stimuli with reinforcement. *Psychological Review*, *82*, 276–298.

MacLachlan, M. (1985) Psychometric contamination in correlational studies of depression and self esteem. *IRCS Medical Science*, *13*, 463–464.

Magoun, H. W. (1958) *The working brain*. Springfield, Ill.: Charles C. Thomas.

Maier, S. F. & Seligman, M. E. P. (1976) Learned helplessness: theory and evidence. *Journal of Experimental Psychology (General)*, *105*, 3–46.

Maller, J. B. & Zubin, J. (1932) The effect of motivation on intelligence test scores. *Journal of Genetic Psychology*, *41*, 136–151.

Malmo, R. B. (1959) Activation: a neuropsychological dimension. *Psychological Review*, *66*, 367–386.

Malmo, R. B. & Shagass, C. (1949) Physiologic study of symptom mechanisms in psychiatric patients under stress. *Psychosomatic Medicine*, *11*, 25.

Maltzman, I. & Wolff, C. (1970) Preference for immediate versus delayed noxious stimulation and the concomitant GSR. *Journal of Experimental Psychology*, *83*, 76–79.

Mandler, G. (1962) Emotion. In R. W. Brown et al. (Eds.), *New directions in psychology*. New York: Holt.

Mandler, G. (1975) *Mind and emotion*. New York: John Wiley.

Mandler, G. & Sarason, S. B. (1952) A study of anxiety and learning. *Journal of Abnormal and Social Psychology*, *47*, 166–173.

Mandler, G. & Watson, D. L. (1966) Anxiety and the interruption of behaviour. In C. D. Spielberger (Ed.), *Anxiety and behaviour*. New York: Academic Press.

Marques, T. & Howell, W. (1979) *Intuitive frequency judgements as a function of prior expectations, observed evidence and individual processing strategies*. Prepublication offprint.

Mason, J. W., Brady, J. V. & Tolliver, G. A. (1968a) Plasma and urinary 17-hydrocorticosteroid responses to 72 hour avoidance sessions in the monkey. *Psychosomatic Medicine*, *30*, 608–630.

Mason, J. W., Tolson, W. W., Brady, J. & Gilmore, L. (1968b) Urinary epinephrine and norepinephrine responses to 72 hour avoidance sessions in the monkey. *Psychosomatic Medicine*, *30*, 640–665.

Masserman, J. H. (1943) *Behaviour and neurosis*. Chicago, Ill: University of Chicago Press.

Matarazzo, J. D., Ulett, G. A. & Saslow, G. (1955) Human maze performance as a function of increasing levels of anxiety. *Journal of General Psychology*, *53*, 79–95.

Matarazzo, R. & Matarazzo, J. D. (1956) Anxiety learning and pursuit meter performance. *Journal of Consulting Psychology*, *20*(1), 70.

Millar, K. (1979) Word recognition in loud noise. *Acta Psychologica*, *43*, 225–237.

Millar, K. (1980) *Loud noise and the retrieval of information*. Dissertation for the degree of Doctor of Philosophy, University of Dundee.

Miller, G., Galanter, E. & Pribram, K. (1960) *Plans and the structure of behavior*. New York: Holt, Rinehart & Winston Inc.

Miller, I. W. & Norman, W. H. (1979) Learned helplessness in humans: A review and attribution theory model. *Psychological Bulletin, 86,* 93–119.

Miller, J. G. (1962) Adjusting to overloads of information. Chapter 7 in D. McRioch & E. Weinstein (Eds.), *Disorders of communication*, Proceedings of the Association. New York: Hafner Publishing Company.

Miller, N. E. (1944) Experimental studies in conflict. In J. McV. Hund (Ed.), *Personality and behaviour disorders*. New York: Ronald.

Miller, N. E. (1963) Animal experiments on emotionally induced ulcers. *Proceedings of the Third World Congress of Psychiatry*, Montreal, Vol. 3, 213–219.

Miller, S. M. (1979) Controllability and human stress: Method, evidence and theory. *Behaviour Research and Therapy, 17,* 287–304.

Miller, W. & Seligman, M. E. P. (1973) Depression and the perception of reinforcement. *Journal of Abnormal Psychology, 82,* 62–73.

Mills, R. T. & Krantz, D. S. (1979) Information, choice and reactions to stress: a field experiment in a blood bank with a laboratory analogue. *Journal of Personality and Social Psychology, 37,* 608–620.

Mirels, H. (1970) Dimensions of internal versus external control. *Journal of Consulting Clinical Psychology, 34,* 226–228.

Moorman, L. J. (1950) Tuberculosis on the Navako Reservation. *American Review of Tuberculosis, 61,* 586.

Mouton, R. (1965) Effects of success and failure on level of aspiration as related to achievement motives. *Journal of Personality and Social Psychology, 1,* 399–406.

Mowrer, O. H. & Viek, P. (1948) An experimental analogue of fear from a sense of helplessness. *Journal of Abnormal and Social Psychology, 43,* 193–200.

Murray, D. J. (1965) The effect of white noise upon recall of vocalised lists. *Canadian Journal of Psychology, 19,* 333–345.

Murray, E. J., Schein, E. H., Erikson, K. T., Hill, W. F. & Cohen, M. (1959) The effects of sleep deprivation on social behaviour. *Journal of Social Psychology, 49,* 229-236.

Näätänen, R. (1973) The inverted-U relationship between activation and performance: a critical review. In S. Kornblum (Ed.), *Attention and performance IV.* New York: Academic Press.

Nakao, H., Balim, H. M. & Gellhornm, E. (1956) The role of the sino aortic receptors in the action of adrenaline, noradrenaline and acetylcholine on the cerebral cortex. *Electroencephalography Clinical Neurophysiology, 8,* 413–420.

Navran, L. (1954) A rationally derived MMPI scale to measure dependence. *Journal of Consulting Psychology, 18,* 192–194.

Neisser, U. & Becklen, R. (1975) Selective looking: Attending to visually specified events. *Cognitive Psychology, 7,* 480–494.

Nilsson, L. G., Wright, E. & Murdock, B. B. Jr. (1975) The effect of visual presentation method on single-trial free recall. *Memory and Cognition, 3,* 427–433.

Norman, D. A. & Bobrow, D. G. (1975) On data-limited and resource-limited processes. *Cognitive Psychology, 7,* 44–64.

Norman, D. A. & Wickelgren, W. A. (1969) Strength theory of decision rules, and latency on retrieval from short term memory. *Journal of Mathematical Psychology, 6,* 192–208.

Nottelmann, E. D. & Hill, K. T. (1977) Test and anxiety and off-task behaviour in evaluative situations. *Child Development, 48,* 225–231.

Ohman, A. (1979) Fear relevance, autonomic conditioning and phobias. In P. O. Sjoden & S. Bates (Eds.), *Trends in behaviour therapy*. New York: Academic Press.

Pachella, R. G. (1972) *Memory scanning under speed stress.* Paper presented at the meeting of the Midwestern Psychological Association, Cleveland, Ohio, May 1972. (Discussed by Pachella, Smith & Stanovich, 1978.)

Pachella, R. (1974) The interpretation of reaction time in information processing research. In B. Kantowitz (Ed.), *Human information processing: Tutorials in performance and cognition.* Hillsdale, N.J.: Lawrence Erlbaum Associates Inc.

Pachella, R., Smith, J. & Stanovich, K. (1978) Qualititive error analysis and speeded classification. Chapter 7 in N. J. Castellan & F. Restle (Eds.), *Cognitive theory,* Vol. 3. Hillsdale, N.J.: Lawrence Erlbaum Associates Inc.

Parducci, A. (1963) Range-frequency compromise in judgement. *Psychological Monographs, 77,* 2.

Parducci, A. (1965) Category judgement: a range frequency model. *Psychological Review, 72,* 407–418.

Parkes, C. M. (1978) *Bereavement.* New York: International Universities Press.

Pascal, G. R. (1949) The effect of relaxation upon recall. *American Journal of Psychology, 62,* 33–47.

Paulhus, D. L. & Christie, R. (1981) Spheres of control: An inter-actionist approach to the assessment of perceived control. In H. Lefcourt (Ed.), *Research with the locus of control construct.* New York, London: Academic Press.

Pearce, D. (1965) *Cool hand Luke.* Greenwich, Conn: Fawcett.

Pennebaker, J. & O'Heeron, R. (1984) Confiding in others and illness rate among spouses of suicide and accidental death victims. *Journal of Abnormal Psychology, 93*(4), 473–476.

Pervin, L. A. (1963) The need to predict and control under conditions of threat. *Journal of Personality, 31,* 570–587.

Peterson, C. (1978) Learning impairment following insoluble problems: Learned helplessness and altered hypothesis pool. *Journal of Experimental Social Psychology, 14,* 53–68.

Peterson, C. (1982) Learned helplessness and attributional intervention in depression. In C. Antaki, & C. Brewin (Eds.), *Attributions and psychological change.* London, New York: Academic Press.

Peterson, C. R. & Beach, L. R. (1967) Man as an intuitive statistician. *Psychological Bulletin, 68*(1), 29–46.

Peterson, C. R. & Miller, A. (1964) Mode, median and mean as optimal strategies. *Journal of Experimental Psychology, 68,* 363–367.

Peterson, C., Schwartz, S. M. & Seligman, M. E. P. (1981) Self-blame and depressive symptoms. *Journal of Personality and Social Psychology, 41*(2), 253–259.

Petrie, A. (1960) Some psychological aspects of pain and the relief of suffering. *Annals of the New York Academy of Science, 86,* 13–27.

Petrie, A., Collins, W. & Solomon, P. (1958) Pain sensitivity, sensory deprivation and susceptability to sensation. *Science, 128,* 1431–1433.

Phares, E. J. (1955) *Changes in expectancy in skill and chance situations.* Unpublished doctoral dissertation, Ohio State University.

Phares, E. J. (1976) *Locus of control in personality.* Morristown, N.J.: General Learning.

Phillips, L. D. & Edwards, W. (1966) Conservatism in a simple probability inference task. *Journal of Experimental Psychology, 72,* 346–354.

Pope, L.T. (1962) *Aerospace Medical Research Laboratory Report,* No. AMRL-TDR-62-97.

Posner, M. I. & Boies, S. (1971) Components of attention. *Psychological Review, 78,* 391–408.

Posner, M. I. & Keele, S. (1969) Attentional demands of movement. In *Proceedings of the 17th Congress of Applied Psychology.*

Posner, M. I., Klein, R., Summers, J. & Buggie, S. (1973) On the selection of signals. *Memory and Cognition, 1,* 2–12.

Poulton, E. C. (1970) *Environment and human efficiency.* Springfield, Ill.: Thomas.

Poulton, E. C. (1976a) Arousing environmental stresses can improve performance whatever people say. *Aviation space and Environmental Medicine, 47,* 1193–1204.

Poulton, E. C. (1976b) Continuous noise interferes with work by masking auditory feedback and inner speech. *Applied Ergonomics, 7,* 79–84.

Poulton, E. C. (1977a) Continuous intense noise masks auditory feedback and inner speech. *Psychological Bulletin, 84,* 977–1001.

Poulton, E. C. (1977b) Arousing stresses increase vigilance. In R. R. Mackie (Ed.), *Vigilance: Theory, operational performance and physiological correlates.* New York: Plenum Press.

Poulton, E. C. (1978a) A note on the masking of acoustic clicks. *Applied Ergonomics, 9,* 103.

Poulton, E. C. (1978b) A new look at the effects of noise: A rejoinder. *Psychological Bulletin, 85,* 1068–1079.

Poulton, E. C. (1979) Composite model for human performance in continuous noise. *Psychological Review, 86*(4), 361–375.

Poulton, E. C. (1981a) Not so! Rejoinder to Hartley on masking by continuous noise. *Psychological Review, 88*(1), 90–92.

Poulton, E. C. (1981b) Masking beneficial arousal and adaptation level: A reply to Hartley. *British Journal of Psychology, 72,* 109–116.

Poulton, E. C. (1982) Influential companions: Effects of one strategy or another in the within-subject designs of cognitive psychology. *Psychological Bulletin, 91,* 673–690.

Poulton, E. C. & Edwards, R. S. (1974) Interactions and range effects in experiments on pairs of stresses: mild heat and low frequency noise. *Journal of Experimental Psychology, 102,* 621–628.

Prucuik, T. J. & Breen, L. J. (1976) Machiavellianism and locus of control. *Journal of Social Psychology, 98,* 141–142.

Rabbitt, P. (1966) Errors and error correction in choice-response tasks. *Journal of Experimental Psychology, 71*(2), 264–272.

Rahe, R. H. (1972) Subjects' recent life changes and their near future illness reports. *Annals of Clinical Research, 4,* 250–265.

Rassmussen, A. F. (1957) Emotions and immunity. *Annals of the New York Academy of Science, 254,* 458–461.

Reid, D. & Ware, E. E. (1974) Multidimensionality of internal versus external control: Addition of a third dimension and non-distinction of self versus others. *Canadian Journal of Behavioural Science, 6,* 131–142.

Rescorla, R. A. (1969) Conditioned inhibition of fear resulting from negative CS–UCS contingencies. *Journal of Comparative and Physiological Psychology, 67,* 504–509.

Rescorla, R. A. (1972) Informational variables in Pavolovian conditioning. In G. H. Bower (Ed.), *The psychology of learning and motivation,* Vol. 6. New York: Academic Press.

Rosenbaum, M. (1983) Learned resourcefulness. In M. Rosenbaum, C. M. Franks and Y. Joffee (Eds.), *Perspectives in behavior therapy in the eighties.* New York: Springer.

Rosenman, R. H. (1982) Role of Type A behaviour pattern in the pathogenesis and prognosis of ischaemic heart disease. In H. Denolin (Ed.), *Psychological problems before and after mycocardial infarction.* Basel: S. Karger.

Rosenman, R. H., Friedman, M., Straus, R., Wurm, M., Kositchek, R., Haan, W. & Werthessen, N. T. (1964) A predictive study of coronary heart disease: the Western Collaborative Group Study. *Journal of the American Medical Association, 189,* 15–22.

Rosenman, R. H., Brand, R. J., Jenkins, C. D., Friedman, M., Straus, R. & Wurm, M. (1975) Coronary heart disease in the Western Collaborative Groups Study: Final follow-up of 8½ years. *Journal of American Medical Association, 233,* 872–877.

Roth, S. (1980) A revised model of learned helplessness in humans. *Journal of Personality, 48,* 103–133.

Rotter, J. B. (1966) Generalised expectancies for internal versus external control of reinforcement. *Psychological Monographs, 80*(1), 609.

Rotter, J. B. (1975) Some problems and misconceptions related to the construct of internal versus external control of reinforcement. *Psychological Monographs, 48,* 56–67.

Rotter, J. B. & Mulry, R. C. (1965) Internal versus external control of reinforcements and decision time. *Journal of Personality and Social Psychology, 2,* 598–604.

Salame, P. & Wittersheim, G. (1978) Selective noise disturbance of the information input in short term memory. *Quarterly Journal of Experimental Psychology, 30,* 693–704.

Sarason, I. (1957) Effects of anxiety and two kinds of failure on serial learning. *Journal of Personality, 27,* 116–124.

Sarason, I. G. (1972) Anxiety and self-preoccupation. In I. G. Sarason and C. D. Spielberger (Eds.), *Stress and anxiety,* Vol. 2. Washington: Hemisphere Publishing Company.

Sarason, I. G. (1973) Test anxiety and cognitive modelling. *Journal of Personality and Social Psychology, 28,* 58–61.

Schactel, E. G. (1954) The development of focal attention and the emergence of reality. *Psychiatry, 17,* 309–324.

Schacter, S. & Singer, J. E. (1962) Cognitive, social and physiological determinants of emotional states. *Psychological Review, 69,* 379–399.

Schönpflug, W. (1983) Coping efficiency and situational demands. In G. R. J. Hockey (Ed.), *Stress and fatigue in human performance.* Chichester and New York: John Wiley & Sons.

Schönpflug, W. & Schafer, M. (1962) Retention und aktivation bei akustischer zusatzreizung. *Zeitschrift für Experimentelle und Angewande Psychologie, 9,* 452–464.

Schouten, J. F. & Bekker, J. A. (1967) Reaction time and accuracy. *Acta Psychologica, 27,* 143–153.

Schwartz, B. (1981) Does helplessness cause depression, or do only depressed people become helpless? Comment on Alloy and Abramson. *Journal of Experimental Psychology (General), 110,* 429–435.

Seeman, M. (1963) Alienation and social learning in a reformatory. *American Journal of Sociology, 69,* 270–284.

Seeman, M. & Evans, J. W. (1962) Alienation and learning in a hospital setting. *American Sociological Review, 27,* 772–783.

Seligman, M. E. P. (1971) Phobias and preparedness. *Behaviour and Therapy, 2,* 307–321.

Seligman, M. E. P. (1975) *Helplessness: On depression development and death.* San Francisco: Freeman.

Seligman, M. E. P., Maier, S. D. & Solomon, R. L. (1971) Unpredictable and uncontrollable aversive events. In F. R. Brush (Ed.), *Aversive conditioning and learning.* New York: Academic Press.

Selye, H. (1956) *The stress of life.* London, New York and Toronto: Longmans Green and Company.

Selye, H. (1974) *Stress without distress.* Philadelphia and New York: Lippencott.

Shannon, I. L. & Isbell, G. M. (1963) Stress in dental patients: Effects of local anesthetic procedures. *Technical Report No. SAM-1DR-63-29,* USAF School of Aerospace Medicine, Brooks Airforce Base, Texas.

Sigerist, H. F. (1932) *Man and medicine* (trans. Margaret Boise) New York: W. W. Norton.

Silverman, R. E. (1954) Anxiety and the mode of response. *Journal of Abnormal and Social Psychology, 49,* 538–542.

Sines, J. O., Cleeland, C. & Adkins, J. (1963) The behaviour of normal and stomach lesion susceptible rats in several learning situations. *Journal of Genetic Psychology, 102,* 91–94.

Sloboda, W. & Smith, E. E. (1968) Disruption effects in human short term memory: Some negative findings. *Perceptual Motor Skills, 27,* 575–582.

Smedslund, J. (1963) The concept of correlation in adults. *Scandinavian Journal of Psychology, 4,* 165–173.

Smith, A. P. (1983a) The effects of noise on strategies of human performance. *Proceedings of the Fourth International Congress on Noise as a Public Health Problem.* Turin, Italy, June 21–25.

Smith, A. P. (1983b) The effects of noise and memory load on a running memory task. *British Journal of Psychology, 74,* 439–445.

Smith, A. P. & Broadbent, D. E. (1982) The effects of noise on recall and recognition of categories. *Acta Psychologica, 51,* 257.

Smith, A. P., Jones, D. H. & Broadbent, D. E. (1981) The effects of noise on recall of categorised lists. *British Journal of Psychology, 72*, 299–316.

Sokolov, E. N. (1963) *Perception and the conditioned reflex* (trans. S. W. Waydenfeld). Oxford: Pergamon.

Spence, K. W. (1956) *Behaviour theory and conditioning*. London: Oxford University Press.

Staub, E. & Kellett, D. S. (1972) Increasing pain tolerance by information about aversive stimuli. *Journal of Personality and Social Psychology, 21*, 198–203.

Steinberg, H. (1959) Effects of drugs on performance and incentives. In B. R. Lawrence (Ed.), *Quantitative methods in human pharmacology and therapeutics*, Oxford: Pergamon.

Stennett, R. G. (1957) The relationship of performance level to level of arousal. *Journal of Experimental Psychology, 54*, 54–61.

Sterling, P. & Eyer, J. (1981) Biological basis of stress related mortality. *Social Science and Medicine, 15E*. 3–42.

Sternbach, R. A. (1968) *Pain: A psychophysiological analysis*. New York: Academic Press.

Sternberg, S. (1969) Memory scanning: mental processes revealed by reaction time experiments. *American Scientist, 57*, 421–457.

Sternberg, S. (1975) Memory scanning: new findings and current controversies. *Quarterly Journal of Experimental Psychology, 27*, 1–32.

Stevens, S. (1972) *The effects of noise on psychomotor efficiency*. U.S.O.S.R.D. Report No. 274, Harvard University.

Stewart, A. & Salt, P. (1981) Life stress, life styles, depression and illness in adult women. *Journal of Personality and Social Psychology, 40*(6), 1063–1069.

Stokols, D., Shumaker, S. A. & Martinez, J. (1983) Residential mobility and personal well being. *Journal of Environmental Psychology, 3*, 5–19.

Stroop, J. R. (1935) Studies of interference in serial verbal reaction. *Journal of Experimental Psychology, 18*, 643–662.

Swensson, R. G. (1972) The elusive trade-off: Speed versus accuracy in visual discrimination tasks. *Perception and Psychophysics, 12*, 16–32.

Symington, T., Currie, A. R., Curran, R. A. & Davidson, J. N. (1955) The reaction of the adrenal cortex in conditions of stress. *Ciba Foundation Colloquia on Endocrinology, 8*, 70–91. Boston: Brown and Company.

Szpiler, F. A. & Epstein, S. (1976) Availability of an avoidance response as related to autonomic arousal. *Journal of Abnormal Psychology, 85*, 73–82.

Thayer, R. E. (1967) Measurement of activation through self report. *Psychological Reports, 20*, 663–678.

Thayer, R. E. (1970) Activation states as by verbal report and for psychophysiological variables. *Psychophysiology, 7*, 86–94.

Theios, J. (1973) Reaction time measurements in the study of memory processes: theory and data. In G. Bower (Ed.), *The psychology of learning and motivation: Advances in research and theory*, Vol. 7. New York: Academic Press.

Theorell, T. (1970) *Psychosocial factors in relation to the onset of myocardial infarction and to some metabolic variables*. Stockholom: Korolinska.

Thompson, S. C. (1981) Will it hurt less if I can control it? A complex answer to a simple question. *Psychological Bulletin, 90*(1), 89–101.

Thorndyke, E. L. (1935) *The psychology of wants, interests and attitudes*. New York: Appleton-Century-Crofts.

Totman, R. (1979) *Social causes of illness*. London: Souvenir Press.

Tversky, A. & Kahneman, D. (1971) Belief in small numbers. *Psychological Bulletin, 76*(2), 105–110.

Tversky, A. & Kahneman, D. (1973) Availability: a heuristic for judging frequency and probability. *Cognitive Psychology, 5*, 207–232.

Uehling, B. & Sprinkle, R. (1968) Recall of a list as a function of arousal and retention interval. *Journal of Experimental Psychology, 78*, 103–106.

Venables, P. H (1964) Input dysfunction in schizophrenia. In B. A. Maher (Ed.), *Progress in experimental personality research*, Vol. 1. London, New York: Academic Press.

Von Holst, E. (1954) Relations between the central nervous system and the peripheral organs. *British Journal of Animal Behaviour*, *2*, 89–94.

Wachtel, P. L. (1967) Conceptions of broad and narrow attention. *Psychological Bulletin*, *68*, 417–429.

Wald, A. (1947) *Sequential analysis*. New York: John Wiley.

Walker, E. L. (1958) Action decrement and its relation to learning. *Psychological Review*, *65*, 129–142.

Wang, T., Sheppard, J. R. & Foker, J. E. (1978) Rise and fall of cyclic AMP required for onset of lymphocyte DNA synthesis. *Science*, *201*, 155–157.

Warburton, D. M. (1975) *Brain drugs and behaviour*. Chichester: John Wiley.

Ward, W. C. & Jenkins, H. M. (1965) The display of information and the judgement of contingency. *Canadian Journal of Psychology*, *19*, 231–241.

Wason, P. C. & Johnson-Laird, P. N. (1972) *Psychology of reasoning: structure and content*. London: Batsford.

Waters, R. H. (1937) The principle of least effort in learning. *Journal of General Psychology*, *16*, 3–20.

Weiner, B., Frieze, J., Kukla, A., Reed, L., Rest, S. & Rosenbaum, R. M. (1971) Perceiving the cause of success and failure. Chapter 6 in E. Jones, D. Kanouse, H. Kelly, R. Nesbitt, S. Valins & B. Weiner (Eds.), *Attribution: Perceiving the causes of behaviour*. New York: General Learning Press.

Weiner, B., Hecklausen, H., Reeger, W. V. & Cook, R. E. (1972) Causal ascriptions and achievement motivation. *Journal of Personality and Social Psychology*, *21*, 239–248.

Weinstein, N. D. (1974) Effect of noise on intellectual performance. *Journal of Applied Psychology*, *59*(5), 548–554.

Weiss, J. M. (1968) Effects of coping responses on stress. *Journal of Comparative Physiological Psychology*, *65*, 251–266.

Weiss, J. M. (1970) Somatic effects of predictable and unpredictable shock. *Psychosomatic Medicine*, *32*, 397–408.

Weiss, J. M. (1971a) Effects of coping behaviour in different warning signal conditions on stress pathology in rats. *Journal of Comparative and Physiological Psychology*, *77*, 1–13·

Weiss, J. M. (1971b) Effects of coping behaviour with and without a feedback signal on stress pathology in rats. *Journal of Comparative and Physiological Psychology*, *77*, 22–30.

Weiss, J. M. (1971c) Effects of punishing the coping response (conflict) on stress pathology in rats. *Journal of Comparative and Physiological Psychology*, *77*, 14–21.

Welford, A. T. (1952) The psychological refractory period and the timing of high speed performance. *British Journal of Psychology*, *43*, 2–19.

Welford, A. T. (1973) Stress and performance, *Ergonomics*, *16*(5), 567–580.

Wherry, R. J. & Curran, P. M. (1965) *A study of some determinants of psychological stress*. US Naval School of Aviation Medicine, Medical Center, Pensacola, Florida, July 1965.

White, R. W. (1959) Motivation re-considered: The concept of competence. *Psychological Review*, *66*, 297–333.

Wilkinson, R. T. (1961) Interaction of lack of sleep with knowledge of results repeated testing and individual differences. *Journal of Experimental Psychology*, *62*, 263–271.

Wilkinson, R. T. (1964) Effects of up to 60 hours deprivation on different types of work. *Ergonomics*, *7*, 175–186.

Wilkinson, R. T. (1965) Sleep deprivation. In O. G. Edholm & A. L. Bacharach (Eds.), *The physiology of human survival*, 399–430. London and New York: Academic Press.

Wilkinson, R. T. (1975) *Noise, incentive and prolonged work: Effects on short term memory*. Paper presented to the Annual Meeting of the American Psychological Association, Chicago.

Wilson, G. D. (1968) Reversal of differential GSR conditioning by instructions. *Journal of Experimental Psychology*, *76*, 491–493.

Wine, J. (1971) Text anxiety and direction of attention. *Psychological Bulletin*, *76*, 92–104.

Wolfe, C. T., Freidman, S. B., Hofer, M. A. & Mason, J. W. (1964) Relationship between psychological defenses and mean urinary 17-hydroxycorticosteroid excretion rates. I: A predictive study by parents of fatally ill children; II: Methodologic and theoretical considerations. *Psychosomatic Medicine*, 26, 592.

Wolff, G. I. (1940) Tuberculosis, mortality and industrialisation. *American Review of Tuberculosis*, 42, 1.

Wolff, H. M. (1953) *Stress and disease*. Chicago, Ill.: C. C. Thomas.

Yellott, J. I. (1971) Correction for fast guessing and the speed accuracy trade-off in choice reaction time. *Journal of Mathematical Psychology*, 8, 159–199.

Yerkes, R. M. & Dodson, J. D. (1908) The relation of strength of stimulus to rapidity of habit formation. *Journal of Comparative Neurological Psychology*, 18, 459–482.

Zeiner, A. & Grings, W. W. (1968) Backward conditioning: A replication with emphasis on conceptualisation by the subject. *Journal of Experimental Psychology*, 76, 232–235.

Zipf, G. K. (1949) (revised 1965) *Human behaviour and the principle of least effort. An introduction to human ecology*. New York: Hafner Publishing Company. (Text refers to 1965 version)

Zuckerman, M. (1979) *Sensation seeking: Beyond the optimum level of arousal*. Hillsdale, N.J.: Lawrence Erlbaum Associates Inc.

Zuckerman, M. (1983) Sensation seeking: A biosocial dimension of personality. In A. Gale and J. Edwards (Eds.), *Physiological correlates of human behaviour*, Vol. 3, 99–115.

Zuckerman, M., Bucksbaum, M. S. & Murphy, D. L. (1980) Sensation seeking and its biological correlates. *Psychological Bulletin*, 88, 187–214.

Author Index

Subject Index

& overload, 145
strategy transfer hypothesis, 152
survival strategies, 194–197
Stress:
  appraisal processes, 11
  attentional deployment, 138–145
  & attentional scanning, 142–144
  & change, 220–225
  Cox's cognitive model, 11
  control, 12, 17, 18, 19
  control model, 12
  coping, 12, Chapters 8, 9, 10, 11
  definitions of, 1–9
  demand & capacity model, 10, 11, 12
  dental injections, 103
  & disease, 219–240, 233
  engineering model, 8
  Fisher's composite model, 130–132
  General Adaptation Syndrome (GAS), 103
  hormones & health, 169–171
  interactional model, 10, 11
  interactions, 108
  low temperature, 103
  meaning, 9
  mechanical effects of stress performance, 137–146
  & memory changes, 145–153
  models of, 8–9, 11
  & non dominant responses, 143
  perceived competence in, 14, 21
  personal control, 12
  physiological responses, 9
  Poulton's composite model, 128–130

  & restricted cue utilisation hypothesis, 142–143
  state models of stress & performance, 125
  strategic hypothesis of stress & performance, 137–138
  strategic processes, 14, 69, 137-138
  tolerance model, 9
  transactional model, 11
  types of, 8
  & ulcers, 18, 31, 229
  variables, 1–9
  warning signals, 19, 20
Stroop effects, 140–141
Suicide, 216
Suspiciousness, 48–50, 54

Task complexity, 96
Test anxiety, 117–118
"TOTE" units, 73, 200
Type A/Type B personality, 206

Ulcers, 18, 31, 229

Vulnerability, 235–236

Waiting time paradox, 231
Worry:
  definitions of, 112
  & parachute jumping, 113–115
  psychological basis of, 116
  strategies for control of, 112
  & surgical operations, 114
  & task irrelevant thoughts, 116
  & test anxiety, 117
  work, 111–119, 237